T0212576

Lecture Notes in Computer Science   10189

Commenced Publication in 1973
Founding and Former Series Editors:
Gerhard Goos, Juris Hartmanis, and Jan van Leeuwen

More information about this series at http://www.springer.com/series/7407

Shaoying Liu · Zhenhua Duan
Cong Tian · Fumiko Nagoya (Eds.)

Structured Object-Oriented Formal Language and Method

6th International Workshop, SOFL+MSVL 2016
Tokyo, Japan, November 15, 2016
Revised Selected Papers

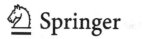

Editors
Shaoying Liu
Hosei University
Tokyo
Japan

Cong Tian
Xidian University
Xi'an
China

Zhenhua Duan
Xidian University
Xi'an, Shaanxi
China

Fumiko Nagoya
Nihon University
Tokyo
Japan

ISSN 0302-9743 ISSN 1611-3349 (electronic)
Lecture Notes in Computer Science
ISBN 978-3-319-57707-4 ISBN 978-3-319-57708-1 (eBook)
DOI 10.1007/978-3-319-57708-1

Library of Congress Control Number: 2017938165

LNCS Sublibrary: SL1 – Theoretical Computer Science and General Issues

Printed on acid-free paper

This Springer imprint is published by Springer Nature
The registered company is Springer International Publishing AG
The registered company address is: Gewerbestrasse 11, 6330 Cham, Switzerland

Preface

In spite of extensive research on formal methods and many efforts on transferring the technology to industry over the last three decades, how to enable practitioners to easily and effectively use formal techniques still remains challenging. The Structured Object-Oriented Formal Language (SOFL) has been developed to address this challenge by providing a comprehensive specification language, a practical modeling method, various verification and validation techniques, and tool support through effective integration of formal methods with conventional software engineering techniques. SOFL integrates data flow diagram, Petri nets, and VDM-SL to offer a visualized and formal notation for constructing specification; a three-step approach to requirements acquisition and system design; specification-based inspection and testing methods for detecting errors in both specifications and programs; and a set of tools to support modeling and verification. The Modeling, Simulation and Verification Language (MSVL) is a parallel programming language. Its supporting toolkit MSV has been developed to enable us to model, simulate, and verify a system in a formal manner.

Following the success of the previous SOFL+MSVL workshops, the 6th international workshop on SOFL+MSVL 2016 was jointly organized in Tokyo by Shaoying Liu's research group at Hosei University, Japan, and Zhenhua Duan's research group at Xidian University, China, with the aim of bringing together industrial, academic, and government experts and practitioners of SOFL or MSVL to communicate and to exchange ideas. Also, one invited keynote talk was on verification of Web applications. The keynote speaker was Prof. Huaikou Miao, Shanghai University, China. The workshop attracted 26 submissions on specification-based testing, specification inspection, model checking, formal verification, formal semantics, and formal analysis. Each submission was rigorously reviewed by two or more Program Committee members on the basis of its technical quality, relevance, significance, and clarity, and 13 papers were accepted for publication in the workshop proceedings. The acceptance rate is 50%.

We would like to thank ICFEM 2016 for supporting the organization of the workshop, all of the Program Committee members for their great efforts and cooperation in reviewing and selecting the papers, and our postgraduate students for their various help. We would also like to thank all of the participants for attending presentation sessions and actively joining discussions at the workshop. Finally, our gratitude goes to Alfred Hofmann and Christine Reiss of Springer for their continuous support in the publication of the workshop proceedings.

November 2016

Cong Tian
Fumiko Nagoya
Shaoying Liu
Zhenhua Duan

Organization

Program Committee

Shaoying Liu (General Chair)	Hosei University, Japan
Zhenhua Duan (General Chair)	Xidian University, China
Cong Tian (Program Co-chair)	Xidian University, China
Fumiko Nagoya (Program Co-chair)	Nihon University, Japan
Gihwon Kwon	Kyonggi University, Korea
Guoqiang Li	Shanghai Jiao Tong University, China
Haitao Zhang	Lanzhou University, China
Hong Zhu	Oxford Brookes University, UK
Huaikou Miao	Shanghai University, China
Jing Sun	The University of Auckland, New Zealand
Jinyun Xue	Jiangxi Normal University, China
Karl Leung	Hong Kong Institute of Vocational Education, SAR China
Kazuhiro Ogata	JAIST, Japan
Richard Lai	La Trobe University, Australia
Shengchao Qin	Teesside University, UK
Shin Nakajima	National Institute of Informatics, Japan
Stefan Gruner	University of Pretoria, South Africa
Weikai Miao	East China Normal University, China
Wuwei Shen	Western Michigan University, USA
Xi Wang	Shanghai University, China
Xiaobing Wang	Xidian University, China
Xiaohong Li	TianJin University, China
Xinfeng Shu	Xi'an University of Posts and Telecommunications, China
Yuting Chen	Shanghai Jiao Tong University, China

A CEGAR Based Approach to Verifying Web Application (Abstract of Invited Talk)

Huaikou Miao[1,2]

[1] School of Computer Engineering and Science,
Shanghai University, Shanghai 200444, China
hkmiao@shu.edu.cn

[2] Shanghai Key Laboratory of Computer Software Testing and Evaluating,
Shanghai 201114, China

Abstract. How to model and verify navigational behaviors of Web application is the key issue to ensure the reliability of Web engineering. The feature of user behaviors includes inputting URLs to Web browser's address bar, clicking the hyperlink in Web page and clicking the *back* or *forward* button of Web browser. The dynamic behaviors should be verified. In recent years, model checking has been used for Web application modeling and verification. But Web application's behaviors and interactions are prone to the states space explosion problem, in which the computation, validation, and complexity will also rapidly increase.

After analyzing the interactive interactions between the user and Web browser, we propose a CEGAR method + On-the-fly approach. We apply On-the-fly strategy and Counterexample-Guided Abstraction Refinement (CEGAR) method to Web application modeling, abstraction refinement and verification. Carrying out the verification in on-the-fly model can implement doing verification while building the model. The verification can be carried out when the part of model is generated, the counterexample can be identified before modeling all behaviors. It can be used to save the memory and time consumption during verification. For example, when the navigation model is constructed on the fly, a verification property based incremental state abstraction approach is used to generate the corresponding abstract navigation model. The CTL is used to describe the safety property. Then, an equivalence classes-based abstraction refinement is introduced to eliminate the spurious counterexample if the abstract counterexample is verified to be false. It models Web pages, and checks the validity of counterexample by using abstraction refinement. In conclusion, our approach can effectively alleviate the state explosion problem of Web application verification. In my talk, a Web application, an audit system, is taken as an example to demonstrate the approach we proposed.

Keywords: Web application · Navigation model · Abstraction refinement · Model checking · Spurious counterexample

This work is supported by National Natural Science Foundation of China (NSFC) under grant No. 61572306.

Contents

Model Checking

Modeling and Specification

Orchestration Combinators in Apla+ Language

Zhen You[1,2(✉)] and Jinyun Xue[1,2]

[1] State International S&T Cooperation Base of Networked Supporting Software,
Jiangxi Normal University, Nanchang 330022, China
youzhenjxnu@163.com, jinyun@vip.sina.com
[2] Provincial Key Lab of High-Performance Computing,
Jiangxi Normal University, Nanchang 330022, China

Abstract. Concurrency has been rapidly gaining a concern for mainstream software development, caused by widespread adoption of multicore processing architectures and cloud computing. This paper elaborates an abstract concurrent mechanism by introducing Bundle and Orchestration Combinators, which conservatively absorbed some features of Orc calculus and Orc language designed by J. Misra et al. This concurrent mechanism would be merged into our abstract sequential programming language Apla, then it evolved into a unified sequential and concurrent language Apla+. A typical concurrent dining philosophers problem are designed by using Apla+ language. Finally, we present some comparison between our work and other related concurrent programming or modelling language.

Keywords: Orchestration combinators · Orc calculus · Orc language · Apla+ language

1 Introduction

The widespread adoption of the Internet and the rapid development of service-oriented architecture and cloud computing has fostered a concurrent and distributed environment, where many components or services are available. There is great demand to orchestration of concurrent and distributed components or services in face of communication, free-deadlock, free-starvation and high-performance. As a result, an increasing number of researchers and developers have to pursue their work on concurrent programming.

But so far, academia and industry are generally considered that theory and technology of concurrent programming is more complex and harder to control. Undoubtedly, developing efficient and reliable concurrent programs is more difficult than the sequential programs, and developing concurrent programs is a hard task even for the expert. This difficulty resulted from the following four aspects: (1) the diversity of concurrent and distributed architectures, (2) more complicated intra-features (such as Non-Determinism, Synchronization and Cooperation, Mutual Exclusion), (3) low-level of synchronization control mechanism about concurrent-units (such as process, thread,

© Springer International Publishing AG 2017
S. Liu et al. (Eds.): SOFL+MSVL 2016, LNCS 10189, pp. 3–14, 2017.
DOI: 10.1007/978-3-319-57708-1_1

task and action), (4) lack of simple and abstract concurrent language and its related development environment or CASE tools.

Therefore, many researchers paid more attention on proposing an abstract, simple, convenient concurrent mechanism and its specification, modelling or programming language. RSL (RAISE Specification Language) [1, 2] was proposed by RAISE Company, and its concurrent mechanism is based on process calculus, such as CCS and CSP. Professor Jim Woodcock designed a concurrent language for refinement Circus [3, 4] and a refinement-oriented formal notation SCJ-Circus [5], which supports the specification and verification of low-level programming models. A concurrent object-oriented programming model SCOOP [6–9] was invented by Bertrand Meyer's research team based on contracts. MSVL language and its tools [10–12] was developed to support the modeling, simulating and verification of concurrent software system. Prof. Jayadev Misra, who once proposed UNITY [13] concurrent programming theory and Seuss [14] programming theory for distributed applications, have done some research on Orc calculus and Orc structured concurrent programming language [16–18].

After comparison of the above abstract concurrent mechanism and analysis of Orc concurrent combinators semantics in our previous paper [19], we make decision that our new orchestration combinators borrow the virtues of Orc. Our Apla+ language provides common, simple, and abstract underlying concurrent mechanism, through which varied styles of concurrent codes and synchronizations, which could smoothly interact and evolve, and easier to understood, designed, verified by programmers.

The primary contributions of our work on Apla+ are summarized as follows. (1) We proposed a new concurrent mechanism based on Orc four combinators; (2) Apla+ extends our abstract sequential programming language by adding the new concurrent mechanism, so it becomes a unified language supported sequential and concurrent programming; (3) A prototype implementation called Apla+2Java Generator is under developing, and this CASE tool can automatically translated abstract Apla + concurrent program into concrete Java multi-threads program.

In this paper, we mainly discuss the orchestration combinators in Apla+ language. The paper is organized as follows. In Sect. 2, we describe our previous work and concurrent primitives of Orc. Section 3 is our major work of elaborating five concurrent orchestration combinators in Apla+ language and a case study. Then we present some comparison of the related works in Sect. 4. Finally, we conclude our works in the last section.

2   Background on Apla and Overview of Orc

Apla+ language is a conservative extension of our abstract sequential programming language Apla, and its concurrent mechanism partly absorbed some features of Orc calculus and Orc language, designed by J. Miras et al. Let us review the background on Apla and the description of Orc.

2.1   PAR Method and PAR Platform

PAR method was first proposed by Prof. Jinyun Xue in 1997 [20]. In the beginning, PAR (partition-and- recur) method is a unified approach for developing, formal deriving and verifying efficient and correct algorithmic programs. The approach convers several well-known algorithm design techniques, e.g. dynamic programming, greedy, divide-and-conquer and enumeration, etc. With twenty-year work of our research team, PAR method and PAR platform (abbreviation as "PAR") [21] become a general programming environment and tools, which can support software development process, including algorithm-design based on recursive-relations, abstract program design, database application, multimedia development, component-based software development.

PAR pay special attention on derivation, verification and generation of software, and it consists of the following six parts.

- Radl Modeling language, used to describe specification and algorithm
- Apla Abstract Programming Language, used to design algorithmic program
- New Definition of Loop Invariant and its two development strategies
- Transformation Rules, used to formal derivation and verification
- Radl2Apla Generator, used to transform Radl algorithm to Apla program
- Apla2C++ Generator, Apla2Java Generator, Apla2C# Generator, used to transform abstract Apla program to concrete C++/Java/C# program.

In the following sections, we mainly presented the concurrent mechanism of orchestration combinators, which would be imported into Apla Language. Hence, Apla is upgraded to a new version language, called Apla+. Firstly, let's review some basic concepts of Apla. **Apla Language** [22] is based-object abstract programming language, and its syntax is similar to control structure of Dijkstra guard command language. Until now, our research group have already successfully used PAR method/PAR platform and its Apla Language to design lots of programs, including Knuth's program that translates a binary fraction to a decimal fraction [23], Hopcroft-Tarjan planarity testing algorithm [24, 25], linear In-situ algorithm for the cyclic permutation [26], bank database management system [27], transport operation system [28], multi-media database system [29], local and distributed transaction processing system [29].

2.2   Overview of Orc

Orc was originally presented as a process calculus and a programming model for task orchestration [15]. It had now evolved into a full structured concurrent programming language [17, 18]. As pointed out by its websites, the power of Orc is that it is not only a general purpose programming language, a web scripting language, but also an executable specification language. A key aspect of Orc is that the orchestrations of components/web-services may be performed concurrently.

2.2.1   Sites

Orc was used to be a computation model as a calculus for wide area computing. An Orc program is conceived as one of orchestrating components or web-services, where each components or web-services is abstracted as a site. A site [18] is a service of any kind that a program can call and from which it may receive responses. It is called like a traditional procedure or function and it responds with some number of values, called publications.

2.2.2   Orc Combinators

An Orc program is an expression. A combinator combines two expressions to form an expression. Expressions are site calls connected by combinators. Orc calculus has four combinators, more details and their semantics could be found in our previous paper [19].

- Parallel combinator $f \mid g$ do f and g in parallel
- Sequential combinator $f > x > g$ for all x from f do g
- Pruning combinator $f < x < g$ for some x from g do f
- Otherwise combinator $f; g$ if f halts without publishing do g

3   Orchestration Combinators in Apla+ Language

Orc is an inherent concurrent programming language from the moment of its birth. Orc calculus and its four combinators all implied explicit concurrency or implicit concurrency.

Different from initial advocating concurrency in Orc, our goal is to extend concurrent function in Apla sequential language, then it upgraded to Apla+ language, which support both sequential and concurrent programming. Hence, we selectively absorb and improve the original Orc four combinators.

3.1   Bundle

The notion of a computational unit is fundamental to computing. Similar to sites in Orc, we import a new concept Bundle for expressing Component/Service. Bundle is an even more general notion of computational unit, which could be a function or procedure, a subprogram, a component, or a web service. In Apla+ language, a Bundle is defined as follows.

```
Bundle:: <procedure/function definition>
Bundle:: <subprogram definition>
Bundle:: <component definition>
Bundle:: <service definition>
```

3.2   Design of Orchestration Combinators

In the new concurrent mechanism, we originally proposed five combinators selectively borrow some properties from Orc. After analysis of orchestration of Bundles, these five combinators could be divided into two kinds, non-communicative combinators and communicative combniators.

- **Non-communicative Combinator:**
  - Sequential Combinator: $F; G$
  - Parallel Combinator: $F \mid G$
  - Otherwise Combinator: $F \downarrow G$
- **Communicative Combinator:**
  - Transfer Combinator: $F\|G(x)$ or $(F_1|F_2|...|F_n) \| G(x)$
  - Pruning Combinator: $F > G(x)$ or $(F_1|F_2|...|F_n) > G(x)$

Bundles could be also classified into two types. (1) **Simple Bundle** without any combinator; (2) **Composed Bundle** combined Bundles with at least one or more combinators. Let us show some details about combinators.

3.2.1 Sequential Combinator

Traditional sequential composition is a special case of expression by using Orc's sequential combinator like this $f \gg g$, which means that if f just publishes a signal when it has completed its execution, then $f \gg g$ behaves like a program in which g follows f.

Different from sequential composition $f \gg g$ in Orc language, Apla is an abstract sequential modeling language. As a mature sequential language, it provided traditional sequential composition $F;G$ means that execute Bundle G after completed the execution of Bundle F. Hence, different meaning from otherwise combinator's notation ";" in Orc, a semicolon indicates the ending symbol in Apla+ program.

3.2.2 Parallel Combinator

The syntax and semantics parallel combinator in Apla+ language are same as parallel combinator in Orc calculus. Parallel composition $F|G$ means that executes Bundle F and Bundle G concurrently and publishes whatever either Bundles. If Bundle F publishes the value of u, and Bundle G publishes the value of v, then $F|G$ publishes the value of $<u, v>$ or $<v,u>$ because of the non-determinism of parallel execution. There is **no direct communication** between Bundle F and Bundle G during the execution.

Example 3.1

$add(1,2) \mid add(3,4)$ publishes $<3,7>$ or $<7,3>$

Parallel combinator in Apla+ language is also is commutative and associative, that is, $F|G$ is equivalent to $G|F$ and $(F|G) |H$ to $F|(G|H)$.

Let's consider the transformation from Apla+ parallel composition to Java multi-threads program. Parallel composition $F|G$ would be translated into two different concurrent-units (such as thread in Java), that executes Bundle F in a concurrent-unit *thread_F* and executes Bundle G in another concurrent-unit *thread_G*. There is **no direct communication** between *thread_F* and *thread_G* during the execution.

3.2.3 Otherwise Combinator

The notion of Orc's otherwise combinator ";" is replaced by symbol "$\downarrow$" in Apla+ language. But their semantics are similar. Otherwise composition $F{\downarrow}G$ means execution of F is firstly started. If F halted without publications, then G is started, and F if ever publishes a value, then is G ignored. If Bundle F publishes the value of u, then $F{\downarrow}G$ publishes the value of u, or If Bundle F halted with no-publications and Bundle G publishes the value of v, then $F{\downarrow}G$ publishes the value of v. There is also **no direct communication** between Bundle F and Bundle G during the execution.

Example 3.2. There are two servers S_1 and S_2, which could provide the same computation. When a client C send a web-request to two servers, where S_1 has a form of priority because of its higher-performance of hardware and its wider bandwidth for transferring data.

$C.send(request, S_1) \downarrow C.send(request, S_2)$

Let's consider the transformation from Apla+ otherwise composition to Java multi-threads program. Otherwise composition $F{\downarrow}G$ would be translated into two different concurrent-unites (such as thread in Java), that firstly executes Bundle F in *thread_F*, if no publication from F, then executes Bundle G in *thread_G*.

3.2.4   Transfer Combinator

Transfer combinator of Apla+ language borrows some features from Orc's sequential combinator, but they have distinguishing syntax and different semantics. The notion of Orc's sequential combinator "$\gg$" is replaced by symbol "$\|$" in Apla+ language. Transfer compositions could be classified into two types: simple transfer composition $F\|G(x)$ and complex transfer composition $(F_1|F_2|...|F_n) \| G(x)$, where x is universal variable, defined by keyword "*Uvar*" in Apla+ language. There is **date communication** from left Bundle to right Bundle during the execution.

1. **Simple Transfer Composition $F \| G(x)$**, means that execute F firstly, and halted with a publication, which is bound to universal variable x, then executes G with x.
2. **Complex Transfer Composition $(F_1|F_2|...|F_n) \| G(x)$**, means executed n Bundles concurrently, then binds each of its publication to a different instance of universal variable x, then executes a separate instance of G for each such binding.

Example 3.3. There are two clients C_1 and C_2, which could send a web-request to a server S. Each request from clients could be bound to universal variable x, and then executes two requests from C_1 and C_2 in a server S.

$(C_1.send(request, S) \mid C_2.send(request, S)) \| S.receive(x)$

Undoubtedly, simple transfer composition is traditional data communication between from Bundle F to Bundle G. Let's consider the transformation from Apla+ complex transfer composition to Java multi-threads program. Complex transfer composition $(F_1|F_2|...|F_n)\|G(x)$ would be translated into n different concurrently executed-unites (*thread_1, thread_2, ...thread_n*), for each *thread_i* $(1 \le i \le n)$ means firstly executes Bundle F_i with its publication bound to variable x, then executes G with each value of x.

3.2.5   Pruning Combinator

Pruning combinator of Apla+ language also absorbs some features from Orc's pruning combinator, and its syntax is similar to the above transfer composition. Pruning combinator also use symbol ">", substitute of "$\ll$" of Orc. Pruning compositions also can be divided into two types: simple pruning composition $F > G(x)$ and complex pruning composition $(F_1|F_2|...|F_n) > G(x)$, where x is universal variable, defined by keyword "*Uvar*". There is **date communication** from left Bundle to right Bundle during the execution.

1. **Simple Pruning Composition $F > G(x)$**, means that execute F firstly, and halted with a publication, which is bound to universal variable x, then executes G with x.
2. **Complex Pruning Composition $(F_1|F_2|...|F_n) > G(x)$**, the left part $F_1|F_2|...|F_n$ means executed n Bundles concurrently, when get the first publication from a Bundle F_k ($1 \leq k \leq n$), then stop execution of other Bundles. Finally, execute G with the universal variable x, which binds to the first publication from left Bundle.

Example 3.4. A client C need to search information from two servers S_1 and S_2. After getting the first result from S_1 or S_2, stop process of searching from another server, then execute computation in client C.

$$(S_1.search(information) \mid S_2.search(information)) > C.computation(x)$$

Similarly, simple pruning composition is traditional data communication between two Bundles. Let's consider the transformation from Apla+ complex pruning composition to Java multi-threads program. For complex pruning composition $(F_1|F_2|...|F_n) > G(x)$, it firstly concurrently starts n different executed-unites (*thread_1, thread_2, ...thread_n*), for each executes a Bundle from left part $F_1|F_2|...|F_n$. After getting the first publication from one thread *thread_k* ($1 \leq k \leq n$), stops execution of other *n-1* threads (if they are not halted), and binds the first publication to variable x, then executes G with first value of x.

3.3   Case Study

In this section, we will design Apla+ programs with above orchestration combinators to solve a typical concurrent problem–Dining Philosophers Problem. In concurrent algorithm design, the dining philosophers' problem could be often used to illustrate synchronization issues. Dining Philosophers Problem was firstly introduced for a ring topology by Dijkstra [30]. Five silent philosophers sit around a circular table with bowls of spaghetti. Forks are placed between each pair of adjacent philosophers. Each philosopher must alternately think and eat. However, a philosopher can only eat spaghetti when he has both left and right forks. Each fork can be held by only one philosopher. After he finishes eating, he needs to put down both forks so they become available to others.

Orc program for dining philosophers problem was given in Orc websites [31], and its TLA + semantics and verification of safety, liveness properties were presented in our previous paper [19]. The following Apla+ program for dining philosophers problem is designed by using our concurrent mechanism, including Bundle and Orchestration Combinators, and its functionality and solution strategy are same as Orc program.

```
Bundle::  procedure pick(left:semaphore(), right:semaphore());
var  ran: integer;
begin
    ran:= Random(2);
    if (Random(2)=0)→(left.acquire();right.acquire();)↓
                     (left.release();pick(left,right);)
    [] (Random(2)=1)→(right.acquire(); left.acquire();)↓
                     (right.release();pick(left,right);)
    fi
end;
Bundle::  procedure drop(left:semaphore(), right:semaphore());
begin
    left.release();   right.release();
end;
Bundle::  procedure thinking();
begin
    sleep(Random());
end;
Bundle::  procedure eating(name:integer);
begin
    writeln(name," Philosopher is eating");
end;
Bundle::  procedure Ph(name:integer, left:semaphore(), right:sema-
phore());
begin
    do true→thinking();
            pick(left, right);
            eating();
            drop(left,right);
    od
end;
program DiningPhilosophers;
var
    cs1,cs2,cs3,cs4,cs5: semaphore(1);
    P1: Bundle Philosopher(1,cs1,cs2);
    P2: Bundle Philosopher(2,cs2,cs3);
    P3: Bundle Philosopher(3,cs3,cs4);
    P4: Bundle Philosopher(4,cs4,cs5);
    P5: Bundle Philosopher(5,cs5,cs1);
begin
    P1.Ph(1,cs1,cs2); | P2.Ph(2,cs2,cs3); |
    P3.Ph(3,cs3,cs4); | P4.Ph(4,cs5,cs5); | P5.Ph(5,cs5,cs1);
end.
```

In the above Apla+ program for dining philosophers problem, we defined five Bundles, which used to describe behavior of philosophers. This problem was designed to illustrate the challenges of avoiding **deadlock**, a system state in which no progress is possible. Besides use of **Semaphore**, which is a constraint condition for mutual-exclusively acquirement of forks, we also adopt to a proposal in Bundle *pick*, which import randomly pick left or right fork firstly and then another one. On the other hand, otherwise composition combined by binary operator "$\downarrow$" successfully broke one of deadlock's necessary condition–**Hold and wait or resource holding**. We formally verified its free-deadlock in previous paper [19] based on the random-picking strategy for avoiding deadlock.

Five philosophers' processes of thinking- > hungry/pick-forks- > eating- > drop-forks would be concurrently executed with share-resources (forks). Parallel composition combined by binary parallel operator "|" could presents concurrent execution of five philosophers.

4 Comparing with Related Work

Until now, there are many research works about general concurrent programming language and abstract concurrent programming/modelling language.

Some general programming languages (such as Java, C, C#, FORTRAN, etc.) also included concurrent library and explicit concurrent units (such as process, thread, task, feature, etc.). This allows programmer to choose between different concurrent tools and library. However, the explicit encoding of concurrency also tends to cause some problems when multiple different concurrent libraries need to work together, diversity resulted in complicated communication and interaction, or low-level control mechanism (such as semaphore, monitor, lock, etc.) could easily lead to unsafe state (such as deadlock, starvation, unfairness, busy waiting, etc.). Different from importing concurrent library and explicit concurrent units in these general programming language, our primary purpose is to design five abstract Apla+ orchestration combinators, which hide low-level details for implicit concurrent execution, increase readability and understandability of concurrent program, and reduce the gap between concurrent design and its formal verification.

Based on process algebras, concurrent combinators of RSL(RAISE Specification Language) [1, 2] is similar to CSP and CCS. Circus (Concurrent Integrated Refinement CalculUS) [3, 4] is a concurrent specification language that integrates imperative CSP, Z, and the refinement calculus in the setting of Hoare and He's UTP. Circus support simultaneous refinement of behavior by process and actions. The distinction between RSL, Circus and Apla+ is that RSL and Circus are used to formal specification and modeling concurrent behavior of software system, but Apla+ is used to develop an abstract concurrent program, which could be translated into executable Java program with aid of Apla+2Java Generator.

SCOOP (Simple Concurrent Object-Oriented Programming) [6–9] is a popular concurrent model, and now it have been successfully added to Eiffel programming language [32, 33] and its Integrated Development Environment—EiffelStudio [34]. The simplicity and platform-independence are pursuing goals of SCOOP model and

Apla+ concurrent mechanism, the main different between them is that SCOOP extends only one keyword "separate" in sequential program to express implicit locak, wait by contracts and wait by necessity, while Apla+ employs five orchestration combinators to express concurrent operation.

There are some similar characteristics between Apla+ concurrent mechanism and Orc calculus/language [16–18]. Bundle of Apla+ is similar to site of Orc. On the other hand, five orchestration combinators of Apla+ is absorbed some functional features from Orc's four combinators. As for their comparison, three differences are summarized as follows. Firstly, Orc originally presented as a calculus and language for task concurrent orchestration. By importing five orchestration combinators, Apla+ is evolved from a sequential programming language Apla, which has mature program structure, abundant data types and supporting tools. Secondly, we abandon the Orc's expression, and make full use of statements and Bundles of Apla. Finally, syntax of combinators is distinguished from each other, and Apla+ reduced the levels of recursive and nested use of orchestration combinators, in order to more-conveniently translate abstract Apla+ program to concrete Java program.

5 Conclusion and Future Work

Many domains lend themselves naturally to concurrency. Concurrent programming provides a different method of conceptualizing program solutions to problems. With the advent of multiple processors on machines, concurrent program would be distributed over several machines, either locally or through the Internet. Concurrent programming language provides an efficient way to speed the execution of programs on machines. In this paper, we firstly proposed Bundle as component or service, and designed five orchestration combinators, and then the new concurrent mechanism were merged into a sequential and concurrent programming language, called Apla+. A typical concurrent program of dining philosophers problem is developed by using Apla+ language.

In the future, we will pursue research about semantics of orchestration combinators, rules of translation from Apla+ implicit concurrent-units to Java multi-threads, development of Apla+2Java Generator, which supporting automatically generating executable Java program from abstract Apla+ concurrent program.

Acknowledgement. This work was financially supported in part by the National Nature Science Foundation of China (Grant No. 61462041, 61462039, 61472167, 61662036) and the Science and Technology Research Project of Jiangxi Province Educational Department (Grant No. 160329). The authors thanks Professor Jayadev Misra, inventor of Orc calculus and Orc language, for discussion about Orc combinators and his tutorial lessons of FACS2013 in Nanchang, China.

References

1. George, C.: The RAISE specification language a tutorial. In: Prehn, S., Toetenel, H. (eds.) VDM 1991. LNCS, vol. 552, pp. 238–319. Springer, Heidelberg (1991). doi:10.1007/BFb0019998
2. Zhao, Y., Bao, T., Han, L., Liu, S., Chen, Q.: A formal framework for domain software analysis based on raise specification language. In: Li, S., Jin, Q., Jiang, X., Park, James J. (Jong Hyuk) (eds.) Frontier and Future Development of Information Technology in Medicine and Education. LNEE, vol. 269, pp. 2699–2705. Springer, Dordrecht (2014). doi:10.1007/978-94-007-7618-0_339
3. Woodcock, J., Cavalcanti, A.: A concurrent language for refinement. In: IWFM 2001: 5th Irish Workshop in Formal Methods, Dublin, Ireland, 16–17 July 2001
4. Sampaio, A., Woodcock, J., Cavalcanti, A.: Refinement in *circus*. In: Eriksson, L.-H., Lindsay, P.A. (eds.) FME 2002. LNCS, vol. 2391, pp. 451–470. Springer, Heidelberg (2002). doi:10.1007/3-540-45614-7_26
5. Miyazawa, A., Cavalcanti, A.: SCJ-Circus: a refinement-oriented formal notation for safety-critical Java. In: Refinement Workshop 2015 (Refine 2015) EPTCS, vol. 209, pp. 71–86 (2016). doi:10.4204/EPTCS.209.6
6. Nienaltowski, P.: Practical framework for contract-based concurrent object-oriented programming, Ph.D. thesis. ETH No. 17061 (2007)
7. Morandi, B., Bauer, Sebastian S., Meyer, B.: SCOOP – A contract-based concurrent object-oriented programming model. In: Müller, P. (ed.) LASER 2007-2008. LNCS, vol. 6029, pp. 41–90. Springer, Heidelberg (2010). doi:10.1007/978-3-642-13010-6_3
8. Morandi, B., Nanz, S., Meyer, B.: Performance analysis of SCOOP programs. J. Syst. Softw. **85**(11), 2519–2530 (2012)
9. Caltais, G., Meyer, B.: On the Verification of SCOOP Programs. Computer Science (2015)
10. Duan, Z.: Temporal Logic and Temporal Logic Programming. Science Press, Beijing (2005)
11. Duan, Z., Tian, C., Zhang, L.: A decision procedure for propositional projection temporal logic with infinite models. Acta Informatica **45**(1), 43–78 (2008)
12. Tian, C., Duan, Z., Zhang, N.: An efficient approach for abstraction refinement in model checking. Theoret. Comput. Sci. **461**, 76–85 (2012)
13. Chandy, K.M., Misra, J.: Parallel Program Design: a Foundation. Addison-Wesley Publishing Co., Boston (1988)
14. Misra, J.: A Discipline of Multiprogramming: A Programming Theory for Distributed Applications. Springer, New York (2001)
15. Misra, J., Cook, W.R.: Computation orchestration: a basis for wide-area computing. Softw. Syst. Model. **6**(1), 10–1007 (2006)
16. Kitchin, D.: Orchestration and Atomicity, Ph.D. dissertation, The University of Texas at Austin, August 2013
17. Kitchin, D., Quark, A., Cook, W., Misra, J.: The orc programming language. In: Lee, D., Lopes, A., Poetzsch-Heffter, A. (eds.) FMOODS/FORTE -2009. LNCS, vol. 5522, pp. 1–25. Springer, Heidelberg (2009). doi:10.1007/978-3-642-02138-1_1
18. Misra, J.: Structured Concurrent Programming (Pre-publication book), 4 December 2014
19. You, Z., Xue, J., Hu, Q., Hong, Y.: Formal semantics of orc based on TLA[+]. In: Liu, S., Duan, Z. (eds.) SOFL+MSVL 2014. LNCS, vol. 8979, pp. 147–163. Springer, Cham (2015). doi:10.1007/978-3-319-17404-4_10
20. Xue, J.: A unified approach for developing efficient algorithm of programs. J. Comput. Sci. Technol. **12**(4), 314–329 (1997)

21. Xue, J.: PAR method and its supporting platform. In: Proceedings of the 1st Asian Working Conference on Verified Software (AWCVS 2006), pp. 29–31 (2006)
22. Xue, J.: Abstract programming language Apla in PAR method and PAR platform. Technical report. Key Laboratory of high performance computing technology, Jiangxi Normal University (2015). (in Chinese)
23. Xue, J., Davis R.: A simple program whose derivation and proof is also. In: Proceedings of the International Conference on Formal Engineering Methods, ICFEM 1997, pp. 132–139 (1997)
24. Gries, D., Xue, J.: The Hopcroft-Tarjan planarity algorithm, presentations and improvements. Technical report 88-906, Computer Science Department, Cornell University (1988)
25. Xie, W.: Implementation of Hopcroft-Tarjan planarity testing algorithm in Apla language. Technical report of Jiangxi Normal University (2009). (in Chinese)
26. Xue, J., Yang, B., Zuo, Z.: A linear in-situ algorithm for the power of cyclic permutation. In: Preparata, Franco P., Wu, X., Yin, J. (eds.) FAW 2008. LNCS, vol. 5059, pp. 113–123. Springer, Heidelberg (2008). doi:10.1007/978-3-540-69311-6_14
27. Yang, B.: Implementation of bank management system in Apla language. Technical report of Jiangxi Normal University (2008). (in Chinese)
28. Wu, G.: The Application and Research of PAR Platform in Software Outsourcing Services. MS. thesis. Nanchang: Jiangxi Normal University (2013). (in Chinese with English abstract)
29. Zhu, X.: Research on Implementation of Several New Software Technologies in Apla-Java Generation System. MS. thesis. Nanchang: Jiangxi Normal University (2016). (in Chinese with English abstract)
30. Dijkstra, E.W.: Hierarchical ordering of sequential processes. In: Operating Systems Techniques, Academic Press (1971)
31. Try Orc! A example of Dining Philosophers. http://orc.csres.edu/tryorc.shtml#tryorc/small-demos/philosopher.orc
32. Rist, R., Terwilliger R.: Object-Oriented Programming in EIFFEL (1993)
33. ECMA. Eiffel: Analysis, Design and Programming Language (Standard ECMA-367, 2nd Edn.) June 2006
34. Effielstudio: Eiffel Software Downloads. https://www.eiffel.org/downloads

On Termination and Boundedness of Nested Updatable Timed Automata

Yuwei Wang, Xiuting Tao, and Guoqiang Li[⊠]

School of Software, Shanghai Jiao Tong University, Shanghai, China
{wangywgg,xiutingtao,li.g}@sjtu.edu.cn

Abstract. We introduce a model named *nested updatable timed automata (NeUTAs)*, which can be regarded as a combination of *nested timed automata (NeTAs)* and *updatable timed automata with one updatable clock (UTA1s)*. The model is suitable for soft real-time system analysis, since the updatable clock representing a deadline can be updated due to environments. A NeUTA behaves as a UTA1, in which all clocks can be tested/updated and a special clock can be incremented/decremented. It also behaves as a pushdown system, in which a UTA1 can be pushed to a stack or popped from a stack. When time elapses, all clocks (clocks in the current running UTA1 or in the stack) proceed uniformly. We show the termination and boundedness of NeUTAs are decidable.

1 Introduction

Recently, numerous extensions of Alur and Dill's *timed automata (TAs)* have been proposed to model and reason real-time systems. They increase the expressive power of TAs in various ways, such as augmenting a stack, adding more operations on clocks, and extending the original deterministic reset operation to a non-deterministic update operation.

Nested timed automata (NeTAs) [1,2] are pushdown systems whose control locations and stack alphabet are TAs. A control location describes a working TA, and the stack presents a pile of interrupted TAs. A NeTA can either behaves as the top TA in the stack, or switches from one TA to another by pushing, popping, or changing the top TA of the stack. It is a natural model for analyzing real-time systems with context switches, e.g., interrupt systems. The reachability problem for NeTAs is shown to be decidable.

Updatable timed automata (UTAs) [3] are extensions of TAs having the ability to update clocks in a more elaborate way (i.e. increment and decrement) besides the normal operations. The reachability problem of UTAs is undecidable, which can be easily verified by encoding two counter machine with UTAs. However, there are still many decidable subclasses of UTAs by restricting the expressive power. Among them, *updatable timed automata with one updatable clock (UTA1s)* [4] is an interesting decidable subclass by restricting the number of updatable clocks to be one.

The aim of this paper is to combine NeTAs and UTA1s as a new model and to study the verification problems. More precisely, we replace TAs in NeTAs with

© Springer International Publishing AG 2017
S. Liu et al. (Eds.): SOFL+MSVL 2016, LNCS 10189, pp. 15–31, 2017.
DOI: 10.1007/978-3-319-57708-1_2

UTA1s and thus get *nested updatable timed automata (NeUTAs)*. Such kind of model is suitable for soft real-time system analysis, since the updatable clock of each UTA1 is used to describe the soft deadline, which is adjusted due to different environment. Termination and boundedness of the model are proved to be decidable, by encoding NeUTAs to *vector pushdown systems*, after digitizing dense time. The properties of the latter model are proved to be decidable by extending the reduced reachability tree proof technique of *pushdown vector addition systems* [5]. Note that pushdown vector addition systems assume the set of locations is a WQO, while the stack alphabet is finite. vector pushdown systems assume the set of locations is finite, while stack alphabet is a WQO.

Related Work. Timed automata (TAs) [6], proposed by Alur and Dill, are finite automata augmented with a finite set of clocks. Clocks can be used to record precisely how much time has elapsed in a dense manner and constrain the behaviour of the model. Although the theory of timed automata is successful in modeling and analyzing real-time systems with a large number of problems having been studied, it is so low-level that it is hard to apply it to verification of systems in reality directly. Actually many researchers are devoted to study subclasses or extensions of timed automata.

Hybrid automata [7–9] can be regarded as a generalization of timed automata. It is a mathematical model for mixed discrete-continuous systems, in which a discrete problem is embedded in continuous changing environments. The decidability of reachability problem is undecidable for general hybrid automata, while initialized rectangular automata form a maximum decidable subclass of hybrid automata that lies in the boundary of decidability.

Dense timed pushdown automata (DTPDAs) [10] play an essential role of the prove in this paper. DTPDAs extend timed automata with an additional stack, where a stack symbol with an age can be pushed to the stack. When time elapses, all clocks together with ages in the stack proceed uniformly. When popping, the value of the age in the top stack frame can be checked. The reachability problem for DTPDAs is shown to be EXPTIME-complete.

Interrupt timed automata (ITAs) [11,12] intend to model timed multi-task systems with different priority levels. As extensions of TAs, each control state in ITAs is in an interrupt level, ranged from 1 to n, with exactly one active clock recording time in each interrupt level. When ITAs are in a given interrupt level, all clocks of lower interrupt levels are suspended and those of higher interrupt levels are undefined. The reachability problem for ITAs is shown to be in NEX-PTIME and PTIME when the number of clocks is fixed. Though both ITAs and NeTAs can be used to model interrupt systems, they are different in what they are focus on. ITAs focus on the interrupt level, while NeTAs focus on context switches.

Paper Organization. The remainder of this paper is structured as follows: In Sect. 2 we introduce basic notations and models. Section 3 defines syntax and the semantics of UDTPDA1s. Section 4 shows that the termination and boundedness of UDTPDA1s are decidable. Section 5 introduces NeUTAs and shows the decidability on termination and boundedness by encoding NeUTAs to UDTPDA1s. Section 6 concludes this paper with summarized results.

2   Preliminaries

Let $\mathbb{R}^{\geq 0}$ and $\mathbb{N}$ be the sets of non-negative real and natural numbers, respectively. Let $\mathbb{N}_\omega := \mathbb{N} \cup \{\omega\}$, where ω is the least limit ordinal. $\mathcal{I}$ denotes the set of *intervals*, which are (a, b), $[a, b]$, $[a, b)$ or $(a, b]$ for $a \in \mathbb{N}$ and $b \in \mathbb{N}_\omega$.

Let $X = \{x_1, \ldots, x_n\}$ be a finite set of *clocks*. A *clock valuation* $\nu : X \to \mathbb{R}^{\geq 0}$, assigns a value to each clock $x \in X$. ν_0 denotes the clock valuation assigning each clock in X to 0. Given a clock valuation ν and a time $t \in \mathbb{R}^{\geq 0}$, $(\nu + t)$ $(x) = \nu(x) + t$, for $x \in X$. A clock assignment function $\nu[y \leftarrow b]$ is defined by $\nu[y \leftarrow b](x) = b$ if $x = y$, and $\nu(x)$ otherwise. Further, multiple clock assignment function $\nu[y_1 \leftarrow b_1, \cdots, y_n \leftarrow b_n]$ is defined by $\nu[y_1 \leftarrow b_1, \cdots, y_n \leftarrow b_n](x) = b_i$ if $x = y_i$ for $1 \leq i \leq n$, and $\nu(x)$ otherwise. $Val(X)$ is used to denote the set of clock valuation of X.

For finite words $w = aw'$, we denote $a = head(w)$ and $w' = tail(w)$. The concatenation of two words w, v is denoted by $w.v$, and ϵ is the empty word. we denote the set of finite multisets over D by $\mathcal{MP}(D)$, and the union of two multisets M, M' by $M \uplus M'$. We regard a finite set as a multiset with the multiplicity 1, and a finite word as a multiset by ignoring the ordering.

2.1   Updatable Timed Automata

Updatable timed automata (UTAs) [13,14] are extensions of timed automata, based on the possibility to update the clocks in a elaborate way such as increment and decrement operations and assignments to arbitrary values. However, generally, the reachability problem of updatable timed automata is undecidable. Several decidable subclasses are investigated, based on restriction on the update abilities [3]. In [4], we proposed another decidable subclass by restricting the number of updatable clocks to be one. We will adopt the restriction in the following content paper.

Definition 1 (Updatable Timed Automata with One Updatable Clock). *An updatable timed automaton with one updatable clock (UTA1) is a tuple $\mathcal{A} = \langle Q, q_0, X, c, \Delta \rangle$, where*

- *Q is a finite set of control locations, with the initial control location $q_0 \in Q$,*
- *$X = \{x_1, \ldots, x_k\}$ is a finite set of normal clocks, and c is the singleton updatable clock,*
- *$\Delta \subseteq Q \times Actions_\mathcal{A}^+ \times Q$ is a finite set of actions. A (discrete) transition $\delta \in \Delta$ is a sequence of actions $(q_1, \phi_1, q_2) \ldots (q_i, \phi_i, q_{i+1})$, written as $q_1 \xrightarrow{\phi_1; \ldots; \phi_i} q_{i+1}$, in which ϕ_j (for $1 \leq j \leq i$) is one of the following*

Local ϵ, *an* empty *operation*,
Test $x \in I?$, *where* $x \in X \cup \{c\}$ *is a clock and* $I \in \mathcal{I}$ *is an interval*,
Assignment $x \leftarrow I$, *where* $x \in X \cup \{c\}$ *and* $I \in \mathcal{I}$,
Increment $c := c + 1$, *and*
Decrement $c := c - 1$.

Similar to the definitions in [2], for an easier encoding later, a transition as a sequence of actions $q_1 \xrightarrow{\phi_1; \cdots; \phi_i} q_{i+1}$ prohibits interleaving time progress. This can be encoded with an extra clock by resetting it to 0 and checking it still 0 after transitions, and introducing fresh control states.

Given a UTA1 $\mathcal{A} \in \mathscr{A}$, we use $Q(\mathcal{A})$, $q_0(\mathcal{A})$, $X(\mathcal{A})$, $c(\mathcal{A})$ and $\Delta(\mathcal{A})$ to represent the set of control locations, the initial location, the set of normal clocks, the updatable clock and the set of actions, respectively. We will use similar notations throughout the paper.

Definition 2 (Semantics of UTA1s). *Given a UTA1* $\mathcal{A} = \langle Q, q_0, X, c, \Delta \rangle$, *a configuration is a pair* (q, ν) *of a control location* $q \in Q$, *and a clock valuation* ν *on* $X \cup \{c\}$. *The transition relation of the UTA1 is represented as follows,*

- *Progress transition:* $(q, \nu) \xrightarrow{t} (q, \nu + t)$, *where* $t \in \mathbb{R}^{\geq 0}$.
- *Discrete transition:* $(q_1, \nu_1) \xrightarrow{\phi} (q_2, \nu_2)$, *if* $q_1 \xrightarrow{\phi} q_2 \in \Delta$, *and one of the following holds,*
  - **Local** $\phi = \epsilon$, *then* $\nu_1 = \nu_2$. *This operation only changes the control location and leaves the clock valuation unaltered.*
  - **Test** $\phi = x \in I?$, $\nu_1 = \nu_2$ *and* $\nu_2(x) \in I$ *holds. The transition can be performed only if the value of* x *belongs to* I.
  - **Assignment** $\phi = x \leftarrow I$, $\nu_2 = \nu_1[x \leftarrow r]$ *where* $r \in I$. *Clock* x *is assigned to a non-deterministic value in* I.
  - **Increment** $\phi = c := c + 1$, $\nu_2 = \nu_1[c \leftarrow \nu_1(c) + 1]$. *The value of the updatable clock* c *is incremented by 1.*
  - **Decrement** $\phi = c := c - 1$, $\nu_2 = \nu_1[c \leftarrow \nu_1(c) - 1]$ *and* $\nu_1(c) \geq 1$ *holds. The value of the updatable clock* c *is decremented by 1.*

The initial configuration is (q_0, ν_0).

Proposition 1. *The reachability problem of UTA1 under diagonal-free constraints is decidable [4].*

2.2   Dense Timed Pushdown Automata

Dense timed pushdown automata [2,10] extend timed pushdown automata with time updating in the stack. Each symbol in the stack is equipped with a local clock named an *age*, and all ages in the stack proceed uniformly. An age in each context is assigned to the value of a clock when a push action occurs. A pop action pops the top symbol to assign the value of its age to a specified clock.

Definition 3 (Dense Timed Pushdown Automata). *A dense timed pushdown automaton is a tuple* $\mathcal{D} = \langle Q, q_0, \Gamma, X, \Delta \rangle \in \mathscr{D}$, *where*

- Q is a finite set of control locations with the initial control location $q_0 \in Q$,
- Γ is a finite stack alphabet,
- X is a finite set of clocks, and
- $\Delta \subseteq Q \times Actions_D^+ \times Q$ is a finite set of actions.

A (discrete) transition $\delta \in \Delta$ is a sequence of actions $(q_1, \varphi_1, q_2), \cdots, (q_i, \varphi_i, q_{i+1})$ written as $q_1 \xrightarrow{\varphi_1; \cdots; \varphi_i} q_{i+1}$, in which φ_j (for $1 \leq j \leq i$) is one of the followings,

- **Local** ϵ, an empty operation,
- **Test** $x \in I?$, where $x \in X$ is a clock and $I \in \mathcal{I}$ is an interval,
- **Assign** $x \leftarrow I$ where $x \in X$ and $I \in \mathcal{I}$,
- **Push** $push(\gamma, x)$, where $\gamma \in \Gamma$ is a stack symbol and $x \in X$, and
- **Pop** $pop(\gamma, x)$, where $\gamma \in \Gamma$ is a stack symbol and $x \in X$.

Definition 4 (Semantics of DTPDAs). For a dense timed pushdown automaton $\langle Q, q_0, \Gamma, X, \Delta \rangle$, a configuration is a triplet (q, w, ν) with a control location $q \in Q$, a stack $w \in (\Gamma \times \mathbb{R}^{\geq 0})^*$, and a clock valuation ν on X. In a stack $w = (\gamma_1, t_1). \cdots .(\gamma_n, t_n)$, γ_i is a stack symbol and t_i is an age. t-time passage on the stack increases all ages in the stack by the same value, which is denoted by $w + t = (\gamma_1, t_1 + t). \cdots .(\gamma_n, t_n + t)$. The transition relation of a DTPDA is represented as follows.

- Progress transition: $(q, w, \nu) \xrightarrow{t}_{\mathscr{D}} (q, w + t, \nu + t)$, where $t \in \mathbb{R}^{\geq 0}$. When time elapses, all clocks together with all ages in the stack proceed uniformly.
- Discrete transition: $(q_1, w_1, \nu_1) \xrightarrow{\varphi}_{\mathscr{D}} (q_2, w_2, \nu_2)$, if $q_1 \xrightarrow{\varphi} q_2$, and one of the following holds,
  - **Local** $\varphi = \epsilon$, then $w_1 = w_2$, and $\nu_1 = \nu_2$.
  - **Test** $\varphi = x \in I?$, then $w_1 = w_2$, $\nu_1 = \nu_2$ and $\nu_1(x) \in I$ holds.
  - **Assign** $\varphi = x \leftarrow I$, then $w_1 = w_2$, $\nu_2 = \nu_1[x \leftarrow r]$ where $r \in I$.
  - **Push** $\varphi = push(\gamma, x)$, then $\nu_1 = \nu_2$, $w_2 = (\gamma, \nu_1(x)).w_1$. The stack symbol γ and an age of the value of clock x are pushed to the stack.
  - **Pop** $\varphi = pop(\gamma, x)$, then $\nu_2 = \nu_1[x \leftarrow t]$, $w_1 = (\gamma, t).w_2$. The top stack frame (γ, t) is popped from the stack and the clock x is assigned with the value of the age t.

The initial configuration $\varrho_0 = (q_0, \epsilon, \nu_0)$.

Remark 1. For simplicity of the later proofs, the definition of DTPDAs follows Definition 1 in [2], slightly modified from the original [10]. The former can encode the later easily.

3   Updatable Dense Timed Pushdown Automata

An updatable dense timed pushdown automaton with one updatable clock (UDTPDA1) is different from Definition 3 at:

- besides the set X of normal clocks (of the fixed number k), an updatable clock c is introduced. We refer to the normal clocks as $x_1, x_2, ..., x_k$ and sometimes we refer to the updatable clock c as x_0 for simplicity.
- a tuple of ages (for simplicity, we fix the length of a tuple to be $k + 1$) is pushed on the stack and/or popped from the stack.

Definition 5 (UDTPDA1s). *A UDTPDA1 is a tuple $\mathcal{U} = \langle S, s_0, \Gamma, X, c, \Delta \rangle \in \mathcal{U}$, where*

- *S is a finite set of control locations with the initial control location $s_0 \in S$,*
- *Γ is a finite stack alphabet,*
- *X is a finite set of local clocks (with $|X| = k$),*
- *c is the singleton updatable clock and*
- *$\Delta \subseteq S \times Action_{\mathcal{U}}^+ \times S$ is a finite set of actions.*

A (discrete) transition $\delta \in \Delta$ is a sequence of actions $(s_1, \varphi_1, s_2), \cdots, (s_i, \varphi_i, s_{i+1})$ written as $s_1 \xrightarrow{\varphi_1; \cdots ; \varphi_i} s_{i+1}$, in which φ_j (for $1 \leq j \leq i$) is one of the followings,

- **Local** *ϵ, an empty operation,*
- **Test** *$x \in I?$, where $x \in X \cup \{c\}$ is a clock and $I \in \mathcal{I}$ is an interval,*
- **Assign** *$x \leftarrow I$ where $x \in X \cup \{c\}$ and $I \in \mathcal{I}$,*
- **Increment** *$c := c + 1$,*
- **Decrement** *$c := c - 1$,*
- **Push** *$push(\gamma)$, where $\gamma \in \Gamma$, and*
- **Pop** *$pop(\gamma)$, where $\gamma \in \Gamma$.*

Definition 6 (Semantics of UDTPDA1s). *For a UDTPDA1 $\langle S, s_0, \Gamma, X, c, \Delta \rangle$, a configuration is a triplet (s, w, ν) with a control location $s \in S$, a stack $w \in (\Gamma \times (\mathbb{R}^{\geq 0})^{k+1})^*$, and a clock valuation ν on $X \cup \{c\}$. In a stack $w = (\gamma_1, \bar{t}_1). \cdots .(\gamma_n, \bar{t}_n)$, γ_i is a stack symbol and $\bar{t}_i = (t_i^0, \cdots, t_i^k)$ is a $k + 1$-tuple of ages. t-time passage on the stack increases all ages in the stack by the same value t, which is denoted by $w + t = (\gamma_1, \bar{t}_1 + t). \cdots .(\gamma_n, \bar{t}_n + t)$ where $\bar{t}_i + t = (t_i^0 + t, \cdots, t_i^k + t)$.*

The transition relation of a UDTPDA1 is represented as follows.

- *Time progress: $(s, w, \nu) \xrightarrow{t}_{\mathcal{U}} (s, w + t, \nu + t)$, where $t \in \mathbb{R}^{\geq 0}$.*
- *Discrete transition: $(s_1, w_1, \nu_1) \xrightarrow{\varphi}_{\mathcal{U}} (s_2, w_2, \nu_2)$, if $s_1 \xrightarrow{\varphi} s_2$, and one of the following holds,*
  - **Local** *$\varphi = \epsilon$, then $w_1 = w_2$, and $\nu_1 = \nu_2$.*
  - **Test** *$\varphi = x \in I?$, then $w_1 = w_2$, $\nu_1 = \nu_2$, and $\nu_1(x) \in I$ holds.*
  - **Assign** *$\varphi = x \leftarrow I$, then $w_1 = w_2$, $\nu_2 = \nu_1[x \leftarrow r]$ where $r \in I$.*
  - **Increment** *$c := c + 1$, then $w_1 = w_2$, and $\nu_2 = \nu_1[c \leftarrow \nu_1(c) + 1]$,*
  - **Decrement** *$c := c - 1$, then $w_1 = w_2$, $\nu_2 = \nu_1[c \leftarrow \nu_1(c) - 1]$ and $\nu_1(c) \geq 1$ holds,*
  - **Push** *$\varphi = push(\gamma)$, then $\nu_2 = \nu_0$, $w_2 = (\gamma, (\nu_1(c), \nu_1(x_1), \cdots, \nu_1(x_k))).w_1$ for $X = \{x_1, \cdots, x_k\}$. The values of $k+1$ clocks are pushed as ages in the stack.*

- **Pop** $\varphi = pop(\gamma)$, then $\nu_2 = \nu_1[c \leftarrow t_0, x_1 \leftarrow t_1, \cdots, x_k \leftarrow t_k]$, $w_1 = (\gamma, (t_0, \cdots, t_k)).w_2$. The values of $k{+}1$ clocks are recovered with ages in the top stack frame.

The initial configuration $\varrho_0 = (s_0, \epsilon, \nu_0)$. We use $\hookrightarrow$ to range over these transitions, and $\hookrightarrow^*$ is the reflexive and transitive closure of $\hookrightarrow$.

Example 1. The figure shows transitions $\varrho_1 \hookrightarrow \varrho_2 \hookrightarrow \varrho_3 \hookrightarrow \varrho_4$ of a UDTPDA1 with $S = \{\bullet\}$ (omitted in the figure), $X = \{x_1, x_2\}$ and $\Gamma = \{a, b, d\}$. All values which are changed in a transition are in bold. At $\varrho_1 \hookrightarrow \varrho_2$, the values of c, x_1 and x_2 (2.3, 0.5 and 3.9) are pushed to the stack with d. After pushing, value of c, x_1 and x_2 will be reset to zero, At $\varrho_2 \hookrightarrow \varrho_3$, time elapses 2.6. At $\varrho_3 \hookrightarrow \varrho_4$, a increment occurs which increases the value of c from 2.6 to 3.6.

	$(d, (\mathbf{2.3}, \mathbf{0.5}, \mathbf{3.9}))$	$(d, (\mathbf{4.9}, \mathbf{3.1}, \mathbf{6.5}))$	$(d, (4.9, 3.1, 6.5))$
$(a, (1.5, 1.9, 4.5))$	$(a, (1.5, 1.9, 4.5))$	$(a, (\mathbf{4.1}, \mathbf{4.5}, \mathbf{7.1}))$	$(a, (4.1, 4.5, 7.1))$
$(b, (3.2, 6.7, 2.9))$	$(b, (3.2, 6.7, 2.9))$	$(b, (\mathbf{5.8}, \mathbf{9.3}, \mathbf{5.5}))$	$(b, (5.8, 9.3, 5.5))$
$(a, (3.3, 3.1, 5.2))$	$(a, (3.3, 3.1, 5.2))$	$(a, (\mathbf{5.9}, \mathbf{5.7}, \mathbf{7.8}))$	$(a, (5.9, 5.7, 7.8))$
$(d, (2.7, 4.2, 3.3))$	$(d, (2.7, 4.2, 3.3))$	$(d, (\mathbf{5.3}, \mathbf{6.8}, \mathbf{5.9}))$	$(d, (5.3, 6.8, 5.9))$

$c \leftarrow 2.3$	$c \leftarrow 0$	$c \leftarrow \mathbf{2.6}$	$c \leftarrow \mathbf{3.6}$
$x_1 \leftarrow 0.5$	$x_1 \leftarrow 0$	$x_1 \leftarrow \mathbf{2.6}$	$x_1 \leftarrow 2.6$
$x_2 \leftarrow 3.9$	$x_2 \leftarrow 0$	$x_2 \leftarrow \mathbf{2.6}$	$x_2 \leftarrow 2.6$

$$\varrho_1 \xrightarrow{\;\;push(d)\;\;}_{\mathcal{U}} \varrho_2 \xrightarrow{\;\;2.6\;\;}_{\mathcal{U}} \varrho_3 \xrightarrow{\;\;c := c+1\;\;}_{\mathcal{U}} \varrho_4$$

4 Termination and Boundedness of UDTPDA1s

In this section, we show that the termination and boundedness of UDTPDA1s are decidable. We first introduce vector pushdown systems and prove its decidability on termination and boundedness. Then we describe the digitization technique in UDTPDA1s using *digitized configuration* and its operations, which intend to simulate configurations and transitions of UDTPDA1s, respectively. Finally, the specific encoding from a UDTPDA1 to a snapshot vector pushdown system is given.

4.1 Vector Pushdown Systems

Definition 7 (Vector Pushdown Systems). *A vector pushdown system is a tuple $\mathcal{P} = (Q, \Gamma, \mathbb{N}^k, \Delta)$, where Q is a finite set of states, Γ is a finite stack alphabet, $\mathbb{N}^k$ is k-dimension natural number vectors, and $\Delta \subseteq P \times (\Gamma \times \mathbb{N}^k)^{\leq 2} \times P \times (\Gamma \times \mathbb{N}^k)^{\leq 2}$. We use $\alpha, \beta, \gamma, \cdots$ to range over $\Gamma \times \mathbb{N}^k$, and $w, v, \cdots$ over words in $(\Gamma \times \mathbb{N}^k)^*$.*

A configuration of $\mathcal{P}$ is a pair $\langle q, w \rangle$, where a state $q \in Q$ and a stack $w \in (\Gamma \times \mathbb{N})^*$. A transition relation $\Longrightarrow$ between configurations of $\mathcal{P}$ is defined by

$$\frac{(p, \gamma \to p', \gamma') \in \Delta}{\langle p, \gamma w \rangle \hookrightarrow \langle p', \gamma' w \rangle} \text{ INTER} \qquad \frac{(p, \gamma \to p', \alpha\beta) \in \Delta}{\langle p, \gamma w \rangle \hookrightarrow \langle p', \alpha\beta w \rangle} \text{ PUSH}$$

$$\frac{(p, \gamma \to p', \epsilon) \in \Delta}{\langle p, \gamma w \rangle \hookrightarrow \langle p', w \rangle} \text{ POP} \qquad \frac{(p, \epsilon \to p', \alpha) \in \Delta}{\langle p, w \rangle \hookrightarrow \langle p', \alpha w \rangle} \text{ SIMPLE-PUSH}$$

$$\frac{(p, \alpha\beta \to p', \gamma) \in \Delta}{\langle p, \alpha\beta w \rangle \hookrightarrow \langle p', \gamma w \rangle} \quad \text{Nonstandard-Pop}$$

Remark 2. In a pushdown system, the Simple-Push and Nonstandard-Pop rules can be encoded by other three rules. However, in a vector pushdown system, since the stack symbols in $\Gamma \times \mathbb{N}^k$ are essential unbounded, thus all of the five rules are necessary.

Let $|w|$ denotes the length of word w and $w[i]$ denotes the i-th symbol in w. The *head* $h(p, w)$ of a configuration $\langle p, w \rangle$ is $(p, w[1])$ if $w \neq \epsilon$; otherwise, $h(p, w) = (p, \perp)$. Since a finite set is well-quasi-ordered and $(\mathbb{N}^k, \leq)$ is well-quasi-ordered, by Dickson's Lemma, we can obtain the set of heads of configurations is well-quasi-ordered.

Besides, we denote $a_1 a_2 \ldots a_m \ll b_1 b_2 \ldots b_n$, if $m = n$ and, for each i, $a_i \leq b_i$ holds, and $w \ll v$ if $w \ll v$ and $w \neq v$.

The *reachability tree* of a VPS $\mathcal{V} = (Q, \Gamma, \mathbb{N}^k, \Delta)$ with an initial configuration c_0 is a rooted unordered tree defined as follows. Each node of the tree is labeled by a configuration of $\mathcal{V}$. The root r is labeled by the initial configuration c_0, denoted by $r : c_0$. Each node $n : c_n$ has a child $m : c_m$ when $c_n \hookrightarrow c_m$. Note that the reachability tree of $\mathcal{V}$ is finitely branching since Δ is finite.

Termination Problem. The termination problem asks whether all runs of a given system are finite, we have the following definition.

Definition 8. *A node $s : \langle p, w \rangle$ pumps a node $t : \langle q, v \rangle$ if*

- *there is a path from s to t, and every node $t' : \langle p', w' \rangle$ on it satisfies $|w'| \geq |w|$.*
- *$h(\langle p, w \rangle) \unlhd h(\langle q, v \rangle)$, i.e., $p \preceq q$ and either $w = \epsilon$ or $w[1] \leq v[1]$.*

We call a node *pumpable* if there exists a node pumping it. The notion of pumpable nodes is similar to *subsumed nodes* in [5], but we consider the increase of heads instead of states. Let *the reduced reachability tree* be the largest prefix of the reachability tree such that every *pumpable node* has no children.

The intuition of pumpable nodes is that if the run from $\langle p, w \rangle$ to $\langle q, v \rangle$ only changes the top element of w, then we can simulate this run from $\langle q, v \rangle$ to some $\langle q', v' \rangle$ by monotonicity, satisfying $p \preceq q \preceq q'$, and $w[1] \leq v[1] \leq v'[1]$. We can construct an infinite run by repeating this process.

Conversely, assume $\langle p_0, w_0 \rangle \hookrightarrow \langle p_1, w_1 \rangle \cdots$ is an infinite run, we can extract an infinite subsequence, say $\langle p_{i_0}, w_{i_0} \rangle, \langle p_{i_1}, w_{i_1} \rangle, \cdots$, such that each node is chosen if it has the minimal depth of the stack in its suffix run. Note that each pair of $\langle p_{i_k}, w_{i_k} \rangle$ and $\langle p_{i_j}, w_{i_j} \rangle$ with $k < j$ in this subsequence satisfies the first condition of *pumpable nodes*. By the fact that the set of heads is well-quasi-ordered, it must contain a *pumpable node*.

Theorem 1. *A VPS has an infinite run if, and only if, its reduced reachability tree contains a pumpable node.*

Boundedness Problem. The boundedness asks whether the reachability set is finite. We know that any infinite run has a pumpable node. If a pumpable node is exactly the same as the one that pumps it, still an infinite run keeps the reachability set finite. Otherwise, a VPS enlarges reachable configurations infinitely.

Definition 9. *A node* $s : \langle p, w \rangle$ *strictly pumps a node* $t : \langle q, v \rangle$ *if* s *pumps* t, *and either* $|w| < |v|$ *or* $h(\langle p, w \rangle) \triangleleft h(\langle q, v \rangle)$.

Theorem 2. *A VPS has an infinite reachability set if, and only if, its reduced reachability tree contains a strictly pumpable node.*

Proof. **(Only-if)** Assume a VPS $\mathcal{V}$ has an infinite reachability set. Let $\mathcal{T}$ be the largest prefix of its reachability tree such that, on each branch, all nodes have distinct labels. The tree $\mathcal{T}$ is infinite since every configuration in the reachability set is a node in $\mathcal{T}$.

By König's lemma, it follows that $\mathcal{T}$ contains finitely many branches in which all nodes are distinct. Since the reduced reachability tree of $\mathcal{V}$ is finite, among finitely many branches, there are two nodes $n : (p, w)$ and $m : (q, v)$ such that they are in the reduced reachability tree and n pumps m.

Thus, $(p, w) \neq (q, v)$ and (p, w) pumps (q, v). By definition of pumpable nodes, we have two cases: (1) $|w| < |v|$, and (2) $|w| = |v|$. In case (2), either $w \ll v$ or $p \prec q$ holds. $w[2, |w|] = v[2, |v|]$ implies either $w[1] < v[1]$ or $p \prec q$. Thus, both cases, n strictly pumps m.

(If) Similar to that of Theorem 1. The path from the root to a strictly pumpable node yields a run

$$(p_0, w_0) \xrightarrow{op_1} \ldots \xrightarrow{op_k} (p_k, w_k) \xrightarrow{op_{k+1}} \ldots \xrightarrow{op_l} (p_l, w_l)$$

such that (p_k, w_k) strictly pumps (p_l, w_l), which leads an infinite run by iterating the sequence of operations $op_{k+1}, ..., op_l$. As the case analysis, if $|w| < |v|$, the resulting infinite run enlarges the length of the stack infinitely; if $w[1] < v[1]$, the resulting infinite run enlarges the top element of the stack infinitely.

4.2   Digitized Configuration and Its Operations

Let $\langle S, s_0, \Gamma, X, c, \Delta \rangle$ be a UDTPDA1, and let n be the largest integer (except for ω) appearing in Δ. For $v \in \mathbb{R}^{\geq 0}$, $proj(v) = \mathbf{r}_i$ if $v \in \mathbf{r}_i \in Intv(n)$, where

$$Intv(n) = \{\mathbf{r}_{2i} = [i, i] \mid 0 \leq i \leq n\} \cup \{\mathbf{r}_{2i+1} = (i, i+1) \mid 0 \leq i < n\} \cup \{\mathbf{r}_{2n+1} = (n, \omega)\}$$

The idea of the next digitization is inspired by [15–17].

Definition 10 (Digitization). *Let* $frac(t) = t - floor(t)$ *for* $t \in \mathbb{R}^{\geq 0}$. *A digitization function* $\mathtt{digi} : \mathcal{MP}((\{c\} \cup X \cup \Gamma) \times \mathbb{R}^{\geq 0}) \to \mathcal{MP}((\{c\} \cup X \cup \Gamma) \times Intv(n))^*$ *is defined as follows.*

For $\bar{y} \in \mathcal{MP}((\{c\} \cup X \cup \Gamma) \times \mathbb{R}^{\geq 0})$, *let* $Y_0, Y_1, \cdots, Y_m$ *be multisets that collect* $(x, proj(t))$'s *having the same* $frac(x, t)$ *for* $(x, t) \in \bar{y}$. *Among them,*

Y_0 *(which is possibly empty) is reserved for the collection of* $(x, proj(t))$ *with* $frac(t) = 0$. *We assume that* Y_i*'s except for* Y_0 *is non-empty (i.e.,* $Y_i = \emptyset$ *with* $i > 0$ *is omitted), and* Y_i*'s are sorted by the increasing order of* $frac(t)$ *(i.e.,* $frac(t) < frac(t')$ *for* $(x, proj(t)) \in Y_i$ *and* $(x', proj(t')) \in Y_{i+1}$*). Thus,* $\mathtt{digi}(\bar{\mathcal{Y}})$ *is a word* $\bar{Y} = Y_0 Y_1 \cdots Y_m$.

For a stack frame $v = (\gamma, (t_0, \cdots, t_k))$ of a UDTPDA1, we denote a word $(\gamma, t_0) \cdots (\gamma, t_k)$ by $dist(v)$. Given a clock valuation ν, we denote a clock word $(c, \nu(c))(x_1, \nu(x_1)) \ldots (x_n, \nu(x_k))$ by $time(\nu)$ where c is the singleton updatable clock and $x_i \in X$ for $1 \leq i \leq k$.

Example 2. In Example 1, we assume $n = 6$ and have 13 intervals illustrated below.

$$0 \ \ r_1 \ 1 \ r_3 \ \ 2 \ r_5 \ \ 3 \ r_7 \ \ 4 \ r_9 \ \ 5 \ r_{11} \ 6 \ \ \ r_{13}$$

$$r_0 \quad\quad r_2 \quad\quad r_4 \quad\quad r_6 \quad\quad r_8 \quad\quad r_{10} \quad\quad r_{12}$$

For the configuration $\varrho_1 = (\bullet, v_4 \cdots v_1, \nu)$ in Example 1, let $\bar{\mathcal{Y}} = dist(v_4) \uplus time(\nu)$ be a word, and $\bar{Y} = \mathtt{digi}(\bar{\mathcal{Y}})$, then

$$\bar{\mathcal{Y}} = \{(a, 1.5), (a, 1.9), (a, 4.5), (c, 2.3), (x_1, 0.5), (x_2, 3.9)\}$$
$$\bar{Y} = \{\}\{(c, r_5)\}\{(x_1, r_1), (a, r_3), (a, r_9)\}\{(x_2, r_7), (a, r_3)\}$$

Definition 11 (Digiword). *A word* $\bar{Y} \in \mathcal{MP}((\{c\} \cup X \cup \Gamma) \times Intv(n))^*$ *is a* digiword *if the following is satisfied:*

- *Let a* $k + 1$*-pointer* $\bar{p}$ *of* $\bar{U}$ *is a tuple of* $k + 1$ *pointers to mutually different* $k + 1$ *elements in* $\bar{U}$. *Then there are a pair of* $k + 1$*-pointers* $(\bar{p}_1, \bar{p}_2)$ *in* $\bar{Y}$ *that point to clocks and ages in the topmost stack frame, respectively.*
- *For every element in* $\bar{Y}$, *either* $\bar{p}_1$ *or* $\bar{p}_2$ *points to it.*

We refer the element $(\gamma, \mathbf{r})$ *pointed by the* i*-th pointer by* $\bar{p}[i]$ *where* $0 \leq i \leq k$. *Let the set Digi contains all digiwords. Digi is a finite set by observing that at most* $2k + 2$ *elements exist in a digiword.*

A digiword $\bar{Y}$ intends to be the digitization of the current clock valuation (pointed by $\bar{p}_1$) and the topmost stack frame (pointed by $\bar{p}_2$) in a UDTPDA1. More precisely, for $0 \leq i \leq k$, $\bar{p}_1[i]$ points to $(x_i, proj(\nu(x_i)))$ for $(x_i, \nu(x_i)) \in time(\nu)$ where ν is the clock valuation and $\bar{p}_2[i]$ points to $(\gamma, proj(t_i))$ for $(\gamma, t_i) \in dist(v)$ where v is the topmost stack frame.

Definition 12 (Digitized Configuration). *A* digitized configuration *is a tuple* $\bar{U} \in Digi \times \mathbb{N}^2$, *which contains a digiword and a pair of natural numbers. The pair of natural numbers intend to roughly record the time passage when the value of updatable clocks in the current clock valuation and the topmost stack frame exceed the maximum integer* n. *Each time the updatable clocks value exceeds* n *and meanwhile its value changes between integer and non-integer with time elapsing, we increase the corresponding natural number by one.*

Example 3. The word $\bar{Y}$ in Example 2 can be extended to a digitized configuration $\bar{U}$ by adding a pair of 3-pointers $(\bar{\rho}_1, \bar{\rho}_2)$ (pointers are marked with the numbered overlines and underlines). and a pair of numbers $(0,0)$.

$$\bar{U} = (\{\}\{\overline{(c, \mathbf{r}_5)}^0\}\{\overline{(x_1, \mathbf{r}_1)}^1, \underline{(a, \mathbf{r}_3)}_0, \underline{(a, \mathbf{r}_9)}_2\}\{\overline{(x_2, \mathbf{r}_7)}^2, \underline{(a, \mathbf{r}_3)}_1\}, 0, 0)$$

Pointers are given more explicitly below:

$\bar{\rho}_1(0) = (c, \mathbf{r}_5) \quad \bar{\rho}_1(1) = (x_1, \mathbf{r}_1) \quad \bar{\rho}_1(2) = (x_2, \mathbf{r}_7)$

$\bar{\rho}_2(0) = (a, \mathbf{r}_3) \quad \bar{\rho}_2(1) = (a, \mathbf{r}_3) \quad \bar{\rho}_2(2) = (a, \mathbf{r}_9)$

Definition 13 (Operations on Digitized Configuration). *Let* $\bar{U} = (Y_0 \cdots Y_m, num_1, num_2), \bar{U}' = (Y_0' \cdots Y_{m'}', num_1', num_2'), \bar{V} = (Y_0'' \cdots Y_m'', num_1'', num_2'') \in Digi \times \mathbb{N}^2$ *are digitized configurations such that* $\bar{U}$ *(resp.* $\bar{U}'$ *and* $\bar{V}$*) has a pair of* $k+1$*-pointers* $(\bar{\rho}_1, \bar{\rho}_2)$ *(resp.* $(\bar{\rho}_1', \bar{\rho}_2')$ *and* $(\bar{\rho}_1'', \bar{\rho}_2'')$*). We define operations as follows which are used to simulate transitions of UDTPDA1s in the next subsection. Note that except for* **Rotate, Map,** *and* **Propogate,** *the* $k+1$*-pointers* $\bar{\rho}_1$ *is changed corresponding to the operation to ensure that properties of digiwords are still satisfied after operations. Namely when an element is removed, the pointer which points to it is set to empty. And when an element* $(x_i, \mathbf{r})$ *for* $x_i \in \{c\} \cup X$ *is added, the pointer* $\bar{\rho}_1[i]$ *is modified to point to that new element.*

- **Insert$_x$:** *insert$_x$($\bar{U}, (x, \mathbf{r}_i)$) for* $x \in X$ *inserts* $(x, \mathbf{r}_i)$ *to* $\bar{U}$ *(may nondeterministically) at*

$$\begin{cases} \text{either put into } Y_j \text{ for } j > 0, \text{ or} \\ \qquad \text{put the singleton set } \{(x, \mathbf{r}_i)\} \text{ at any place after } Y_0 \quad \text{if } i \text{ is odd} \\ \text{put into } Y_0 \qquad\qquad\qquad\qquad\qquad\qquad\qquad\qquad\quad \text{if } i \text{ is even} \end{cases}$$

- **Insert$_c$:** *insert$_c$($\bar{U}, (c, \mathbf{r}_i)$) for the updatable clock* c *inserts* $(c, \mathbf{r}_i)$ *to* $\bar{U}$ *and updates natural number* num_1 *in one of three following ways:*

$$\begin{cases} (1) \text{ either put } (c, \mathbf{r}_i) \text{ into } Y_j \text{ for } j > 0, \text{ or} \\ \quad \text{put the singleton set } \{(c, \mathbf{r}_i)\} \text{ at any place after } Y_0 \\ \quad \text{and } num_1 = 0 \qquad\qquad\qquad\qquad\qquad\quad \text{if } i \leq 2n \text{ and } i \text{ is odd} \\ (2) \text{ put } (x, \mathbf{r}_i) \text{ into } Y_0 \text{ and } num_1 = 0 \qquad \text{if } i \leq 2n \text{ and } i \text{ is even} \\ (3) \text{ either put } (c, \mathbf{r}_i) \text{ into } Y_j \text{ for } j \geq 0, \text{ or} \\ \quad \text{put the singleton set } \{(c, \mathbf{r}_i)\} \text{ at any place after } Y_0 \\ \quad \text{and } num_1 = d, \text{ where } d \text{ is a positive integer} \\ \quad \text{and } d \text{ is odd if } (c, \mathbf{r}_i) \text{ is put into } Y_0 \text{ otherwise even} \quad \text{if } i = 2n + 1 \end{cases}$$

- **Init:** *For* $\bar{U} = (Y_0 \cdots Y_m, num_1, num_2)$*, init($\bar{U}$) is obtained by updating* Y_0 *with* $Y_0 \uplus \{(x_i, \mathbf{r}_0) \mid x_i \in \{c\} \cup X\}$ *and* num_1 *with 0.*
- **Delete:** *delete($\bar{U}, x$) for* $x \in \{c\} \cup X$ *is obtained from* $\bar{U}$ *by deleting the element* $(x, \mathbf{r})$ *indexed by* x*.*
- **Increase:** *increase($\bar{U}$) is obtained from* $\bar{U}$ *by replacing the element* $(c, \mathbf{r}_i)$ *indexed by* c *with element* $(c, \mathbf{r}_{min\{i+2, 2n+1\}})$ *and updating* num_1 *as follows:*

$$\begin{cases} num_1 := num_1 & \text{if } i < 2n - 1 \\ num_1 := num_1 + 1 & \text{if } i = 2n - 1 \\ num_1 := num_1 + 2 & \text{otherwise} \end{cases}$$

- **Decrease:** $decrease(\bar{U})$ *is obtained from* $\bar{U}$ *by replacing the element* $(c, \mathbf{r}_i)$ *indexed by c with element* $(c, \mathbf{r}_j)$ *and updating* num_1 *as follows:*

$$\begin{cases} j = max(i-2, 0) & and \quad num_1 := num_1 & if \; num_1 \leq 1 \\ j = i - 1 \; and \; num_1 := 0 & & else \; if \; num_1 = 2 \\ j = i \; and \; num_1 := num_1 - 2 & & otherwise \end{cases}$$

- **Rotate:** *Rotate intends to simulate the time progress transition. A rotation* $\bar{U} = (Y_0 \cdots Y_m, num_1, num_2) \Rightarrow \bar{U}' = (Y_0' \cdots Y_{m'}', num_1', num_2')$ *is defined as follows.*

$$\begin{cases} \bar{U}' = (Y_0' \cdots Y_{m+1}', \; if \; Y_0 \neq \emptyset, \; Y_0' = \emptyset, \; Y_1' = \{(\gamma, \mathbf{r}_{min\{i+1, 2n+1\}}) \\ \quad num_1', num_2') \mid (\gamma, \mathbf{r}_i) \in Y_0\}, \; Y_j' = Y_{j-1} \; for \; j \in [2..m+1], \\ \quad num_1' = num_1 + 1 \; if \; (c, \mathbf{r}_i) \in Y_0 \; and \; i \geq 2n \\ \quad otherwise \; num_1, \; and \; num_2' = num_2 + 1 \; if \\ \quad \bar{\rho}_1[0] = (\gamma, \mathbf{r}_i) \in Y_0 \; and \; i \geq 2n, \; otherwise \\ \quad num_2 + 1. \\ \bar{U}' = (Y_0' \cdots Y_{m-1}', \; otherwise, \; Y_0' = \{(\gamma, \mathbf{r}_{min\{i+1, 2n+1\}}) \mid (\gamma, \mathbf{r}_i) \in Y_m\}, \\ \quad num_1', num_2') \; Y_j' = Y_j \; for \; j \in [1..m-1], \; num_1' = num_1 + 1, \\ \quad if \; (c, \mathbf{r}_i) \in Y_m \; and \; i \geq 2n, \; otherwise \; num_1, \\ \quad and \; num_2' = num_2 + 1 \; if \; \bar{\rho}_1[0] = (\gamma, \mathbf{r}_i) \in Y_m \\ \quad and \; i \geq 2n, \; otherwise \; num_2. \end{cases}$$

$(\bar{\rho}_1, \bar{\rho}_2)$ *are updated to correspond to the permutation accordingly. As convention, we define* $\Rightarrow^*$ *as reflexive transitive closure of* $\Rightarrow$.

- **Map:** *Map intends to simulate the push transition.* $map(\bar{U}, \gamma)$ *for* $\gamma \in \Gamma$ *is obtained from* $\bar{U}$ *by the following operations. First delete all elements pointed by* $\bar{\rho}_2$. *Then replace* $(x, \mathbf{r}_j)$ *pointed by* $\bar{\rho}_1$ *for* $x \in \{c\} \cup X$ *with* $(\gamma, \mathbf{r}_j)$ *and set* $\bar{\rho}_2$ *to point to that. Finally assign value of* num_1 *to* num_2.

- **Propogate:** *Propogate intends to simulate the pop transition.* $propogate(\bar{U}, \bar{U}', \gamma)$ *for* $\gamma \in \Gamma$ *is set to be* $\bar{V}$ *which is obtained by finding a rotation* $\bar{U}' \Rightarrow^* \bar{V}$ *such that* $\bar{\rho}_1''$ *of* $\bar{V}$ *matches the original* $\bar{\rho}_2$ *of* $\bar{U}$. *That is to say, for* $0 \leq i \leq k$, $\bar{\rho}_1''[i] = (x, \mathbf{r}_m)$ *and* $\bar{\rho}_2[i] = (\gamma, \mathbf{r}_n)$, *we have* $m = n$.

Example 4. We begin with the digitized configuration $\bar{U}$ in Example 3, to simulate transitions $\varrho_1 \hookrightarrow^* \varrho_4$ in Example 1.

- $push(d)$ is simulated by $\bar{U}_1 = init(map(\bar{U}, d))$.
  $\bar{U}_1 = (\{\overline{(c, \mathbf{r}_0)}^0, \overline{(x_1, \mathbf{r}_0)}^1, \overline{(x_2, \mathbf{r}_0)}^2\}\{(d, \mathbf{r}_5)\}_0\{(d, \mathbf{r}_1)\}_1\{(d, \mathbf{r}_7)\}_2\}, 0, 0)$
- Time elapse of 2.6 time units is simulated by $\bar{U}_1 \Rightarrow^* \bar{U}_2$
  $\bar{U}_2 = (\{\}\{(d, \mathbf{r}_7)\}_1\{(d, \mathbf{r}_{13})\}_2\{\overline{(c, \mathbf{r}_5)}^0, \overline{(x_1, \mathbf{r}_5)}^1, \overline{(x_2, \mathbf{r}_5)}^2\}\{(d, \mathbf{r}_9)\}_0\}, 0, 0)$
- $c := c + 1$ is simulated by $\bar{U}_3 = increase(\bar{U}_2)$.
  $\bar{U}_3 = (\{\}\{(d, \mathbf{r}_7)\}_1\{(d, \mathbf{r}_{13})\}_2\{\overline{(c, \mathbf{r}_7)}^0, \overline{(x_1, \mathbf{r}_5)}^1, \overline{(x_2, \mathbf{r}_5)}^2\}\{(d, \mathbf{r}_9)\}_0\}, 0, 0)$

4.3   Snapshot Vector Pushdown System

A *snapshot vector pushdown system* (snapshot VPS) keeps the digitization of clock valuation and ages in the top stack frame and a pair of natural numbers that record roughly how much the current updatable clock pointed by $\bar{\rho}_1[0]$ and the age of element pointed by $\bar{\rho}_2[0]$ exceed the maximum integer n in the top stack frame, as a *digitized configuration*.

We show that a UDTPDA1 is encoded into its digitization, called a *snapshot VPS*. The keys of the encoding are, when a pop occurs, the time progress recorded at the top stack symbol is propagated to the next stack symbol after finding a series of rotations by matching between $k + 1$-pointers $\bar{\rho}_2$ and $\bar{\rho}'_1$. Using digitized configuration and its operations defined in the last subsection, the encoding is quite natural.

Definition 14. *Let* $\pi : \varrho_0 = (s_0, \epsilon, \nu_0) \hookrightarrow^* \varrho = (s, w, \nu)$ *be a transition sequence of a UDTPDA1 from the initial configuration. If* π *is not empty, we refer the last step as* $\lambda : \varrho' \hookrightarrow \varrho$, *and the preceding sequence by* $\pi' : \varrho_0 \hookrightarrow^* \varrho'$. *Let* $w = v_m \cdots v_1$. *A* snapshot *is a digitized configuration* $snap(\pi) = (\bar{Y}, num_1, num_2)$, *where* $num_1 = 2 \times (floor(\nu(c)) - n) + ceiling(frac(\nu(c)))$, $num_2 = 2 \times (floor(t_0) - n) + ceiling(frac(t_0))$ *if* w *is not empty and* $v_m = (\gamma, t_0, \cdots, t_k)$, *otherwise* $num_2 = 0$, *and* $\bar{Y} = \mathtt{digi}(dist(v_m) \uplus time(\nu))$.

In $snap(\pi)$, *we define the* $k + 1$-pointer $\bar{\rho}_1[i] = (x_i, \nu(x_i))$ *for* $0 \leq i \leq k$. *We also define* $\bar{\rho}_2[i] = (\gamma, proj(t_i))$ *for* $(\gamma, t_i) \in dist(v_m)$ *if* w *is not empty, otherwise* $\bar{\rho}_2$ *is left undefined. A* snapshot configuration $Snap(\pi)$ *is inductively defined from* $Snap(\pi')$.

$$
\begin{cases}
(s_0, snap(\epsilon)) & if \ \pi = \epsilon. \\
(s', snap(\pi) \, tail(Snap(\pi'))) & if \ \lambda \ is \ \textbf{Timeprogress}, \textbf{Local}, \textbf{Test}, \\
& \quad \textbf{Assign}, \textbf{Increment} \ and \ \textbf{Decrement}. \\
(s', snap(\pi) \, Snap(\pi')) & if \ \lambda \ is \ \textbf{Push}. \\
(s', snap(\pi) \, tail(tail(Snap(\pi')))) & if \ \lambda \ is \ \textbf{Pop}.
\end{cases}
$$

Definition 15. *For a UDTPDA1* $\langle S, s_0, \Gamma, X, c, \Delta \rangle$, *we define the corresponding encoded snapshot VPS* $\langle S, s_0, Digi, \mathbb{N}^2, \Delta_d \rangle$ *with the initial configuration* $\langle s_0, snap(\epsilon) \rangle$. *Then* Δ_d *consists of:*

Time progress $\langle s, \bar{U} \rangle \hookrightarrow_S \langle s, \bar{U}' \rangle$ *for* $\bar{U} \Rightarrow^* \bar{U}'$.

Local $(s \xrightarrow{\epsilon} s' \in \Delta)$ $\langle s, \bar{U} \rangle \hookrightarrow_S \langle s', \bar{U} \rangle$.

Test $(s \xrightarrow{x \in I?} s' \in \Delta$ *with* $x \in X \cup \{c\})$ *If* $\mathbf{r}_i \subseteq I$ *and* $(x, \mathbf{r}_i) \in \bar{Y}$, *where* $\bar{U} = (\bar{Y}, num_1, num_2)$, $\langle s, \bar{U} \rangle \hookrightarrow_S \langle s', \bar{U} \rangle$.

Assign $(s \xrightarrow{x \leftarrow I} s' \in \Delta$ *with* $x \in X)$ *For* $\mathbf{r}_i \subseteq I$,
$\langle s, \bar{U} \rangle \hookrightarrow_S \langle s', (insert_x(delete(\bar{U}, x), (x, \mathbf{r}_i))) \rangle$.

Assign $(s \xrightarrow{c \leftarrow I} s' \in \Delta)$ *For* $\mathbf{r}_i \subseteq I$,
$\langle s, \bar{U} \rangle \hookrightarrow_S \langle s', (insert_c(delete(\bar{U}, c), (c, \mathbf{r}_i))) \rangle$.

Increment $(s \xrightarrow{c := c+1} s' \in \Delta)$
$\langle s, \bar{U} \rangle \hookrightarrow_S \langle s', increase(\bar{U}) \rangle$.

Decrement $(s \xrightarrow{c := c-1} s' \in \Delta)$
$\langle s, \bar{U} \rangle \hookrightarrow_{\mathcal{S}} \langle s', decrease(\bar{U}) \rangle.$
Push $(s \xrightarrow{push(\gamma)} s' \in \Delta)$
$\langle s, \bar{U} \rangle \hookrightarrow_{\mathcal{S}} \langle s', (init(map(\bar{U}, \gamma)))\bar{U} \rangle.$
Pop $(s \xrightarrow{pop(\gamma)} s' \in \Delta)$
$\langle s, \bar{U}\bar{U}' \rangle \hookrightarrow_{\mathcal{S}} \langle s', propagate(\bar{U}, \bar{U}', \gamma) \rangle.$

By induction on the number of steps of transitions, the encoding relation between a UDTPDA1 with a single updatable clock and a snapshot VPS is observed.

Lemma 1. *Let us denote ϱ_0 and ϱ (resp. $\langle s_0, \tilde{w}_0 \rangle$ and $\langle s, \tilde{w} \rangle$) for the initial configuration and a configuration of a UDTPDA1 (resp. its snapshot VPS $\mathcal{S}$).*

(Preservation) *If $\pi : \varrho_0 \hookrightarrow^* \varrho$, there exists $\langle s, \tilde{w} \rangle$ such that $\langle s_0, \tilde{w}_0 \rangle \hookrightarrow^*_{\mathcal{S}} \langle s, \tilde{w} \rangle$ and $Snap(\pi) = \langle s, \tilde{w} \rangle$.*
(Reflection) *If $\langle s_0, \tilde{w}_0 \rangle \hookrightarrow^*_{\mathcal{S}} \langle s, \tilde{w} \rangle$, there exists $\pi : \varrho_0 \hookrightarrow^* \varrho$ with $Snap(\pi) = \langle s, \tilde{w} \rangle$.*

5   Nested Updatable Timed Automata

5.1   Nested Updatable Timed Automata

Nested Updatable Timed Automata(NeUTAs) extend NeTAs [1,2] by replacing every TA in NeTAs to a UTA1. A NeUTA has internal transitions, in which it will behave as a individual UTA1 having local, test, assign, increment and decrement transitions, and push and pop transitions. The stack of a NeUTA contains a pile of UTA1s which have been pushed.

Definition 16 (Nested Updatable Timed Automata). *A nested updatable timed automaton (NeUTA) is a quadruplet $\mathcal{N} = (T, \mathcal{A}_0, X, c, \Delta)$, where*

- *T is a finite set $\{\mathcal{A}_0, \mathcal{A}_1, \cdots, \mathcal{A}_m\}$ of UTA1s, with the initial UTA1 $\mathcal{A}_0 \in T$. We assume the sets of states of $\mathcal{A}_i$, denoted by $S(\mathcal{A}_i)$, are mutually disjoint, i.e., $S(\mathcal{A}_i) \cap S(\mathcal{A}_j) = \emptyset$ for $i \neq j$. We denote the initial state of $\mathcal{A}_i$ by $q_0(\mathcal{A}_i)$.*
- *X is the finite set of k local clocks and c is the updatable clock.*
- *$\Delta \subseteq Q \times (Q \cup \{\varepsilon\}) \times Actions \times Q \times (Q \cup \{\varepsilon\})$ describes transition rules below, where $Q = \cup_{\mathcal{A}_i \in T} S(\mathcal{A}_i)$.*

Internal $(q, \varepsilon, internal, q', \varepsilon)$, *which describes an internal transition in the working UTA1 (placed at a control location) with $q, q' \in \mathcal{A}_i$.*
Push $(q, \varepsilon, push, q_0(\mathcal{A}_{i'}), q)$, *which interrupts the currently working UTA1 $\mathcal{A}_i$ at $q \in S(\mathcal{A}_i)$. Then, a UTA1 $\mathcal{A}_{i'}$ newly starts.*
Pop $(q, q', pop, q', \varepsilon)$, *which restarts $\mathcal{A}_{i'}$ in the stack from $q' \in S(\mathcal{A}_{i'})$ after $\mathcal{A}_i$ has finished at $q \in S(\mathcal{A}_i)$.*

Definition 17 (Semantics of NeUTAs). *Given a NeUTA* $(T, \mathcal{A}_0, X, c, \Delta)$, *the current control state is referred by* q. *Let* $Val_X = \{\nu : X \cup \{c\} \to \mathbb{R}^{\geq 0}\}$. *A configuration of a NeUTA is an element in* $(Q \times Val_X, (Q \times Val_X)^*)$.

- *Time progress transitions:* $(\langle q, \nu \rangle, v) \xrightarrow{t} (\langle q, \nu + t \rangle, v + t)$ *for* $t \in \mathbb{R}^{\geq 0}$, *where* $v + t$ *set* $\nu' := \nu' + t$ *of each* $\langle q', \nu' \rangle$ *in the stack.*
- *Discrete transitions:* $\kappa \xrightarrow{\varphi} \kappa'$ *is defined as follows.*
  - **Internal** $(\langle q, \nu \rangle, v) \xrightarrow{\varphi} (\langle q', \nu' \rangle, v)$, *if* $\langle q, \nu \rangle \xrightarrow{\varphi} \langle q', \nu' \rangle$ *is in Definition 2.*
  - **Push** $(\langle q, \nu \rangle, v) \xrightarrow{push} (\langle q_0(\mathcal{A}_{i'}), \nu_0 \rangle, \langle q, \nu \rangle . v)$. *The current working UTA1 (including its control location and clock valuation) is pushed to the stack.*
  - **Pop** $(\langle q, \nu \rangle, \langle q', \nu' \rangle . w) \xrightarrow{pop} (\langle q', \nu' \rangle, w)$. *The current working UTA1 is replaced with the topmost UTA1 in the stack and the topmost stack frame is removed.*

The initial configuration of NeUTA is $(\langle q_0(\mathcal{A}_0), \nu_0 \rangle, \varepsilon)$, *where* $\nu_0(x) = 0$ *for* $x \in X \cup \{c\}$. *We use* $\longrightarrow$ *to range over these transitions, and* $\longrightarrow^*$ *is the reflexive and transitive closure of* $\longrightarrow$.

5.2 Termination and Boundedness of NeUTAs

In this subsection we present a trivial encoding from NeUTAs to UDTPDA1s and so the termination and boundedness of NeUTAs are decidable.

Let $\mathcal{N} = (T, \mathcal{A}_0, X, c, \Delta)$ be a NeUTA. We define a corresponding UDTPDA1 $\mathcal{E}(\mathcal{N}) = \langle S, s_0, \Gamma, X, c, \nabla \rangle$, such that

- $S = \Gamma = \bigcup_{\mathcal{A}_i \in T} S(\mathcal{A}_i)$ is the set of all locations of UTA1s in T, with
- $s_0 = q_0(\mathcal{A}_0)$ is the initial location of the initial UTA $\mathcal{A}_0$ of $\mathcal{N}$.
- $X = \{x_1, \ldots, x_k\}$ is the set of k local clocks, and c is the singleton updatable clock.
- ∇ is the union $\bigcup_{\mathcal{A}_i \in T} \Delta(\mathcal{A}_i) \bigcup \mathcal{H}(\mathcal{N})$ where
  $$\begin{cases} \Delta(\mathcal{A}_i) = \{\textbf{Local}, \textbf{Test}, \textbf{Assign}, \textbf{Increment}, \textbf{Decrement}\}, \\ \mathcal{H}(\mathcal{N}) \text{ consists of rules below.} \end{cases}$$

$$\textbf{Push } q \xrightarrow{push(q)} q_0(\mathcal{A}_{i'}) \text{ if } (q, \varepsilon, push, q_0(\mathcal{A}_{i'}), q) \in \Delta(\mathcal{N})$$
$$\textbf{Pop } \ q \xrightarrow{pop(q')} q' \qquad \text{ if } (q, q', pop, q', \varepsilon)) \in \Delta(\mathcal{N})$$

Definition 18. *Let* $\mathcal{N}$ *be a NeUTA* $(T, \mathcal{A}_0, X, c, \Delta)$ *and let* $\mathcal{E}(\mathcal{N})$ *be a UDTPDA1* $\langle S, s_0, \Gamma, X, c, \nabla \rangle$. *For a configuration* $\kappa = (\langle \mathcal{A}, q, \nu \rangle, v)$ *of* $\mathcal{N}$ *such that* $v = (\mathcal{A}_1, q_1, \nu_1) \ldots (\mathcal{A}_n, q_n, \nu_n)$, $[\![\kappa]\!]$ *denotes a configuration* $(q, \overline{w}(\kappa), \nu)$ *of* $\mathcal{E}(\mathcal{N})$ *where* $\overline{w}(\kappa) = w_1 \cdots w_n$ *with* $w_i = (q_i, \nu_i)$.

Lemma 2. *For a NeUTA* $\mathcal{N}$, *a UDTPDA1* $\mathcal{E}(\mathcal{N})$, *and configurations* κ, κ' *of* $\mathcal{N}$,

    (Preservation) *if* $\kappa \longrightarrow_{\mathcal{N}} \kappa'$, *then* $[\![\kappa]\!] \hookrightarrow^*_{\mathcal{E}(\mathcal{N})} [\![\kappa']\!]$, *and*

    (Reflection) *if* $[\![\kappa]\!] \hookrightarrow^*_{\mathcal{N}} \varrho$, *there exists* κ' *with* $\varrho \longrightarrow^*_{\mathcal{E}(\mathcal{N})} [\![\kappa']\!]$ *and* $\kappa \longrightarrow^*_{\mathcal{N}} \kappa'$.

By this encoding, we have our main result in Theorem 3.

Theorem 3. *The termination and boundedness of a NeUTA* $(T, \mathcal{A}_0, X, c, \Delta)$ *are decidable.*

6   Conclusion

This paper investigates termination and boundedness of NeUTAs, which extend NeTAs by replacing TAs with UTA1s. The proof of decidability can be seen as two phases of encoding, first an encoding NeUTAs to UDTPDA1s, then the one from UDTPDA1s to snapshot vector pushdown systems which extends the idea of digitization. Finally, the decidability of termination and boundedness of vector pushdown systems is obtained by the reduced reachability tree technique. The future work includes consider more verification problems of NeUTAs, as well as vector pushdown systems, such as coverability, reachability, and temporal logic model checking [18–21] et al..

Acknowledgements. This work is supported by National Natural Science Foundation of China with grant No. 61472240, 91318301, 61261130589, and the NSFC-JSPS bilateral joint research project with grant No. 61511140100.

References

1. Li, G., Cai, X., Ogawa, M., Yuen, S.: Nested timed automata. In: Braberman, V., Fribourg, L. (eds.) FORMATS 2013. LNCS, vol. 8053, pp. 168–182. Springer, Heidelberg (2013). doi:10.1007/978-3-642-40229-6_12
2. Li, G., Ogawa, M., Yuen, S.: Nested timed automata with frozen clocks. In: Sankaranarayanan, S., Vicario, E. (eds.) FORMATS 2015. LNCS, vol. 9268, pp. 189–205. Springer, Cham (2015). doi:10.1007/978-3-319-22975-1_13
3. Bouyer, P., Dufourd, C., Fleury, E., Petit, A.: Updatable timed automata. Theoret. Comput. Sci. **321**(2–3), 291–345 (2004)
4. Wen, Y., Li, G., Yuen, S.: On reachability analysis of updatable timed automata with one updatable clock. In: Liu, S., Duan, Z. (eds.) SOFL+MSVL 2015. LNCS, vol. 9559, pp. 147–161. Springer, Cham (2016). doi:10.1007/978-3-319-31220-0_11
5. Leroux, J., Praveen, M., Sutre, G.: Hyper-ackermannian bounds for pushdown vector addition systems. In: Proceeding of the 29th Annual ACM/IEEE Symposium on Logic in Computer Science (LICS 2014), pp. 63:1–63:10. ACM (2014)
6. Alur, R., Dill, D.L.: A theory of timed automata. Theoret. Comput. Sci. **126**(2), 183–235 (1994)
7. Alur, R., Courcoubetis, C., Henzinger, T.A., Ho, P.-H.: Hybrid automata: an algorithmic approach to the specification and verification of hybrid systems. In: Grossman, R.L., Nerode, A., Ravn, A.P., Rischel, H. (eds.) HS 1991-1992. LNCS, vol. 736, pp. 209–229. Springer, Heidelberg (1993). doi:10.1007/3-540-57318-6_30
8. Henzinger, T.A., Kopke, P.W., Puri, A., Varaiya, P.: What's decidable about hybrid automata? J. Comput. Syst. Sci. **57**, 94–124 (1998)
9. Henzinger, T.A.: The theory of hybrid automata. In: Inan, M.K., Kurshan, R.P. (eds.) Verification of Digital and Hybrid Systems. NATO ASI Series, vol. 170, pp. 265–292. Springer, Heidelberg (2000). doi:10.1007/978-3-642-59615-5_13
10. Abdulla, P.A., Atig, M.F., Stenman, J.: Dense-timed pushdown automata. In: Proceedings of the 27th Annual IEEE Symposium on Logic in Computer Science (LICS 2012), pp. 35–44. IEEE Computer Society (2012)
11. Bérard, B., Haddad, S., Sassolas, M.: Interrupt timed automata: verification and expressiveness. Formal Methods Syst. Des. **40**(1), 41–87 (2012)

12. Bérard, B., Haddad, S.: Interrupt timed automata. In: Alfaro, L. (ed.) FoSSaCS 2009. LNCS, vol. 5504, pp. 197–211. Springer, Heidelberg (2009). doi:10.1007/978-3-642-00596-1_15

13. Bouyer, P., Dufourd, C., Fleury, E., Petit, A.: Are timed automata updatable? In: Emerson, E.A., Sistla, A.P. (eds.) CAV 2000. LNCS, vol. 1855, pp. 464–479. Springer, Heidelberg (2000). doi:10.1007/10722167_35

14. Bouyer, P., Dufourd, C., Fleury, E., Petit, A.: Expressiveness of updatable timed automata. In: Nielsen, M., Rovan, B. (eds.) MFCS 2000. LNCS, vol. 1893, pp. 232–242. Springer, Heidelberg (2000). doi:10.1007/3-540-44612-5_19

15. Ouaknine, J., Worrell, J.: On the language inclusion problem for timed automata: closing a decidability gap. In: Proceedings of the 19th IEEE Symposium on Logic in Computer Science (LICS 2004), pp. 54–63. IEEE Computer Society (2004)

16. Abdulla, P.A., Jonsson, B.: Verifying networks of timed processes. In: Steffen, B. (ed.) TACAS 1998. LNCS, vol. 1384, pp. 298–312. Springer, Heidelberg (1998). doi:10.1007/BFb0054179

17. Abdulla, P., Jonsson, B.: Model checking of systems with many identical time processes. Theoret. Comput. Sci. 290(1), 241–264 (2003)

18. Duan, Z.: Temporal Logic and Temporal Logic Programming. Science Press, Beijing (2005)

19. Duan, Z., Tian, C., Zhang, L.: A decision procedure for propositional projection temporal logic with infinite models. Acta Informatica 45(1), 43–78 (2008)

20. Duan, Z., Yang, X., Koutny, M.: Framed temporal logic programming. Sci. Comput. Program. 70(1), 31–61 (2008)

21. Tian, C., Duan, Z., Zhang, N.: An efficient approach for abstraction-refinement in model checking. Theoret. Comput. Sci. 461, 76–85 (2012)

Instant-Based and State-Based Analysis
of Infinite Logical Clock

Qingguo Xu[1,2(✉)], Huaikou Miao[1,2], Robert de Simone[3],
and Julien DeAntoni[3]

[1] School of Computer Engineering and Science, Shanghai University,
No. 99 Shangda Rd., Shanghai 200444, People's Republic of China
qgxu@t.shu.edu.cn, hkmiao@shu.edu.cn
[2] Shanghai Key Laboratory of Computer Software Testing and Evaluating,
Shanghai 201114, China
[3] INRIA Sophia Antipolis Méditerranée AOSTE,
University of Nice Sophia Antipolis, I3S, 06902 Sophia Antipolis Cedex, France
Robert.de_Simone@inria.fr,
Julien.Deantoni@polytech.unice.fr

Abstract. The Clock Constraint Specification Language (CCSL), first introduced as a companion language for Modeling and Analysis of Real-Time and
Embedded systems (MARTE), has now evolved beyond the time specification
of MARTE, and has become a full-fledged domain specific modeling language
widely used in many domains. This paper shows the clock model, for infinite
clock, interpreted over natural number domain based on instant as well as state.
The differences and the relations between the two representations are discussed.
A state-transition system and its abstract form is proposed in order to analyze
CCSL specification's features, such as potential deadlock, inconsistencies
caused by introducing new constraints, and periodicity of admissible behavior.
Finally, we examine some interesting features on a simple application by
improving specification step by step.

Keywords: CCSL · Clock model · State transition system · Infinite clock

1 Introduction

The UML Profile for Modeling and Analysis of Real-Time and Embedded systems
(MARTE) [1], adopted in November 2009, has introduced a Time Model [2] that
extends the informal simple time of the Unified Modeling Language (UML 2.x). This
time model is general enough to support different forms of time (discrete or dense,
chronometric or logical). Its so-called clocks allow enforcing as well as observing the
occurrences of events and the behavior of annotated UML elements. The Time Model
comes with a companion language named the Clock Constraint Specification Language

---

This work is supported by the Natural Science Foundation of China (Grant No. 61572306,
61502294).

S. Liu et al. (Eds.): SOFL+MSVL 2016, LNCS 10189, pp. 32–51, 2017.
DOI: 10.1007/978-3-319-57708-1_3

(CCSL) [3] defined in an annex of the MARTE specification. Initially devised as a language for expressing constraints between clocks of a MARTE model, CCSL has evolved and has been developed independently of the UML. CCSL is now equipped with a formal semantics [3] and is supported by a software environment (TimeSquare [4]) that allows for the specification, solving, and visualization of clock constraints.

MARTE promises a general modeling framework to design and analyze systems. Lots of works have been published on the modeling capabilities offered by MARTE, much less on verification techniques supported. Inspired by the works about state-based semantics interpretation for the kernel CCSL operators [5]. This paper further show a kind of clock model, integrating the interpretations based on instant and state. For the sake of clarity and simplicity, we only take the infinite clock into account. This clock model owns the advantages for proving some properties expressed in different views.

Section 2 gives some preliminaries about logical clock and instant. Sections 3 and 4 introduce clock structure and state-based semantics for CCSL. Section 5 analyzes several kinds of CCSL via state-transition system associated with specification. This analysis technique gives some analysis result on a case study in Sect. 6. Finally, Sect. 7 makes a comparison with related work, and Sect. 8 concludes the contribution and outlines some future work.

2   Preliminaries

This section briefly introduces the time model [2] of MARTE and the Clock Constraint Specification Language (CCSL). MARTE Time model deals with both discrete and dense time. In MARTE, a clock gives access to a time structure. A clock can be either chronometric or logical. The former is related to "physical time" while the latter is not. This paper focuses on discrete-time logical clocks—referred to as logical clocks—and time is qualified as logic.

The notion of multiform logical time has first been used in the theory of synchronous languages [6] and its polychronous extensions. CCSL provides a concrete syntax to make the polychronous clocks first-class citizens of UML-like models. Logical clocks in CCSL are used to measure times of occurrences of events in a system. A clock c can be seen as a totally ordered set of instants, $\mathcal{I}_c$. In the following, i and j are instants. A time structure is a set of clocks $\mathcal{C}$ and a set of relations over instants set $\mathcal{I} = \bigcup_{c \in \mathcal{C}} \mathcal{I}_c$. CCSL considers two kinds of relations: causal and temporal ones. The basic causal relation is causality/dependency, a binary relation on $\mathcal{I} : \preccurlyeq \subset \mathcal{I} \times \mathcal{I}$. $i \preccurlyeq j$ means i causes j or j depends on i. $\preccurlyeq$ is a pre-order on $\mathcal{I}$, i.e., it is reflexive and transitive. The basic temporal relations are precedence ($\prec$), coincidence ($\equiv$), and exclusion (#), three binary relations on $\mathcal{I}$. For any pair of instants $(i, j) \in \mathcal{I} \times \mathcal{I}$ in a time structure, $i \prec j$ means that the only acceptable execution traces are those where i occurs strictly before j (i precedes i). $\prec$ is transitive and asymmetric. $i \equiv j$ imposes instants i and j to be coincident, i.e., they must occur at the same execution step, both of them or none of them. $\equiv$ is an equivalence relation, i.e., it is reflexive, symmetric and transitive. $i \# j$ forbids the coincidence of the two instants, i.e., they cannot occur at the same execution step. # is irreflexive and symmetric. A consistency rule is enforced between causal and temporal relations. $i \preccurlyeq j$ can be refined either as $i \prec j$ or $i \equiv j$, but j can never precede i. CCSL defines a concrete syntax to specify instant relation or more generally clock relations, which represent infinitely many instant relations. Section 3 introduces semantics of some CCSL relations/constraints.

In this paper, we consider discrete sets of instants only, so that the instants of a clock can be indexed by natural numbers. For a clock $c \in C$, and for any $k \in \mathbb{N} > 0$, $c[k]$ denotes the kth instant of c.

3 Stated-Based Time Structure

A clock belongs to a clock set C. During the execution of a system, an execution step is defined and at a given step, every clock in C can tick or not according to the constraints used in the specification. A schedule captures what happens during one particular execution.

Definition 1 (Schedule). Given a clock set C, a *schedule* σ over C is a function $\mathbb{N}_{>0} \to 2^{C} \setminus \emptyset$.   ∎

Given an execution step $i \in \mathbb{N}_{>0}$, and a schedule σ, $\sigma(i)$ denotes the set of clocks that tick at step i. $\forall i, \sigma(i) \neq \emptyset$ asserts that all the stuttering steps without ticking any clock is unallowed along σ.

For a given schedule, the configurations of the clocks tell us the advance of the clocks, relative to the others.

Definition 2 (Clock configuration). For a given schedule σ, clock $c \in C$ and a natural number $n \in \mathbb{N}$, the configuration $\chi_\sigma : C \times \mathbb{N} \to \mathbb{N}$ is defined recursively as:

$$\chi_\sigma(c, n) = \begin{cases} 0 & \text{if } n = 0 \\ \chi_\sigma(c, n-1) & \text{if } c \notin \sigma(n) \\ \chi_\sigma(c, n-1) + 1, & \text{if } c \in \sigma(n) \end{cases} \tag{1}$$

∎

Lemma 1 (Non-decreasing Configuration). $\forall c \in C, \ i, \ j \in \mathbb{N}, \ i \leq j \implies \chi_\sigma(c, i) \leq \chi_\sigma(c, j)$.   ∎

Lemma 1 is easily proved by induction on j via transitivity of $\leq$ over $\mathbb{N}$.

Lemma 2 (Invariant Configuration). During the interval in which clock c doesn't tick, the corresponding configuration keeps unchanged:

$$\forall i, j \in \mathbb{N}, i \leq j, (\chi_\sigma(c, i) = \chi_\sigma(c, j) \text{ if and only if } \forall k \in [i+1..j], c \notin \sigma(k)). \quad ∎$$

Proof of Lemma 2:

(i) *If* direction: It is easily proved by induction on k with the definition of χ_σ as well as transitivity of $=$ over $\mathbb{N}$.

(ii) *Only if* direction: i.e. assume $\forall i, j \in \mathbb{N}, \ i \leq j, \chi_\sigma(c, i) = \chi_\sigma(c, j)$, we want prove $\forall k \in [i + 1..j], \ c \notin \sigma(k)$. We suppose the contrary:
$\exists k \in [i + 1..j], c \in \sigma(k)$, which implies $\chi_\sigma(c, k) = \chi_\sigma(c, k-1) + 1$ by Definition 1.

By Lemma 1, we have $\chi_\sigma(c, j) \geq \chi_\sigma(c, k) > \chi_\sigma(c, k-1) \geq \chi_\sigma(c, i)$ implied by $j \geq k > k-1 \geq i$.

Then we have $\chi_\sigma(c, j) > \chi_\sigma(c, i)$, which contradicts the assumption $\chi_\sigma(c, i) = \sigma(c, j)$. Therefore the supposition is incorrect, so $\forall k \in [i + 1..j]$, $c \notin \sigma(k)$. ∎

Lemma 2 tells us there are no more ticks between the successive two ticks of a given clock.

For a clock $c \in \mathcal{C}$, and a step $n \in \mathbb{N}$, $\chi_\sigma(c,n)$ counts the number of times the clock c has ticked at step n for the given schedule σ. Therefore, the value of $\chi_\sigma(c,n)$ denotes the index of a certain instant for clock c. Over a schedule σ, c can tick $k > 0$ times if and only if $\exists n \in \mathbb{N} > 0$, $\chi_\sigma(c,n) = k$.

For a given schedule σ, and a clock $c \in \mathcal{C}$, here we interpret $\mathcal{I}_c$ as $\mathbb{I}_{c,\sigma} = \{i : \mathbb{N}_{>0} | c \in \sigma(\langle\rangle)\}$, which is a subset of $\mathbb{N}_{>0}$, containing and only containing the step i such that $\sigma(i)$. includes the clock c. A step $i \in \mathbb{I}_{c,\sigma}$ coincides with the $\chi_\sigma(c, i)^{\text{th}}$ instant $c[\chi_\sigma(c, i)]$, i.e., $i \equiv c[\chi_\sigma(c, i)]$ if $i \in \mathbb{I}_{c,\sigma}$.

Definition 3 (Time Structure). For a given clock set $\mathcal{C}$ and a schedule σ over $\mathcal{C}$, $(\mathbb{I}_{c,\sigma}, \leq)$ is a time structure, where $\mathbb{I}_{\mathcal{C},\sigma} = \bigcup_{c \in \mathcal{C}} \mathbb{I}_{c,\sigma}$. ∎

Based on Definition 3 inspired by [7], the clock instant set in Definition 3 can be modeled as a subset of nonnegative natural number set, the three basic temporal relations precedence($\prec$), coincidence($\equiv$) and exclusion(#) are correspondingly interpreted as $<$, $=$ and $\neq$ over $\mathbb{N}_{>0}$, i.e., $\prec \triangleq <$, $\equiv \triangleq =$, and $\# \triangleq \neq$. It is so-called timed structure because of causality finiteness: the set $\{i' \in \mathbb{I}_{c,\sigma} | i' \prec i\}$ is finite for all $i \in \mathbb{I}_{c,\sigma}$.

Lemma 3 (Instant Index). For a clock $c \in \mathcal{C}$ and a given schedule σ over $\mathcal{C}$, the index of any instant $i_c \in \mathbb{I}_{c,\sigma} \subseteq \mathbb{I}_{\mathcal{C},\sigma}$ of clock c, denotes as $Idx_{\sigma,c}(i_c)$, is computed by χ_σ. Meanwhile, the $\chi_\sigma(c, i_c)^{\text{th}}$ instant is i_c.

$$Idx_{\sigma,c}(i_c) = \chi_\sigma(c, i_c)$$
$$c_\sigma[\chi_\sigma(c, i_c)] = i_c \qquad ∎$$

Proof of Lemma 3 is direct from Definition 2 and omitted here.

We can easily deduce that $Idx_{\sigma,c} : \mathbb{I}_{c,\sigma} \to \mathbb{N}_{>0}$ is an injective, monotonically strictly increasing function, whose domain is set of the time slots in which clock c ticks. This paper only care about the infinite clocks, this requires that every clock in $\mathcal{C}$ will tick forever, i.e., $\forall c \in \mathcal{C}, \chi_\sigma(c, n)$ is boundless with n increases. The fact boundlessness of $\chi_\sigma(c,n)$ is fated by the infinity of c's instant set: $\forall i \in \mathbb{N}_{>0}, \exists j > i, c \in \sigma(j)$. Therefore, the clock constraints involving the termination clock is not in our discussion scope. It is noted that $Idx_{\sigma,c}$ becomes a bijective (one-to-one correspondence) function under such assumption. Meanwhile, clock c's instant access operator $c_\sigma[] : \mathbb{N}_{>0} \to \mathbb{I}_{c,\sigma}$ is the inverse function of $Idx_{\sigma,c}$.

Lemmas 1, 2, 3 can be proved via the proof assistor PVS based on the written PVS specification in our previous work [8].

It is possible for one concrete instant belongs to not only one clock. In such case, the instant of these different clocks coincide each other.

4 Clock Constraint

4.1 Specification and Its Component

Definition 4 (CCSL specification). A CCSL specification $\mathcal{SPEC}$ is a pair $<\mathcal{C}, \Re>$, where $\mathcal{C}$ is a set of clocks, clock constraint $\Re$ is a formula (see Definition 6 below) used to specify the relations among the clocks over the set $\mathcal{C}$. ∎
CCSL specification is used to specify a set of valid schedules. There are usually an infinite number of schedules that satisfy a given specification. If there is no satisfying schedule, then we say the specification is unsatisfiable. The detail properties about the schedules again the given specification is investigated in [9].

Definition 5 (Clock set). An element in the clock set $\mathcal{C}$ can be given by the specifier explicitly (**explicit clock**), or by one of the following **clock expressions** (**implicit clock**) (We don't give the clock expression (such as *upto, await*, etc.) that generates finite clock because of this paper's working scope.):

$$Clock := a+b \mid a*b \mid a\backslash b \mid sup(a, b) \mid inf(a, b) \mid SampledOn(a, b) \mid DelayFor(a, b, d)$$
$$\mid Filtered\,By(a, u, v) \tag{2}$$

where $a, b \in \mathcal{C}$ are clocks, $u, v \in (0 + 1)^*$ are finite binary words, and $d \in \mathbb{N}_{>0}$ is a positive natural number. ∎
   Once we write one a clock expression in the form of (2), a new clock is added into the clock set $\mathcal{C}$. For example, if we give the **explicit clock** set $\mathcal{C} = \{a, b\}$, and a clock expression set $\{c' := a+b, c'' := DelayFor(a, c', 1)\}$, then we get two additional **implicit clocks** c' and c'' as new elements in $\mathcal{C}$. The considered clock set is $\mathcal{C} \cup \{c', c''\} = \{a, b, c', c''\}$ in the corresponding specification. Note that there may not be any given name for the implicit of the clock expression (e.g. if it occurs in one clock relation) (see Definition 6 below). It should be noted that the new clock will be scheduled depending on the input clock(s) that occur in that expression.
   The CCSL constraint is defined over the clock set includes both the **explicit** clocks and **implicit** ones.

Definition 6 (CCSL Constraints). For a clock set $\mathcal{C}$, the corresponding clock constraint set $\Phi(\mathcal{C})$ over $\mathcal{C}$ is defined recursively as:

$$\psi := a \subset b \mid a \,\#\, b \mid a \prec b \mid a \preccurlyeq b \mid \psi_1 \wedge \psi_2$$

where $a, b \in \mathcal{C}$. When ψ is in the form of $\psi_1 \wedge \psi_2$, we say ψ_1 and ψ_2 are sub-clauses of ψ. Otherwise we say ψ involves two clocks $right(\psi) = a$ and $left(\psi) = b$. ∎
   Every clock constraint in the set $\Phi(\mathcal{C})$, which is also be called a **clock relation**, is a primitive formulae relates a clock pair or their conjunction. We call the four primitive relations are **Precedence($\prec$)**, **Causality($\preccurlyeq$)**, **Subclock($\subset$)** and **Exclusion(#)**.

4.2   Clock Constraint Interpretation

In order to get to know how the clock constraints in Definition 6 effect the clock's behaviors in a certain schedule, we should extend the constraints over the clocks into those over their instants.

Definition 7 (CCSL specification satisfaction). For a given CCSL specification $\mathcal{SPEC} = <\mathcal{C}, \mathcal{R}>$, A schedule σ over $\mathcal{C}$ satisfies $\mathcal{SPEC}$, denotes $\sigma \vDash \mathcal{SPEC}$, if and only if $\sigma \vDash \mathcal{R}$ defined below:

$\sigma \vDash \mathcal{R}$ *if and only if cases* $\mathcal{R}$*'s form of*

$$
\begin{array}{lll}
a \subset b : \forall n \in \mathbb{N}_{>0}, & a \in \sigma(n) \Rightarrow b \in \sigma(n) & \textbf{(Subclock)} \\
a \,\#\, b : \forall n \in \mathbb{N}_{>0}, & a \notin \sigma(n) \vee b \notin \sigma(n) & \textbf{(Exclusion)} \\
a \prec b : \forall n \in \mathbb{N}, & \chi_\sigma(a, n) = \chi_\sigma(b, n) \Rightarrow b \notin \sigma(n+1) & \textbf{(Precedence)} \\
a \preccurlyeq b : \forall n \in \mathbb{N}, & \chi_\sigma(a, n) \geq \chi_\sigma(b, n) & \textbf{(Causality)} \\
\psi_1 \wedge \psi_2 : \sigma \vDash \psi_1 \wedge \sigma \vDash \psi_2 & & \textbf{(Conjuction)}
\end{array}
$$

where $a, b \in \mathcal{C}$. We also say such a σ is a model of $\mathcal{SPEC}$.   ■

It's straightforward to prove that both *Causality* and *Subclock* are pre-orders on $\mathcal{C}$, i.e., they are reflexive and transitive. For simplicity, we can write $a \preccurlyeq b \preccurlyeq c$ for $a \preccurlyeq b \wedge b \preccurlyeq c$, and so do other transitive clock relation. It is also easy to prove that *Exclusion* is neither reflexive nor transitive relation.

From the view of system evolving, among the four primitive relations in Definition 7, the first two (**Subclock** and **Exclusion**) are "present-based" relations, while the last two (**Precedence** and **Causality**) are "past-based" ones. For a primitive "present-based" clock relation ψ involves clocks a and b, one can deduce whether a may(must) tick or not from the information only about b's tick at current step over a schedule. While "past-based" relation are so called means deciding whether the involved clocks tick or not depends on not only the clock tick's information at current step, but also these two clock tick times accumulated from the beginning. For example, along a schedule σ over a given clock set $\mathcal{C}$ including two clocks a and b under the constrain $a \preccurlyeq b$, one can deduce b must not tick at step $n + 1$ provided that $\chi_\sigma(a, n) = \chi_\sigma(b, n)$ and $a \notin \sigma(n + 1)$ because otherwise it will result in

$$
\chi_\sigma(a, n+1) = \chi_\sigma(a, n) + 1, \; \chi_\sigma(b, n+1) = \chi_\sigma(b, n)
$$

which does not hold at step $n + 1$ for the constrain $a \preccurlyeq b$. Here the fact b must not tick at step $n + 1$ require both the current behavior ($a \notin \sigma(n + 1)$) and the "past" information ($\chi_\sigma(a, n) = \chi_\sigma(b, n)$).

Some logic conclusions can be directly from Definition 7.

Lemma 4 (Precedence implies causality). The **Precedence** is a stronger form of **Causality**:

$$
\sigma \vDash a \prec b \Rightarrow \sigma \vDash a \preccurlyeq b
$$

■

Lemma 5 (Subclock implies causality). When a is a **Subclock** of b, then b is faster than a:

$$\sigma \vDash a \subset b \Rightarrow \sigma \vDash b \preccurlyeq a \qquad \blacksquare$$

Proofs about Lemmas 4 and 5 can be found in Frédéric's report [5].

Definition 7 gives us the semantic for clock relation based on state transition system. There is another interpretation framework for clock constraints in Charles and Frédéric's work [10] when we have no information about the "past" because of without introducing configuration χ_σ. For example, Definition 8 give us the **Precedence** relation based on finding function over time structure defined in Definition 3.

Definition 8 (Instant-based Precedence). Giving two clocks $a, b \in C$ and a schedule σ, $a \prec b$ means that each instant in $\mathbb{I}_{b,\sigma}$ (immediately) follows at least one instant in $\mathbb{I}_{a,\sigma}$. More formally:

$(\sigma \vDash a \prec b)$ if and only if $\exists h : \mathbb{I}_{b,\sigma} \to \mathbb{I}_{a,\sigma}$ such that

(1) h is injective
(2) h is order preserving:

$$(\forall i, j \in \mathbb{I}_{b,\sigma})(i < j) \Rightarrow (h(i) < h(j))$$

(3) an instant of $\mathbb{I}_{b,\sigma}$ and its image are ordered:

$$(\forall i \in \mathbb{I}_{b,\sigma})h(i) < i \qquad \blacksquare$$

In fact, instant-based Precedence is equivalent with that based on state.

Lemma 6 (Precedence Equivalence). Giving two clocks $a, b \in C$ and a schedule σ, $\exists h$, h satisfies all the conditions (1), (2) and (3) in Definition 8, if and only if

$$\forall n \in \mathbb{N}, \chi_\sigma(a, n) = \chi_\sigma(b, n) \Rightarrow b \notin \sigma(n+1) \qquad \blacksquare$$

Proof of Lemma 6:

(i) *If* direction (state-based $\Longrightarrow$ instant-based):

Let us construct an $h : \mathbb{I}_{b,\sigma} \to \mathbb{I}_{a,\sigma}, \forall i_b \in \mathbb{I}_{b,\sigma}, h(i_b) = i_a$ such that $\chi_\sigma(a, i_a) = \chi_\sigma(b, i_b)$, the left is to prove such a function h satisfies all the conditions (1), (2) and (3) in Definition 8.

(i-1) condition (1) requires us to prove $\forall i_{b1}, i_{b2} \in \mathbb{I}_{b,\sigma}, h(i_{b1}) = h(i_{b2}) \Rightarrow i_{b1} = i_{b2}$

suppose $i_{b1} \neq i_{b2}$, then
$\chi_\sigma(b, i_{b1}) \neq \chi_\sigma(b, i_{b2})$, by $i_{b1}, i_{b2} \in \mathbb{I}_{b,\sigma}$ (This means that $b \in \sigma(i_{b1}) \wedge b \in \sigma(i_{b2})$.) and Definition 2

$\Rightarrow \chi_\sigma(a, h(\iota_{b1})) \neq \chi_\sigma(a, h(\iota_{b2}))$, by h's construction

$\Rightarrow h(\iota_{b1}) \neq h(\iota_{b2})$, by $h(\iota_{b1}), h(\iota_{b2}) \in \mathbb{I}_{a,\sigma}$ (This means that $a \in \sigma(h(\iota_{b1})) \wedge a \in \sigma$ $(h(\iota_{b2}))$.) and Definition 2

This contradicts the assumption. So condition (1) holds

(i-2)   condition (2) require us to prove $\forall \iota_{b1}, \iota_{b2} \in \mathbb{I}_{b,\sigma}, \iota_{b1} < \iota_{b2} \Rightarrow h(\iota_{b1}) < h(\iota_{b2})$.

$\iota_{b1} < \iota_{b2} \Rightarrow \chi_\sigma(b, \iota_{b1}) < \chi_\sigma(b, \iota_{b2})$ by $\iota_{b1}, \iota_{b2} \in \mathbb{I}_{b,\sigma}$, Lemma 1 and Definition 2

$$\Rightarrow \chi_\sigma(b, \iota_{b1}) = \chi_\sigma(a, h(\iota_{b1})) < \chi_\sigma(a, h(\iota_{b2})) = \chi_\sigma(b, \iota_{b2})$$

$\Rightarrow h(\iota_{b1}) < h(\iota_{b2})$, by $h(\iota_{b1}), h(\iota_{b2}) \in \mathbb{I}_{a,\sigma}$, Lemma 1 a and Definition 2.

(i-3)   condition (3) require us to prove $(\forall \iota_b \in \mathbb{I}_{b,\sigma}) \iota_a = h(\iota_b) < \iota_b$.

We have $\sigma \vDash a \preccurlyeq b$, by Lemma 4
$\Rightarrow \chi_\sigma(a, \iota_b) \geq \chi_\sigma(b, \iota_b)$, by Definition 4
Suppose $\iota_a = h(\iota_b) \geq \iota_b$, i.e., $\iota_a > \iota_b \vee \iota_a = \iota_b$,
$\iota_a > \iota_b \Rightarrow \chi_\sigma(a, \iota_a) > \chi_\sigma(a, \iota_b) \geq \chi_\sigma(b, \iota_b)$, by $\iota_a \in \mathbb{I}_{a,\sigma}$ and Lemma 1
This contradicts $\chi_\sigma(a, \iota_a) = \chi_\sigma(b, \iota_b)$ postulated by h's construction.
$\iota_a = \iota_b \Rightarrow \chi_\sigma(a, \iota_a) = \chi_\sigma(b, \iota_b)$, by h's construction
$\Rightarrow \chi_\sigma(a, \iota_a - 1) = \chi_\sigma(b, \iota_b - 1)$,   by $a, b \in \sigma(\iota_b)$ and Definition 2
$\Rightarrow b \notin \sigma(\iota_b)$, by **Precedence** in Definition 7
This contradicts $b \in \sigma(\iota_b)$.

(ii)   *Only if* direction (instant-based $\Rightarrow$ state-based):

Now we prove this by induction on sorted $\mathbb{I}_{b,\sigma}$.
$\chi_\sigma(a, n) = \chi_\sigma(b, n) = 0 \notin b \notin \sigma(n+1)$ is obvious. Otherwise one cannot find $(n + 1)$'s image $h(n+1) < n + 1$ because there isn't an element, which is less than $n + 1$, in h's range $\mathbb{I}_{a,\sigma}$.
Assume $\forall \iota_b \in \mathbb{I}_{b,\sigma}, \iota_b < \chi_\sigma(b, n)$, the conclusion is true.
Let $\iota_b = \chi_\sigma(b, n) = \chi_\sigma(a, n)$,
$\Rightarrow |\{\iota : \mathbb{I}_{a,\sigma} | \iota < n+1\}| = |\{\iota : \mathbb{I}_{b,\sigma} | \iota < n+1\}| = \iota_b$, by Lemma 3
Suppose $b \in \sigma(n+1)$.
$\Rightarrow h(n+1) < (n+1)$, by condition (3) in Definition 8
This is impossible because

$$\forall \iota_a \in \{\iota : \mathbb{I}_{a,\sigma} | \iota < n+1\}, \exists \iota_b \in \{\iota : \mathbb{I}_{b,\sigma} | \iota < n+1\}, \iota_a = h(\iota_b)$$

So there is no additional instant in $\{\iota : \mathbb{I}_{a,\sigma} | \iota < n+1\}$ as $(n + 1)$'s image for the sake of injection of h. ∎

Based on Lemma 3 inspired by Charles' report [11], Definition 9 intuitively exhibits another way of **Precedence** definition:

Definition 9 (Index-based Precedence). Giving two clocks $a, b \in C$ and a schedule σ, $a \prec b$ means that b's each instant in $\mathbb{I}_{b,\sigma}$, with index k, strictly slower than the clock a's instant in $\mathbb{I}_{a,\sigma}$ with the same index k:

$$(\sigma \models a \prec b) \quad \text{if and only if} \quad \forall k : a_\sigma[k] < b_\sigma[k]. \qquad \blacksquare$$

Definition 9 is not convenient in checking specification behavior because deciding the instant's index requires countering tick time from beginning, although it is easily understood by reader.

In fact, Stated-based **Precedence** in Definition 7, Instant-based one in Definition 8 and Index-based one in Definition 9, are pairwise equivalent. This provides a possibility to present the one clock constraint from different view. For example, it is very tedious to prove the transitivity of Stated-based **Precedence**. But it is obvious in the way of both Instant-based and Index-based.

Table 1 show us the definitions of four primitive types of clock relations from three different views (state, instant and index-based). Reader can establish the equivalence between them and Definition 7 following Lemma 6. Here we don't give the detail because of text length.

Table 1. Interpretations of primitive clock constraints in different views

Primitive relation	Stated-based	Instant-based	Index-based	Instant set constraint
$\sigma \models a \subset b$	$\forall i \in \mathbb{N}_{>0}, a \in \sigma(i) \implies b \in \sigma(i)$	$\exists h, h(i) = i$	$\forall k, \exists l, a_\sigma[k] = b_\sigma[l]$	$\mathbb{I}_{b,\sigma} \subset \mathbb{I}_{a,\sigma}$
$\sigma \models a \# b$	$\forall i \in \mathbb{N}_{>0}, a \notin \sigma(i) \vee b \notin \sigma(i)$		$\forall k,l, a_\sigma[k] \neq b_\sigma[l]$	$\mathbb{I}_{b,\sigma} \cap \mathbb{I}_{a,\sigma} = \emptyset$
$\sigma \models a \preccurlyeq b$	$\forall i \in \mathbb{N}, \chi_\sigma(a, n) \geq \chi_\sigma(b, n)$	$\exists h, h(i) \leq i$	$\forall k, a_\sigma[k] \leq b_\sigma[k]$	$|\mathbb{I}_{b,\sigma}| \leq |\mathbb{I}_{a,\sigma}|$
$\sigma \models a \prec b$	$\forall i \in \mathbb{N}, \chi_\sigma(a, n) = \chi_\sigma(b, n) \implies b \notin \sigma(i+1)$	$\exists h, h(i) < i$	$\forall k, a_\sigma[k] < b_\sigma[k]$	$|\mathbb{I}_{b,\sigma}| \leq |\mathbb{I}_{a,\sigma}|$

Note: (1) h: $\mathbb{I}_{b,\sigma} \to \mathbb{I}_{a,\sigma}$ is a monotonically strictly increasing injective function, $i \in \mathbb{I}_{b,\sigma}$.
(2) k and l are index of clock a or b. Assumes that $a_\sigma[k] \in \mathbb{I}_{a,\sigma}$ and $b_\sigma[l], b_\sigma[k] \in \mathbb{I}_{b,\sigma}$.

The *implicit clocks* defined using clock expressions (2), are constrained according to the parameters of the clock expression. In other words, a clock expression is a clock generator where the output clock ticks or not according to the input clock(s) state and other arguments, if any.

Definition 10 (Clock Expression Interpretation). Whether a new clock can tick or not is determined by the behaviors of the input clock(s). we say σ, over clock set C containing a, b, *and* c, is a model of that clock expression, if the following corresponding condition hold:

$c := a + b$ iff $\forall n \in \mathbb{N}_{>0},$ $c \in \sigma(n)$ iff $a \in \sigma(n) \vee b \in \sigma(n)$ **(Union)**

$c := a * b$ iff $\forall n \in \mathbb{N}_{>0},$ $c \in \sigma(n)$ iff $a \in \sigma(n) \wedge b \in \sigma(n)$ **(Intersection)**

$c := a \backslash b$ iff $\forall n \in \mathbb{N}_{>0},$ $c \in \sigma(n)$ iff $a \in \sigma(n) \wedge b \notin \sigma(n)$ **(Minus)**

$c := sup(a, b)$ iff $\forall n \in \mathbb{N},$ $\chi_\sigma(c, n) = \min(\chi_\sigma(a, n), \chi_\sigma(b, n))$ **(Supremum)**

$c := inf(a, b)$ iff $\forall n \in \mathbb{N},$ $\chi_\sigma(c, n) = \max(\chi_\sigma(a, n), \chi_\sigma(b, n))$ **(Infimum)**

$c := DelayFor(a, b, d)$ iff $(\forall n \in \mathbb{N}_{>0}, c \in \sigma(n)$ iff

$(b \in \sigma(n) \wedge (\exists j \in [1..n-1], a \in \sigma(j) \wedge \chi_\sigma(b, n) - \chi_\sigma(b, j) = d)))$ **(Delayfor)**

$c := SampledOn(a, b)$ iff $(\forall n \in \mathbb{N}_{>0}, c \in \sigma(n)$ iff

$(b \in \sigma(n) \wedge (\exists j \in [1..n], a \in \sigma(j) \wedge \forall m : [j..n-1], b \notin \sigma(m))))$ **(SampledOn)**

$c := FilteredBy(a, u, v) : \forall n \in \mathbb{N}_{>0}, c \in \sigma(n)$ iff

$(a \in \sigma(n) \wedge (\text{if } k < |u| \text{ then } u[k] = 1 \text{ else } v[(k - |u|) \bmod |v|] = 1), \text{where } k = \chi_\sigma(a, n))$ **(FilteredBy)**

where $a, b \in \mathcal{C}, u, v \in (0+1)^*, d \in \mathbb{N}_{>0}. |u|$ represents the length of binary word u to count the number of binary bits in u. ∎

The first three clock expressions are based on **Subclock**. **Union** builds the slowest super clock of two given clocks. **Intersection** builds the fastest clock that is a **Subclock** of two given clocks. **Minus** $a\backslash b$ builds the clock that ticks whenever a ticks but b does not.

The next two clock expressions are based on **Causality**. **Infimum** builds the slowest clock that is faster than two given clocks. **Supremum** builds the fastest clock that is slower than two given clocks.

The next expression $Delayfor(a, b, d)$ produces a clock which ticks in coincidence with the next d^{th} tick of b after once tick of a. The sampling expression $SampledOn(a, b)$ produces a clock that ticks in coincidence with the tick of the base clock a immediately following a tick of the trigger clock b. These two clock expressions, which are based on both **Subclock** and **Causality**, can be called mixed-based form.

Filtering expression $FilteredBy(a, u, v)$ is also written in the form of $a \blacktriangledown (u.(v)^\omega)$, where u is a prefix, and v a periodical pattern. It defines the clock as a **Subclock** of a according to two binary words u and v.

Table 2 show us the direct and indirect clock constraints between new clock and the original one(s) implied by different clock expressions. Column 2 in Table 2 exhibits the interpretation based on instant set for each clock expression.

We can introduce alias for some special clock expression:

$a \$ d := DelayFor(a, a, d)$ **(Delay)**
$StrictSampledOn(a, b) := DelayFor(a, b, 1)$ **(StrictSampledOn)**

Although $DelayFor$ is an expression of mixed form, **Delay** expression $a \$ d$, as one of its special case, has been become a Subclock-based one because the two input clocks are the same one, produces a sub-clock that is always a given number of ticks d late compared to its original clock a. A new clock generated by **Delay** expression $a \$ d$ impose the constraints $\forall n \in \mathbb{N}, \chi_\sigma(a \$ d, n) = \max(\chi_\sigma(a, n) - d, 0)$ on all the corresponding schedule σ.

By composing the relation and the expressions provided in Definitions 5 and 6, it is necessary to define new clock relations, for example:

Table 2. Attributes of Clock Expressions (new clock is c)

Clock expression	Instant/Index constraint	Relations implied	Further causality	Remark
$a + b$	$\mathbb{I}_{c,\sigma} = \mathbb{I}_{a,\sigma} \cup \mathbb{I}_{b,\sigma}$	$a \subset c, b \subset c$	$c \preccurlyeq a, c \preccurlyeq b$	Subclock-based
$a * b$	$\mathbb{I}_{c,\sigma} = \mathbb{I}_{a,\sigma} \cap \mathbb{I}_{b,\sigma}$	$c \subset a, c \subset b$	$a \preccurlyeq c, b \preccurlyeq c$	Subclock-based
$a \setminus b$	$\mathbb{I}_{c,\sigma} = \mathbb{I}_{a,\sigma} \setminus \mathbb{I}_{b,\sigma}$	$c \subset a, c \,\#\, b$	$a \preccurlyeq c$	Subclock-based
$sup(a, b)$	$\forall k, c_\sigma[k] = a_\sigma[k]$, if $a_\sigma[k] \geq b_\sigma[k]$, $c_\sigma[k] = b_\sigma[k]$, else	$a \preccurlyeq c, b \preccurlyeq c$		Causality-based
$inf(a, b)$	$\forall k, c_\sigma[k] = a_\sigma[k]$, if $a_\sigma[k] \leq b_\sigma[k]^\dagger$, $c_\sigma[k] = b_\sigma[k]$, else	$c \preccurlyeq a, c \preccurlyeq b$		Causality-based
$DelayFor$ (a, b, d)	$\forall k, \exists j < k, \exists l > k + d,$ $c_\sigma[k] = b_\sigma[l] \wedge b_\sigma[l - d] \leq a_\sigma[j] < b_\sigma[l - d + 1]$	$c \subset b, a \preccurlyeq c$	$a \preccurlyeq c, b \preccurlyeq c$	Mixed
$SampledOn$ (a, b)	$\forall k, \exists j \leq k, \exists l \geq k,$ $c_\sigma[k] = b_\sigma[l] \wedge b_\sigma[l - 1]^\ddagger < a_\sigma[j] \leq b_\sigma[l]$	$c \subset b, a \preccurlyeq c$	$b \preccurlyeq c$	Mixed
$a \blacktriangledown (u.$ $(v)^\omega)$	$\forall k, c_\sigma[k] = a_\sigma[u.(v)^\omega \uparrow k]$	$c \subset a$	$a \preccurlyeq c$	Subclock-based

Note: (1) σ occurs in column 2 is a model of corresponding clock expression.

    (2) $^\dagger b_\sigma[k]$ does not exist is allowed here.

    (3) ‡Here we assume $b_\sigma[l-1] = 0$ if $l = 1$.

    (4) $u.(v)^\omega \uparrow k$ denotes the index of the kth '1' in the binary word $u.(v)^\omega$.

$$a \sim b := a \prec b \prec a \,\$ 1 \quad \textbf{(Alternation)} \tag{3}$$

$$a \prec_n b := a \prec b \prec a \,\$ n \quad \textbf{(Bounded precedence)} \tag{4}$$

$$a \equiv b := a \preccurlyeq b \bigwedge b \preccurlyeq a \quad \textbf{(Coincidence)} \tag{5}$$

$$a \bowtie b := (a \prec b \,\$ 1) \bigwedge (b \prec a \,\$ 1) \quad \textbf{(Synchronization)} \tag{6}$$

Alternation, used frequently in CCSL specification, is a special case of **Bounded precedence**.

5   Analysis of CCSL Specification

5.1   Transition System Based on State

A transition system is a tuple $<Q, q^0, \Sigma, \rightarrow>$, where Q is a set of states, $q^0 \in Q$ is an initial state, Σ is a state of labels, and $\rightarrow \subseteq Q \times \Sigma \times Q$ is a set of transition. We write a transition $<q, a, q'>$ in $\rightarrow$ as $q \xrightarrow{a} q'$. The system starts from the initial state q^0, and then can change its state form q to q' if $q \xrightarrow{a} q'$. We write $q \rightarrow q'$ if $q \xrightarrow{a} q'$ for some label $a \in \Sigma$. $q \rightarrow *q'$ denotes that state q' is **reachable** from the state q.

The state space $\mathcal{S}$, for a given CCSL specification $\mathcal{SPEC} = <\mathcal{C}, \mathcal{R}>$, is the set of function $v : \mathcal{C} \rightarrow \mathbb{N}$ that assigns a natural number for every clock in $\mathcal{C}$. v_0 is a special function denotes $v_0(c) = 0$ for all clock $c \in \mathcal{C}$. Thus we can define the semantics of $\mathcal{SPEC}$ by associating a transition system $TS_{\mathcal{SPEC}}$ with it.

Definition 11 (CCSL Transition System). For a given CCSL specification $\mathcal{SPEC} = <\mathcal{C}, \mathcal{R}>$, $TS_{\mathcal{SPEC}}$ is the transition system $<\mathcal{S}, v_0, 2^{\mathcal{C}} \backslash \emptyset, \rightarrow>$ with definition of $\rightarrow$: $v \xrightarrow{\lambda} v'$ if $v'(c) = v(c) + 1$ for a clock $c \in \lambda$ otherwise $v'(c) = v(c)$, for simplicity we write $v' = v + \lambda$. ∎

According to Definition 2, if we let $\lambda_i = \sigma(i)$, $v_i(c) = \chi_\sigma(c, i)$ for every clock $c \in \mathcal{C}$ and $i \in \mathbb{N}$, then $v_0 \xrightarrow{\lambda 1} \ldots \xrightarrow{\lambda i} v_i \xrightarrow{\lambda i + 1} \cdots$ is one trace of $TS_{\mathcal{SPEC}}$. It is noted that every label $\lambda \neq \emptyset$ implies that there is no self-loop transition from one state to itself in transition set. This corresponds that stuttering transitions are not allowed along a schedule. Therefore, we can say that $TS_{\mathcal{SPEC}}$ characterizes all the schedules σ such that $\sigma \vDash \mathcal{SPEC}$.

The reachable state set of $TS_{\mathcal{SPEC}}$ is $\{v | v_0 \rightarrow *v\}$. We say one clock c is an **enabled clock** at state v, if $v \xrightarrow{\lambda} v'$ for some state v' and $c \in \lambda. \cup_i \{\lambda_i | \exists v', v \xrightarrow{\lambda i} v'\}$ is called **enabled clock set** at state v, and denoted as **enabled**(v). A clock c is **disabled** at state v if we cannot find a state v' such that $v \xrightarrow{\lambda} v'$ and $c \in \lambda$, all the disabled clocks at state v forms the **disabled clock set,** and denoted as **disabled**(v). Obviously, a clock $c \in \mathcal{C}$ in **disabled**(v) or **disabled**(v), but not both. This is implied by **disabled**(v) = $\mathcal{C}\backslash$**enabled**(v).

It is hard to analysis the transition system with infinite state space. To address this problem, one can abstract the transition system for some specification, such as periodic one defined in Definition 14 below, as its stable quotient with respect to an equivalence relation $\approx$ over state space. $\approx$ is stable if and only if whenever $q \approx u$ and $q \xrightarrow{\lambda} q'$, there exists a state u' such that $u \xrightarrow{\lambda} u'$ and $q' \approx u'$.

5.2   Different Kinds of Specification

Definition 12 (Potential Deadlock Specification). A CCSL specification $\mathcal{SPEC} = <\mathcal{C}, \mathcal{R}>$ is potential deadlock, if there is a reachable set v of $TS_{\mathcal{SPEC}}$, such that **enabled**$(v) = \emptyset$. ∎

According to the previously mentioned relation between a schedule σ such that $\sigma \vDash \mathcal{SPEC}$ and $TS_{\mathcal{SPEC}}$, potential deadlock is caused by the possible inconsistence in specification when we computing satisfaction of $\mathcal{SPEC}$ the based on Definition 7 or interpreting the clock expression based on Definition 10.

Definition 13 (Inconsistent Specification). A CCSL specification $\mathcal{SPEC} = <\mathcal{C}, \mathcal{R}>$ is inconsistent, if we cannot find a schedule σ **over** $\mathcal{C}$ such that $\sigma \vDash \mathcal{SPEC}$. This can be checked by $\forall \sigma$, $\sigma \nvDash \psi$ for some sub-clause ψ of $\mathcal{R}$. ■

We also call inconsistent specification unsatisfied one. There are several possible types unsatisfactions based on the different form of ψ occurs in Definition 13 according to Definitions 7 and 10:

- **TYPE 1** ψ is a conflict primitive formula such as $c \# c$ or $c \prec c^1$ for some clock c. Obviously we cannot find a schedule satisfies ψ.
- **TYPE 2** ψ is in the form of $\psi_1 \wedge \psi_2$ for some mutually contradictory sub-clauses ψ_1 and ψ_2 of $\mathcal{R}$, i.e., $\forall \sigma$, $\sigma \vDash \psi_1 \implies \sigma \nvDash \psi_2$. For example, $\psi_1 = a \prec b$, $\psi_2 = b \preccurlyeq a$. Note that ψ_1 or ψ_2 may also be the conjunction of other clauses.
- **TYPE 3** We can find at least two mutually contradictory instant/index constraints by Tables 1 and 2 for sub-clause ψ of $\mathcal{R}$ or some implicated clock in $\mathcal{C}$.

A specification, which is *not* inconsistent, is said to be a consistent one. Here we define a special kind of consistent specification, which will be illustrated on an example in case study section.

Definition 14 (Periodic Specification). A CCSL specification $\mathcal{SPEC} = <\mathcal{C}, \mathcal{R}>$ is periodic for a user-defined nonempty clock subset $\mathcal{U} \subseteq \mathcal{C}$, if for each σ over $\mathcal{U}$, $\sigma \vDash \mathcal{SPEC} \Rightarrow$ there exists an sequence $\{n_i\}$ such that $\forall c \in \mathcal{U}$, $\{\chi_\sigma(c, n_i)\}$ is an arithmetic sequence with the positive common difference $\delta_i^c = \chi_\sigma(c, n_{i+1}) - \chi_\sigma(c, n_i)$. $[n_{i+1} .. n_{i+1}]$ is a cycle of σ, and $MT = \max_{c \in \mathcal{U}} \{\delta_i^c\}$ is the maximum tick times within a cycle. $\mathcal{SPEC}$ is simply said to be periodic if $\mathcal{U} = \mathcal{C}$. ■

Definition 14 states that the schedule, which satisfies the periodic specification $\mathcal{SPEC}$ for the user-defined clock set $\mathcal{U} \subseteq (\mathcal{SPEC})$, has the periodical behavior in each cycle with respect to the clock set $\mathcal{U}$. If we assign every time slot for each tick of every clock in $\mathcal{U}$, it is enough to assign at most $MT \times |\mathcal{U}|$ slots for characterizing the complete behavior. Therefore, we say periodic specification is allocate-able since the associated execution platform only has the finite memory. Of course, we suppose that there is no prominent significance about the ticks of the clock in $\mathcal{C} \backslash \mathcal{U}$. Hence $\mathcal{U}$ must be chosen carefully to *abstract* the system specified by $\mathcal{SPEC}$.

---

[1] We don't allow such a schedule σ that $\forall i > 0$, $c \notin \sigma(i)$ to avoid to check the inconsistence caused by $c \prec c$ or $c \# c$ because here σ is **over** $\mathcal{C}$ including c.

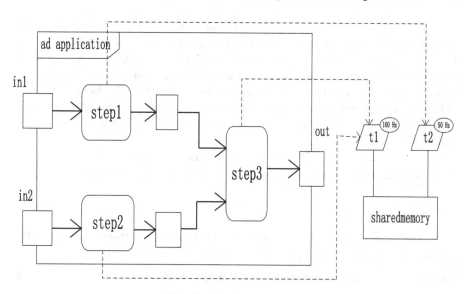

Fig. 1. Simple application

6 Case Study

To illustrate the approach, we take an example inspired by [12], that was used for flow latency analysis on Architecture Analysis and Design Language(AADL) specifications. However, with CCSL we are conducting different kinds of analyses.

Figure 1 considers a simple application described as a UML as structured class. This application captures two inputs *in1* and *in2*, performs some calculations (*step1, step2* and *step3*) and then produces a result *out*. This application has the possibility to compute *step1* and *step2* concurrently depending on the chosen execution platform. This application runs in a streaming-like fashion by continuously capturing new inputs and producing outputs. To abstract this application as a CCSL specification, we assign one clock to each action. The clock has the exact same name as the associated action (e.g., *step1*). We also associate one clock with each input, this represents the capturing time of the inputs, and one clock with the production of the output (*out*). The successive instants of the clocks represent successive executions of the actions or input sensing time or output release time. The basic CCSL specification is $\mathcal{SPEC}_{\text{simp}} = <\mathcal{C}, \mathcal{R}>$, where $\mathcal{C} = \{in1, in2, step1, step2, step3, out\}$, $\mathcal{R}$ is conjunction of the following clock constraints, i.e., $\mathcal{R} = (7)\wedge(8)\wedge(9)$:

$$in1 \preccurlyeq step1 \bigwedge step1 \prec step3 \tag{7}$$

$$in2 \preccurlyeq step2 \bigwedge step2 \prec step3 \tag{8}$$

$$step3 \preccurlyeq out \tag{9}$$

(7) specifies that step1 may begin as soon as an input *in1* is available. Executing *step3* also requires step1 to have produced its output. (8) is similar for *in2* and *step2*. (9) states that an output can be produced as soon as *step3* has executed. $\mathcal{SPEC}_{\text{simp}}$ is not potential deadlock specification because clock *in1* or *in2* is always enabled in every reachable state of. Therefore, such a specification is **free of deadlock**. Furtherly, $\mathcal{SPEC}_{\text{simp}}$ is a **consistent** specification since there aren't mutually contradictories in $\mathcal{R}$. Nevertheless, $\mathcal{SPEC}_{\text{simp}}$ is adapted to capture infinite FIFOs denoted on the figure as object nodes.

One way to transform $\mathcal{SPEC}_{\text{simp}}$ into finite state one, denotes $\mathcal{SPEC}_{\text{simp}'} = <\mathcal{C}'$, $\mathcal{R}' >$, is to add a CCSL constraint like (10) as a new sub-clause of $\mathcal{R}$.

$$in1 + in2 \sim out \tag{10}$$

Now $\mathcal{R}' = \mathcal{R}\wedge(10)$. By expanding the definition of **Alternation** in (3) and using Definition 5, we get $\mathcal{C}' = \mathcal{C}\bigcup\{in_{12}, in_{12}\$1\}$ where $in_{12} = in1 + in2$.

Theorem 1. $\mathcal{SPEC}_{\text{simp}'}$ is a potential deadlock specification.   ■

Proof of Theorem 1: According to potential deadlock in Definition 12, Under the condition that the first instant of *in1* and *in2* is not coincident, for example, *in1* [1] $>$ *in2* [1], we can find a reachable state v in $TS_{\mathcal{SPEC}simp'}$ such that $v(in1) = v(step1) = v(in_{12}) = 1$, $\forall c \in \mathcal{C}'\backslash\{in1, in_{12}, step1\}$, $v(c) = 0$ and **enabled**$(v) = \emptyset$. We say v is reachable since $v_0 \overset{\{in1, step1, in_{12}\}}{\rightarrow} v'$. We say all the clock is disabled at v because (10) prevents in_{12} from ticking again before *out* ticks. But since *in2* was not produced and therefore *step2* was not executed, then *step3* cannot execute either since it requires both *step1* and *step2*. If *step3* cannot execute, then *out* cannot be produced, which then results in a deadlock. In fact, deadlock exists in this specification unless $in1 \equiv in2$.   ■

$\mathcal{SPEC}_{\text{simp}'}$ is consistent under the condition $in1 \equiv in2$. Otherwise we can find the deadlock caused by the inconsistence stated that mutually contradictory sub-clauses $in_{12} \prec out$ and $out \prec in_{12} \$ 1$ when trying to fire *out* after step k such that $in1[k] \neq in2[k]$ first time. $\mathcal{SPEC}_{\text{simp}'}$ become inconsistent because of introducing (10). We can eliminate the inconsistence caused by (10) via substituting (10) by (11).

$$inf(in1, in2) \sim out \tag{11}$$

Let $inf_{in12} = inf(in1, in2)$, now we get another specification $\mathcal{SPEC}_{\text{simp}''} = <\mathcal{C}'', \mathcal{R}'' >$ where $\mathcal{R}'' = \mathcal{R}\wedge(11)$, $\mathcal{C}'' = \mathcal{C}\bigcup\{inf_{in12}, inf_{in12}\$1\}$ correspondingly.

Theorem 2. $\mathcal{SPEC}_{\text{simp}''}$ is a consistent periodic specification.   ■

Proof of Theorem 2: Suppose a schedule σ over $\mathcal{C}''$ such that $\sigma \models \mathcal{SPEC}_{\text{simp}''}$, we can find a sequence $\{n_i\}$ such that $\chi_\sigma(c, n_i) = i + 1$ for every clock $c \in \mathcal{C}''$ no matter what feasible choice is made throughout σ. Obviously, $\forall c \in \mathcal{C}''$, $\{\chi_\sigma(c, n_i)\} = \{i + 1\}$ is an arithmetic sequence with positive common difference 1. This is periodicity's requirement of Definition 14 indeed. The consistence of $\mathcal{SPEC}_{\text{simp}''}$ is guaranteed by the existence of some σ according to Definition 13.   ■

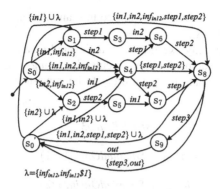

Fig. 2. Abstract transition system for $\mathcal{SPEC}_{\text{simp}''}$

Because of the periodicity of $\mathcal{SPEC}_{\text{simp}''}$, Fig. 2 shows the abstracted transition system $[TS_{\mathcal{SPEC}simp''}] \approx$ with the definition of $\approx$ over $\mathcal{S}$:

$$\forall v, v' \in \mathcal{S}, v \approx v' \text{ if and only if } \forall c, c' \in C'', v(c) = v(c') \Leftrightarrow v'(c) = v'(c').$$

For simplicity, singleton set is depicted by its element on some edges of Fig. 2. The reachable set of $TS_{\mathcal{SPEC}simp''}$ can be expressed as

$$\{v \mid v(\inf_{in12}\$1) + 1 \geq v(\inf_{in12}) \geq v(in1) \geq v(step1) > v(step3)$$
$$\bigwedge v(\inf_{in12}) \geq v(in2) \geq v(step2) > v(step3) \geq v(out) \geq v(\inf_{in12}\$1)\}.$$

In fact, every inequality follows Definitions 7 and 10.

CCSL can also be used to capture the execution platform. Figure 1 (right part) shows the selected execution platform: two tasks with different activation periods. First, the execution platform requires introducing two implicit clocks $t1$ and $t2$ to describe two threads run in *sharedMemory*:

$$t1 = ms \blacktriangledown (1.0^9)^\omega \tag{12}$$

$$t2 = t1 \blacktriangledown (1.0)^\omega \tag{13}$$

where *ms* is a particular clock that denotes milliseconds, and ticks once every millisecond. Being periodic on *ms* with a period of 10 makes $t1$ a 100 Hz clock and therefore $t2$ a 50 Hz clock.

When the execution platform is specified, the remaining task is to map the application onto the execution platform. In MARTE, this is done through an allocation. In CCSL, this is done by refining the two specifications with new constraints that specify this allocation. Since both *step2* and *step3* are allocated on the same thread, then their execution is exclusive described by (14). Then, two implicit clocks are used to describe that the inputs are sampled according to the period of activation of the threads (15) and (16). Then *step3* needs inputs from both *step1* and *step2* before executing but it can execute only according to the sampling period of *t1* since *step3* is allocated to *t1*((17) and (18).

Finally, all steps can only execute when their input data have been sampled (19). Similar to (11), the two sampled inputs execute alternating with the final output (20). (It is $\prec$ rather than $\preceq$ as that of [5], in order to be consistent with the constraints in (7) and (8).)

$$step2 \,\#\, step3 \tag{14}$$

$$in1\_s = SampledOn(in1, t1) \tag{15}$$

$$in2\_s = SampledOn(in2, t2) \tag{16}$$

$$sup_{st12} = sup(step1, step2) \tag{17}$$

$$d3\_s = SampledOn(sup_{st12}, t1) \tag{18}$$

$$in1\_s \preceq step1 \land in2\_s \preceq step2 \land d3\_s \prec step3 \tag{19}$$

$$inf(in1\_s, in2\_s) \sim out \tag{20}$$

Now we have a CCSL specification $\mathcal{SPEC}_{simp\_alloc} = <\mathcal{C}''', \mathcal{R}'''>$, where $\mathcal{R}'''$ = (12)∧(13)∧(14)∧(19)∧(9)∧(20), and $\mathcal{C}''' = \{ms, t1, t2, in1, in2, in1\_s, in2\_s, step1, step2, sup_{st12}, d3\_s, step3, inf_{in12\_s}, out, inf_{in12\_s} \$1\}$ with $inf_{in12\_s} = inf(in1\_s, in2\_s)$.

$\mathcal{SPEC}_{simp\_alloc}$ is obviously not periodic like $\mathcal{SPEC}_{simp''}$ because the calculation may be preformed as soon as there are the sampled inputs, which is not periodic with respect to the physical time denoted by the particular clock *ms*. Fortunately, every calculation process has the periodicity with respect to the sampled inputs.

Theorem 3. $\mathcal{SPEC}_{simp\_alloc}$ is a periodic specification for $\mathcal{U} = \{in1\_s, in2\_s, step1, step2, sup_{st12}, d3\_s, step3, inf_{in12\_s}, out, inf_{in12\_s}\$1\}$. ∎

Proof of Theorem 3: Similar to that of **Theorem 2**. For every schedule σ over $\mathcal{U}$ such that $\sigma \vDash \mathcal{SPEC}_{simp\_alloc}$, an sequence $\{n_i\}$, such that $\chi_\sigma(c, n_i) = i + 1$ for every clock $c \in \mathcal{U}$, can be found and then checked it is indeed an expect one. ∎

$\mathcal{U}$ is chosen to reduce the complexity and without losing the necessary behaviors. First, only associated logical clocks are considered since $\mathcal{SPEC}_{simp\_alloc}$ is not a physical time-related specification. Therefore, clocks *ms*, *t1* and *t2*, which are used to measure the physical time despite that they are in the logical form, are not candidate in $\mathcal{U}$. Second, according to Definition 10, once one tick of input clock (*in1* or *in2*) is triggered, the corresponding sampled signal (*in1_s* or *in2_s*) must then be captured. Therefore, the resulting calculation depend on *in1_s* and *in2_s* rather than *in1* and *in2*. Thus, $\mathcal{U} = \mathcal{C}''' \backslash \{ms, t1, t2, in1, in2\}$. We can get the finite-state abstracted transition system $[TS_{\mathcal{SPEC}simp\_alloc}]_{\approx}$, with definition an equivalence relation $\approx$ over $\mathcal{S}$:

$$\forall v, v' \in \mathcal{S}, v \approx v' \text{ if and only if } \forall c, c' \in \mathcal{U}, v(c) = v(c') \Leftrightarrow v'(c) = v'(c').$$

$[TS_{\mathcal{SPEC}\text{simp\_alloc}}]_{\approx}$ is similar to Fig. 2 and omitted here. The following is the reachable set of the transition system $TS_{\mathcal{SPEC}\text{simp\_alloc}}$:

$$\{v : C''' \rightarrow \mathbb{N} | v(inf_{in12\_s}\$1) + 1 \geq v(inf_{in12\_s}) \geq v(in1\_s) \geq v(step1) \geq v(sup_{st12})$$
$$\bigwedge v(inf_{in12\_s}) \geq v(in2\_s) \geq v(step2) \geq v(sup_{st12}) \geq v(d3\_s) > v(step3) \geq v(out) \geq v(inf_{in12\_s}\$1)\}.$$

In fact, $\mathcal{SPEC}_{\text{simp\_alloc}}$ can be viewed as calculation unit to response the two inputs *in1* and *in2*. Once the two inputs are given by external environment, $\mathcal{SPEC}_{\text{simp\_alloc}}$ will sample the inputs and finally give the output. It keeps idle otherwise.

7 Related Work

Some techniques were provided as an effort to analyze CCSL specifications. F. Mallet etc. [13] implemented the automatic analysis by translating CCSL into signal, for the purpose of generating executable specifications through discrete controller synthesis. However, this work did not consider the Infimum and Supremum operators that introduce unbounded counters. Exhaustive analysis of CCSL through a transformation into labeled transition systems has already been attempted in [14]. However, in those attempts, the CCSL operators were bounded because the underlying model-checkers cannot deal with infinite labeled transition systems. In [15], the authors showed that even though the primitive constraints were unbounded, the composition of these primitive constraints could lead to a system where only a finite number of states were accessible. [16] defines a notion of safety for CCSL and establish a condition to decide whether a specification is safe on the transformed marked graph from CCSL. We have tried to define a applicable data structure to detect divergence in CCSL specification [17].

All the above works share one common point: the specification analysis were done by some transformation and performed on the transformed target. The results were dependent on the correctness and efficiency of the mechanized transformation.

I. Zaretska etc. introduces a notion of time structure with clocks to refine describing denotational semantics for a pure relational subset of CCSL [18]. Our work in Sect. 3 is inspired by work in [18]. Yin etc. analyzes the schedule ability with the help of distinguishing clock halt from proper termination for some clock [10]. Clock halt, means abnormal termination of a clock, is similar to deadlock in Definition 12. The clocks' proper termination isn't in this paper's scope because we don't care about the finite clock.

Our contribution here is to represent all the feasible schedules by a state-transition system with the configurations as state spaces.

8   Conclusion and Future Works

Based on the state-based semantics of a kernel subset of CCSL, this paper gives one time structure in which we can relate the clock instant set with the state space. We also discuss some interesting properties about this time structure. A state-transition system and its abstract form is proposed in order to analyze CCSL specification's possible features, such as potential deadlock, inconsistences caused by introducing new constraints, and periodicity of postulated behavior. Finally, we investigate some interesting features on a simple application by a improved specification step by step.

As a future work, we plan to design the algorithm to compute the reachable state set of the state-transition system. How to abstract the state-transition system without losing the necessary traces may also be an interesting research area.

References

1. OMG: UML Profile for MARTE v1.0. Object Management Group, November 2009 edn., 2009 formal/2009-11-02 (2009)
2. André, C., Mallet, F., Simone, R.D.: Modeling time(s). In: Presented at the Proceedings of the 10th International Conference on Model Driven Engineering Languages and Systems, Nashville, TN (2007)
3. André, C.: Syntax and semantics of the clock constraint specification language (CCSL). Inria I3S Sophia Antipolis, 15 June 2009
4. DeAntoni, J., Mallet, F.: TimeSquare: treat your models with logical time. In: Furia, Carlo A., Nanz, S. (eds.) TOOLS 2012. LNCS, vol. 7304, pp. 34–41. Springer, Heidelberg (2012). doi:10.1007/978-3-642-30561-0_4
5. Mallet, F., Millo, J.-V., Romenska, Y.: State-based representation of CCSL operators, 19 July 2013
6. Benveniste, A., Caspi, P., Edwards, S.A., Halbwachs, N., Le Guernic, P., de Simone, R.: The synchronous languages 12 years later. Proc. IEEE **91**, 64–83 (2003)
7. Mallet, F.: Logical Time @ Work for the Modeling and Analysis of Embedded Systems. LAP LAMBERT Academic Publishing, Saarbrücken (2011)
8. Xu, Q., De Simone, R., Deantoni, J.: Logical clock constraint specification in PVS. Inria Sophia Antipolis, 25 June 2015
9. Ling, Y., Jing, L., Zuohua, D., Mallet, F., de Simone, R.: Schedulability analysis with CCSL specifications. In: 2013 20th Asia-Pacific Software Engineering Conference (APSEC 2013), pp. 414–421 (2013)
10. André, C., Mallet, F.: Combining CCSL and Esterel to specify and verify time requirements. Research report (2009)
11. André, C.: Verification of clock constraints: CCSL observers in Esterel. Research report, February 2010
12. Feiler, P.H., Hansson, J.: Flow latency analysis with the architecture analysis and design language (AADL). CMU technical note CMU/SEI-2007-TN-010 (2007)
13. Mallet, F., Andre, C.: UML/MARTE CCSL. Signal and Petri nets (2008)
14. Gascon, R., Mallet, F., DeAntoni, J.: Logical time and temporal logics: comparing UML MARTE/CCSL and PSL. In: 2011 Eighteenth International Symposium on Temporal Representation and Reasoning (TIME), pp. 141–148 (2011)

15. Mallet, F., Millo, J.-V.: Boundness issues in CCSL specifications. In: ICFEM 2013 - 15th International Conference on Formal Engineering Methods, pp. 20–35 (2013)
16. Mallet, F., Millo, J.-V., De Simone, R.: Safe CCSL specifications and marked graphs. In: MEMOCODE - 11th IEEE/ACM International Conference on Formal Methods and Models for Codesign, pp. 157–166 (2013)
17. Xu, Q., Simone, R., DeAntoni, J.: Divergence detection for CCSL specification via clock causality chain. In: Fränzle, M., Kapur, D., Zhan, N. (eds.) SETTA 2016. LNCS, vol. 9984, pp. 18–37. Springer, Cham (2016). doi:10.1007/978-3-319-47677-3_2
18. Zaretska, I., Zholtkevych, G., Zholtkevych, G., Mallet, F.: Clocks model for specification and analysis of timing in real-time embedded systems. In: ICTERI 2013, pp. 475–489 (2013)

Animation and Prototyping

Automated Safety Analysis on Scenario-Based Requirements for Train Control System

Xi Wang[1,2(✉)], Huaikou Miao[1,2], and Weikai Miao[3]

[1] School of Computer Engineering and Science, Shanghai University, Shanghai, China
wangxi@t.shu.edu.cn
[2] Shanghai Key Laboratory of Computer Software Testing and Evaluating,
Shanghai, China
[3] School of Computer Science and Software Engineering,
East China Normal University, Shanghai, China

Abstract. Train control system is a kernel component of railway transportation which acts as the controller of the involved equipment. With the popularization of train-based transportation, how to guarantee the safety of train control system becomes an important problem to be solved. This paper proposes a safety analysis method for train control system. It provides a scenario language for practitioners to describe their requirements on the train control system in terms of physical scenarios of the train operations. With the specification written in the scenario language, its implied hazards will be automatically identified by verifying its satisfaction of the given safety properties. In contrast to the traditional textual representation of the analysis result, animation technique is adopted to demonstrate the unsafe requirement in an intuitive way. A software tool has been developed to support the approach. It identifies the hazards of a given scenario specification and animates the physical scenarios that lead to the hazards. We also carried out a case study on the tool and the result shows the efficacy of the proposed approach.

1 Introduction

Serving as one of the kernel components of train-based transportation, train control system determines the running operations of the involved trains [1]. As a typical safety-critical system, its quality needs to be guaranteed to prevent fatal train accident that might lead to a huge loss of both life and wealth.

Safety analysis is one of the major activities for improving the quality of safety-critical systems [2]. It usually starts from hazard analysis that identifies the potential hazards of the system and results in safety requirements or properties that the system must hold to avoid hazard from happening. By checking the system specification against the safety properties, the developer is able to discover and reconstruct the unsafe requirements. Traditional methods adopt natural language to describe the safety properties and mainly depend on manual effort to verify the satisfaction of these properties. They facilitate the involvement of the domain experts in safety analysis since natural language is easy to use, but lack tool support due to the difficulty in natural language processing.

S. Liu et al. (Eds.): SOFL+MSVL 2016, LNCS 10189, pp. 55–73, 2017.
DOI: 10.1007/978-3-319-57708-1_4

To improve the automation level of safety analysis, formal methods has been introduced and regarded as a promising technique for software quality assurance [3]. Instead of traditional natural language, formal notation is used for describing both system specification and safety properties in formal methods. Its mathematical representation and formal semantics can effectively support precise description and rigorous verification. Many companies have tried formal methods to analyze the safety of the train control system under development, but failed to integrate it into the original development process [4]. One of the major reasons is that the appropriate application of formal methods requires for strong mathematical background and sufficient experience in using formal notations; most of the developers are not familiar with formal methods and feel difficult to apply it in practice [5]. Besides, the analysis result is usually represented in textual data without intuitive explanation. Due to the lack of semantic link between the textual data and physical scenarios of train operations, it is not easy for developers or domain experts to understand the analysis result, locate the unsafe requirements and reconstruct the specification accordingly.

In this paper, we propose a safety analysis method for train control system where a scenario language is provided for domain experts to describe their expected requirements in terms of physical scenarios of the train operations and a classification of train operation hazards is given to guide the verification of consistency between the physical scenarios and safety properties. The simplicity and understandability of the scenario language allow domain experts to focus on the design of train operations without the need of considering formal notation details. Hazard classification helps clarify the safety properties that must be satisfied by the train operations and facilitates automatic safety analysis on the scenario-based requirements. For each kind of hazards, a set of safety properties are given where the satisfaction of the properties can be automatically checked by a proposed algorithm. With a specification written by domain experts or developers in the scenario language, the implied hazards can be found by verifying whether the specification satisfies the given safety properties.

In contrast to the traditional textual representation of the analysis result, animation technique is adopted in our approach to demonstrate the unsafe requirement in a straightforward way. For each requirement that violates the safety properties, its corresponding physical scenario, which is consist of a sequence of train operations, will be automatically animated. Specifically, we studied the key elements of physical scenario and built mappings from each kind of element to an animation. By applying the animation mappings and combining related animations, an algorithm is given for transforming textual physical scenarios into animated ones. Such kind of analysis result clearly shows the cause and effect of the involved hazards, which provides effective guidance for the location of unsafe requirements and reconstruction of the original specification.

A supporting tool has been developed to demonstrate the feasibility of the proposed approach. It is composed of 4 components: *text processor* for analyzing the input textual scenario specification and transforming the scenario information into pre-defined data structure, *property library* for the management of our derived safety properties of train control systems, *hazard analyzer* for identifying hazards in the specification by checking the satisfaction of the properties in the *property library* and generating physical scenarios that lead to the occurrence of the identified hazards, *animation engine* for animating the generated physical scenarios. We have carried out a case study on the tool for validating the efficacy of the approach. The result shows that the approach can improve the efficacy of safety analysis for train control systems.

The rest of the paper is organized as follows. Section 2 overviews the latest techniques for safety analysis and the related work on safety analysis for train control system. Section 3 presents the proposed safety analysis approach for train control system and explains its technique details. A supporting tool is described in Sect. 4 and a case study on the tool is given that shows the efficacy of our approach. Finally, Sect. 5 concludes the paper and points out the futures works.

2   Related Work

With the increase of demand for software products in safety-critical systems, safety analysis on system specifications has raised much attention in software engineering. It mainly includes modeling method for describing safety-critical systems and safety properties in specifications and analysis method for checking the satisfaction of safety properties by system specifications.

Several modeling languages have been applied in the specification of the requirements of train control system. In [6], the authors propose a three-phases approach to formalizing the requirements of The European Train Control System. using UML language. They have also developed a set of tools to support each phase of the approach. In [7], train control system is firstly described in a UML model which will then be transformed into PSL model to facilitate the test of related properties. In [8], a modeling language ScOLA (Scenario Oriented Molding Language) is defined to formalize the specifications of railway systems. In [9], B method is applied to model data requirements for railway safety-related systems and the requirements will be used to carry out data validation. In [10], CSP is applied to model the control flow of system process with complex data types and timing parameters. However, the above languages are either lack of formal semantics or difficult to use in real practice. Besides, most of these languages are designed from functional perspective, making it difficult to understand the corresponding physical scenarios of a system specification. Our approach provides an easy-to-use language for describing physical scenarios of train operations, which improves the quality of safety analysis by carrying out the involved activities based on the real world.

There are mainly 4 kinds of methods for safety analysis of train control system: *review method, testing method, animation method* and *formal method. Review method* requires developers to review the system specification against given safety properties and provides specific guidance or criteria for facilitating the review process. In [11], the authors use mental model technique to analyze the behaviors and mental states of customers and provide clear criteria to guide the review process of system specifications. In [12], the authors propose an approach to analyzing requirements specification based on the notion of querying a model and describe a case study on a real-world application. In [13], the authors propose a review method that transforms system specifications into virtual prototype to be interacted with stakeholders to validate the satisfaction of given requirements. Although *review method* is widely used in industry since review activity can be easily carried out by practitioners, it is lack of rigorous verification technique and effective tool support. Besides, the execution of the review activities largely depends on the individual practitioners; its quality is hard to be guaranteed.

Testing method generates safety-related test cases and "executes" the test cases on the specification. Then the actual output of the execution will be compared with the expected output and the existence of unsafe requirements can be determined when difference is found. In [14], a specification testing method is proposed for reviewing task trees where a test case generation strategy is given for each kind of task trees. In [15], VDMTools is used to execute VDM specifications for IC Chip Firmware when analyzing the expected behaviors of the software. In [16], dynamic slicing technology has been adopted to build tool support for testing design specifications. *Testing method* emphasizes on the dynamic aspect of safety analysis and detects unsafe requirements by walking through the system specification. The disadvantage lies in the fact that it is difficult to cover all the unsafe requirements using testing and the safety of the system cannot be ensured.

Animation method usually applies model checking and specification execution to animate specifications. In [17], an animation-based inspection approach is proposed where the inspection process of the specification is guided by animating the relations between input and output of the selected functional scenarios. In [18], an animation approach is proposed for analyzing SCR tabular specification. In [19], a tool called UPPAAL is described which can automatically animate the target system using model checking. *Animation method* provides a more intuitive way to demonstrate various aspects of the target system and enables practitioners to carry out safety analysis based on a better understanding of the concerned functions. However, most of the existing methods can only animate on the model level without showing the relation between the model and the corresponding physical scenario, which makes it difficult for practitioners to analyze real system behaviors based on the specification.

Formal method differs from the former 3 methods in the way of mathematical verification which guarantees the correctness and completeness of safety analysis. Through model checking and formal proof, the satisfaction of the given properties by the target formal specification can be automatically verified. In [20], the authors propose a System-theory Process Analysis method for safety analysis of CTCS-3 Systems. It describes the system in PHAVer models and applies PHAVer tool to perform model checking on the PHAVer models. In [21], the authors applies RAISE approach to the development of distributed railway control system where RSL language is adopted to describe the system, as well as the safety constraints, and formal proof is used to prove the safety of the system.

In [22], theorem proving is adopted in verifying whether the given HCSP model of the target train control system satisfies the given properties. Despite the effectiveness in safety analysis, *formal method* requires for manual construction and good understanding of complex mathematical formulas. Its integration into the real software development process is still a challenging problem.

To take the advantage of both formal method and animation method, we use formal language to describe the physical scenario for train control system and automatically identify different kinds of hazards by verifying the system against different sets of safety properties. Based on the analysis result, the animation of the unsafe scenarios that lead to the identified hazards will be provided to facilitate unsafe requirements location and specification reconstruction.

3 Safety Analysis and Animation on Train Control System

Requirements specification is the key to the success of a software project. It serves as the foundation for the design and coding phases, as well as the benchmarks for testing and other software verification activities. Therefore, we carry out safety analysis on the requirements specification of train control system to guarantee the safety of the system to be developed based on the specification. The outline of the safety analysis approach is shown in Fig. 1.

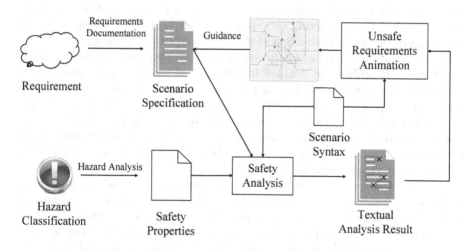

Fig. 1. The outline of the safety analysis approach for train control system

The approach includes two major steps: *safety analysis* for identifying the hazards implied by the scenario specification by checking the satisfaction of the given safety properties and *unsafe requirements animation* for animating the physical scenarios that lead to the occurrence of the identified hazards.

Safety analysis requires for 3 inputs before it can be carried out. The first input is a scenario specification of the target train control system which describes the physical scenarios of the train operations. A scenario language is designed for constructing the specification consisting of a railway route map and the behaviors of the trains running on the routes. Developers and domain experts should cooperate to evolve their original requirements in mind and produce a scenario specification by documenting the evolved requirements using the pre-defined scenario language. The specification will guide the following development phrases and its safety is therefore necessary to be verified.

The second input is a set of safety properties where each property needs to be satisfied to prevent hazards from happening when the target system is running. These properties are obtained by classifying hazards and analyzing each kind of hazards. Hazard classification provides a systematic way to summarize and organize implied hazards of train control system that might cause harm or damage. We divide hazards into single-train ones and multi-train ones. The former includes all the hazards caused by the operations of a single train while the latter includes all the hazards caused by the combination of operations of more than one train. These two categories are divided into concrete hazards that cannot be further decomposed into lower level hazards. For each concrete hazard, a set of safety properties can be obtained by analyzing the various causes of the hazard. The violation of any property in the set will lead to the occurrence of the hazard.

The third input is the syntax of the scenario language. Since automation is one of the main goals of our approach, the syntax of the specification to be ana-lyzed is needed for abstracting various kinds of elements from the specification and supporting the understanding of their semantics by machines.

With the above 3 inputs, *safety analysis* step will produce a textual analysis result which describes the detailed information of the detected hazards. It is carried out through 2 steps. The first step is to analyze the input specification based on the provided syntax of the scenario language and transform it into pre-defined data structures. The second step is to verify the processed specifica-tion with respect to each input safety property by the proposed algorithm and output the textual analysis result which includes the detailed information of the scenarios that violate certain properties.

Unsafe requirements animation takes the produced textual analysis result as input and animates the physical scenarios violating certain safety properties with the provided detailed information in the analysis result. Static elements of a scenario are mapped to animation objects while dynamic behaviors are linked with animated movements of the involved trains. An algorithm is given to integrate the mapped objects and movements into a complete animation.

To present the detail of the approach, we will explain the critical techniques respectively.

3.1   The Scenario Language

Scenario-based requirements need to be constructed by domain experts or developers who are not familiar with software requirements modeling languages, a simple notation that is easy to use and understand will greatly facilitate the construction process. On the other hand, ambiguity will strongly influence the effectiveness of automatic analysis, which indicates the importance of language precision. After an in-depth study and thorough analysis on the railway transportation system, we developed a language that describes physical scenario of the system in two parts: *static map* and *train movement*.

Static map part depicts the railway route map of the target train control system in a hierarchical structure which is shown in Fig. 2. A map is composed of a set of intersecting railway lines where each line is composed of a set of blocks. The lengths of all the blocks in the map are the same and each block can be attached with an offset indicating an exact position on the block. Stations in the map are supposed to be located on one block and those ones that lie across more than one block are not considered in this paper.

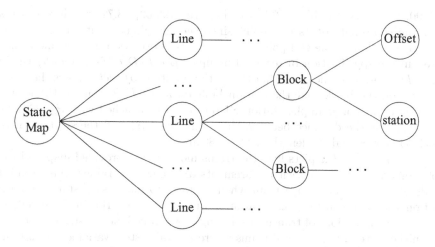

Fig. 2. The hierarchy structure of *static map*

An example *static map* is shown in Fig. 3 where Fig. 3(a) is the scenario specification of the map and Fig. 3(b) is the graphical representation of the map. There are two railway lines in the map where line A is composed of 6 blocks from $b1$ to $b6$ and line B is composed of 4 blocks from $b7$ to $b10$. Each block is attached with coordinate information for determining its position in the map. In addition to the first block that needs to be attached with the coordinates of both start point and end point, for any other block bi in a line, only the coordinate of its end point is needed since its start point is the same as the end point of block $b(i-1)$. For example, the first block $b1$ in line A is attached with $(0,0,100,0)$ indicating that the coordinate of its start point is $(0,0)$ and that of its end point

---

Map
   Line A
      Block b1(0, 0, 20, 0) Block b2(40, 0) Block b3(60, 0) Block b4(80, 0) Block b5(100, 0)

      Block b6(120, 0) Block b7(140, 20) Block b8(160, 20) ......
   Line B
      Block b14(140, 20, 160, 40) Block b15(180, 60) Block b16(200, 60) Block b17(220, 40)
      Block b18(240, 20) Block b19(220, 60) Block b20(240, 60) Block b21(260, 60)

   ......
Train t1(160, +)

      start(#(b1,0),360)   acc(1,20)   run(#(b44,0))   stop(#(b45,0)) ......
Train t2(160, +)

      start(#(b31,0),0)   acc(1,10)   acc(2,10)   run(#(36,0)) ......
Train t3(160, +)

      start(#(b23,0),300)   accTo(#(b24,0),20)   run(#(b26,0))   stop(#(b45,0)) ......

Fig. 3. The scenario specification and graphical representation of the example *static map*

is $(100, 0)$. The second block $b2$ is attached with $(99.62, -8.72)$ which represents only the coordinate of its end point since the coordinate of its start point is the same as that of the end point of $b1$. Station information of each line is also given in the specification in terms of a tuple $(BlockID, offset, length)$ where $BlockID$ represents the block that the station built on, $offset$ denotes the exact position on the block that the station built on and $length$ denotes the length of the station. For example, station $S1$ on line A is attached with $(b4, 20, 180)$ meaning that the distance between the midpoint of $S1$ and the start point of block $b4$ is 90 m and the length of $s1$ is 180 m.

   Train movement depicts how the trains move on the provided map and the notations for describing such requirements are shown in Table 1. There are 3 kinds of moving states for a train when it starts to move: stop state, uniform motion state and constant acceleration motion state. Scenarios in the specifications are combinations of transitions among these three kinds of states based on the initial state of the involved trains where several system variables are initialized including the initial location of the trains and the length of each train. Since a train needs to be accelerated from stationary state to run on the railway, the first two statements of *train movement* must be *start(Coordinate, Dwelltime)* expression and accelerating motion statement.

   An example *train movement* description is given as follows:

$$Train\ t1(160, +)$$
$$start(\#(b1, 0), 60)$$
$$acc(1, 10)$$
$$run(\#(b3, 60))$$
$$stop(\#(b4, 20))$$

Table 1. Notations for describing *train movement*

Notation	Explanation
$\#(BlockID, offset)$	For denoting the location of a concerned train. The distance between the head of the concerned train and the start point of block $BlockID$ is $offset$
$start(Coordinate, Dwelltime = 0)$	The concerned train starts to move from the location $Coordinate$ after waiting for $Dwelltime$ where the default value of $Dwelltime$ is 0
$stop(Coordinate)$	The concerned train stops at the location $Coordinate$
$run(ExpectedCoordinate)$	The concerned train runs at the speed same as the final speed on the previous state and stops at the location $ExpectedCoordinate$
$acc(Acceleration, ExpectedSpeed)$	The concerned train runs with the constant acceleration of $Acceleration$ and reaches the speed of $ExpectedSpeed$ at the end of the movement
$accTo(ExpectedCoordinate, ExpectedSpeed)$	The concerned train runs with a constant acceleration. At the end of the movement, its speed reaches $ExpectedSpeed$ and its location becomes $ExpectedCoordinate$ at the end of the movement

It depicts the operations of a train $t1$ of 160 m long running from start point to end point of each block of the route. After 60 s of waiting, $t1$ will start from the start point of block $b1$ and run with the constant acceleration of $1 \, \text{m/s}^2$ until reaching the speed of $10 \, \text{m/s}$. Then $t1$ will run at the constant speed of $10 \, \text{m/s}$ until reaching the location that is 60 m away from the start point of the block $b3$. Finally, $t3$ will decelerate until stopping at the location that is 20 m away from the start point of the block $b4$.

3.2 Hazard Classification and Analysis

After collecting and analyzing the accident materials in train-based transportation, we categorize the hazards led by train control system into two kinds: *single-train* hazards that are caused by a single train and *multi-train* hazards that are caused by the operations of more than one train.

Single-train hazards are further divided into 2 concrete hazards: derailment accident and passenger detention. Multi-train hazards contain only one concrete hazard: collision accident. These 3 concrete hazards correspond to 5 safety properties. We will present the analysis of each concrete hazard respectively.

Derailment Accident. Derailment accidents are usually seriously hazardous to human health and safety, their detection is one of the main tasks in safety analysis of train control system. There are several causes accounting for derailment accident, such as a collision with another object and so on. Since this paper focuses on safety analysis on train control system, we only consider the causes made by such kind of system.

Two causes were found for derailment accident. The first one is exceeding the speed limit and the corresponding safety property can be written as follows.

Property 1. Given a railway map m where the length of each block is l_b, for each train of length l_t running on the route $b_1 \rightarrow b_2 \rightarrow ... \rightarrow b_n$ with the speed limit of linear movement set as V_{max} and the speed limit of turning movement on each pair of adjacent blocks (b_i, b_{i+1}) set as V_i, its velocity v and location $\#(b_t, offset_t)$ must satisfy:

$$\{(b_j, b_{j+1}) \mid i < t \wedge i * l_b > (t - 1) * l_b + offset_t - l_t\} = \varnothing \wedge v \leq V_{max}$$
$$\vee \ \forall_{(b_p, b_{p+1}) \in \ \{(b_j, b_{j+1}) \mid i < t \wedge i * l_b > (t-1)*l_b + offset_t - l_t\}} \cdot v \leq v_p$$

Since speed limits of linear movement and turning movement are different, the velocity of each train should be restricted based on its location. When a train is running within one block, its velocity must be no more than the speed limit of linear movement. But when a train is running across blocks, its velocity must be no more than the speed limit of the involved adjacent blocks.

The second cause is running out of map border and the satisfaction of the following property will prevent it from happening.

Property 2. For each train running on the route $b_1 \rightarrow b_2 \rightarrow ... \rightarrow b_n$, its location $\#(b_t, offset_t)$ must always satisfy $1 \leq t \leq n \wedge 0 \leq offset_t \leq l_b$ where l_b denotes the length of the blocks in the route.

If the train always runs within the blocks of its route, it will not derail because of running out of the map border.

Passenger Detention. Passengers will get on and off the train when it enters and stops at the railway stations. If they have been detained in the station, more and more people will be gathered in small spaces which will likely result in stampede accidents. We found two main causes for passenger detention. The first one is running out of station border and the corresponding safety property can be written as follows.

Property 3. For each train t running on the route $b_1 \rightarrow b_2 \rightarrow ... \rightarrow b_n$ with a set of stations $\{s_1, ..., s_n\}$ where each station s_i is of length l_{s_i} and located at

$\#(b_{s_i}, offset_{s_i})$, the train's location $\#(b_t, offset_t)$ must satisfy:

$$v = 0 \Rightarrow \exists_{s \in \{s_1, \ldots, s_n\}} \cdot t * l_b + offset_t \leq s * l_b + offset_s + l_s$$
$$\wedge t * l_b + offset_t - l_t \geq s * l_b + offset_s$$

where l_b denotes the length of each block in the route and l_t denotes the length of t.

For each train running on the map, it must stay within one of the stations when it stops so that the passengers can get on board.

The second cause is exceeding the specified time range and the corresponding safety property can be written as follows.

Property 4. For each train t running on the route with a set of stations $\{s_1, \ldots, s_n\}$ where each station s_i is attached with a specified time range $[tr_i, tr_{i'}]$ for t, the time ts_i of t stopping at s_i must satisfy $tr_i \leq ts_i \leq tr_{i'}$.

Each station in the railway map will be given a time range for each train which specifies the time that the train should arrive at the station. Each train must enter and stop at each station within the corresponding time range.

Collision Accident. If more than one train is running on a railway map, collision accident may occur when the trains meet at their routes. Such an accident will probably lead to serious consequences and is caused by the fact that two or more trains reach the same location at the same time. The corresponding safety property is as follows.

Property 5. Given a railway map m and a set of trains $\{t_1, \ldots, t_n\}$ running on m at continuous time $T = \{time_1, \ldots, time_k\}$, the location of the trains must satisfy:

$$\forall_{t_i, t_j \in \{t_1, \ldots, t_n\}} \cdot \forall_{time \in T} \cdot distance(t_i, t_j, time) \geq (l_{t_i} + l_{t_j})/2$$

where $distance(t_i, t_j, time)$ denotes the distance between the midpoints of the trains t_i and t_j at time $time$ and l_{train} denotes the length of the train $train$.

Trains meet when they overlap on the map. Therefore, in order to prevent collision accident, we need to ensure that the distance between any two trains is greater than 0 at any time.

3.3 Safety Analysis

With a scenario specification of the target train control system, safety analysis is carried out by verifying the satisfaction of the provided 5 properties by the specification and generating the scenarios that lead to the violation of the properties. We give an algorithm for safety analysis as shown in Fig. 4 where $v(t, (b_j, offset))$ denotes the maximum velocity of the train t when running on

$\#(b_j, offset)$, $v(t, (b_j, b_{j+1}))$ denotes the maximum velocity of t when running on the angle between blocks b_j and b_{j+1}, $move_i^t(b_{j+1}, offset)$ denotes the scenarios of $move_i$ before the train t reaches the location $\#(b_j, offset)$, $coordinate(s)$ denotes the location $\#(b_j, offset)$, $direction(t)$ denotes the running direction of t and $route_t$ denotes the sequence of blocks that train t goes through. The input of the algorithm is the scenario specification stored in pre-defined data structures, including the static map m with a set of stations S and the movements of each train. The output of the train is a report for hazard identification and the scenarios that cause the hazards.

The algorithm verifies the safety properties for single-train hazards by analyzing the blocks that each movement of a single train performs on. When the violation of certain property is detected on a block, the corresponding cause and scenario information will be added to the final report. Multi-train hazards are identified by calculating the overlapping blocks of the routes of each two trains and the time points that the two trains run on the blocks. If the same time point on the same location is found, a collision hazard, as well as the cause and scenario information, will be added to the final report.

3.4   Unsafe Requirements Animation

Although textual analysis result is produced by the safety analysis algorithm, it still requires for much experience and considerable effort to understand the corresponding physical scenario and locate the cause of the detected hazards. Therefore, we adopt animation technique to provide a more intuitive way to demonstrate the safety analysis result.

The animation process takes the unsafe scenario requirements provided by safety analysis as input and produces the animation of the corresponding physical scenarios. Specifically, it transforms textual requirements into animation based on two kinds of mappings. The first kind is the static mappings from the elements in *static map* into static objects in the animation, including the mappings from blocks with coordinate information into railway lines and stations with coordinate information into station images in the animation. The second kind is the mappings from *train movement* to dynamic behaviors shown in the animation, i.e., the mappings from each kind of movement into the animated running operations of the trains.

With a textual scenario specification of the unsafe requirements consisting of a static map m and a set of movements $Move$ of the involved p trains where $Move = \{move_1^{t1}, move_2^{t1}, ..., move_n^{t1}, move_1^{t2}, ..., move_q^{tp}\}$ and each $move_j^{ti}$ denotes the jth movements performed by the train ti, an algorithm is given to produce the animation as shown in Fig. 5 where $Mapping1(x1, y1, x2, y2)$ denotes the mapped line connecting two points $(x1, y1)$ and $(x1, y1)$ for representing the block attached with the coordinate information $(x1, y1, x2, y2)$, $Mapping1(b, o, l)$ denotes the mapped image of the station attached with the coordinate information (b, o, l) and $Mapping2(t, originX, originY, destX, destY, para)$ denotes the mapped animation of the *para*-type movement of train t from point $(originX, originY)$ to

---

Algorithm   safetyAnalysis

For each train t {
  For each movement $move_i$ {
    For each block b_j that $move_i$ goes through {
      if $\exists_{offset>0} \bullet v(t, (b_j, offset)) > v_{max}$ {
        get minimum *offset* satisfying: $v(t, (b_j, offset)) > v_{max}$;
        add to the report: t over speed at $(b_j, offset)$
                 Scenarios: $move^t_1 \to \ldots \to move^t_i (b_j, offset)$
      }
      if b_j is not the last block {
        if $v(t, (b_j, b_{j+1})) > v_j$ **then** add Over speed at the angle between b_j and b_{j+1}
                 Scenarios: $move^t_1 \to \ldots \to move^t_i (b_{j+1}, 0)$
      }
      if $\forall_{line \ \in m} \bullet \neg\exists_{k \in N} \bullet b_k \in line \wedge k = j$
      then add Out of map border at $(b_j, offset)$ Scenarios: $move^t_1 \to \ldots \to move^t_i (b_j, offset)$
      if $\exists_{offset \ \in N} \bullet v(t,(b_j, offset)) = 0$ {
        if $\exists_{s \in S, p, offset \ \in N} \bullet coordinate(s) = (b_p, offset \ ) \wedge (direction(t) = + \wedge$
        $p*l_b + offset \ + l_s/2 \geq j*l_b + offset \wedge j*l_b + offset - l_t \geq p*l_b + offset - l_s/2 \vee direction(t) = -$
        $\wedge \ j*l_b + offset \geq p*l_b + offset \ - l_s/2 \wedge p*l_b + offset \ + l_s/2 \geq j*l_b + offset - l_t)$ {
          Calculate the time *time* that t spent from the start point to $\#(b_j, offset)$;
          if $time < tr_s \vee time > tr_s$ **then** add Exceeding time range at station s
                   Scenarios: $move^t_1 \to \ldots \to move^t_i (b_j, offset)$
        }
        else add to the report: Out of station border at station s
               Scenarios: $move^t_1 \to \ldots \to move^t_i (b_j, offset)$
      }
      $route_t = route_t + b_j$;
    }
  }
}
For each two trains t and t {
  Calculate the overlapping blocks of $route_t$ and $route_{t\bar{y}}$;
  For each overlapping block b_q {
    For each offset o in b_q {
      Calculate the time points tp and tp that t and t arrive at $\#(b_q, o)$ repectively;
      if $tp = tp$ **then** add Collision of t and t at (b_q, o)
                Scenarios: $move^t_1 \to \ldots \to move^t_i (b_q, o)$
                  $\cup move^t_1 \to \ldots \to move^t_i (b_q, o)$
    }
  }
}

Fig. 4. The algorithm for verifying the satisfaction of the 5 safety properties by a given scenario specification

---

Algorithm   reqAnimation

For each line *line*∈*m*{
   Draw *Mapping1(x1,y1,x2,y2)* where *(x1,y1,x2,y2)* is attached to the first block *b*∈*line*;
   preX = x1; preY = y1;
   For each block b$_i$∈*line-{b}* attached with *(x,y)*{
      Draw *Mapping1(preX, preY, x, y)*;
      preX = x; preY = y;
   }
}
For each station *s* attached with *(b, o, l)*{ Draw *Mapping1(b, o, l)*;}
For each movement *move$^{ti}_j$*∈ *Move*{
   Calculate the coordinates of the start point *(originX, originY)* and end point *(destX, destY)* of *move$^{ti}_j$*;
   if *move$^{ti}_j$* is a movement with constant speed *v*
   then Draw *Mapping2(t, originX, originY, destX, destY, v)*
   else if *move$^{ti}_j$* is a movement with constant acceleration *a*
   then Draw *Mapping2(t, originX, originY, destX, destY, a)*
   else if *move$^{ti}_j$* is *start(Coordinate, Dwelltime)*
   then Draw *Mapping2(t, originX, originY, destX, destY, Dwelltime)*
   else set *originX* and *OriginY* according to *Coordinate*
}

Fig. 5. The algorithm for scenario specification animation

point $(destX, destY)$ where $para = v$ indicating movement with constant speed v, $para = a$ indicating movement with constant acceleration a and $para = Dwelltime$ indicating stop for the time duration of $Dwelltime$.

The algorithm animates the static map first by drawing each block and station in the map based on their coordinate information and the static mapping knowledge. Then dynamic behaviors will be animated by analyzing each movement performed by each train and producing the animation of the movement based on the dynamic mapping knowledge and the detailed information of the movement including the coordinates of its start point and end point and the type of the movement. By combining the static objects and dynamic behaviors, a complete animation of the target scenario specification can be generated automatically.

4   Tool Design and Implementation

The main goal of our proposed approach is to automate the safety analysis on scenario specification for train control system. To validate the approach and demonstrate its efficiency, we implement it into a prototype tool. It takes textual scenario requirements of the target train control system as input and performs safety analysis on the specification to produce a hazard identification report, as well as the animation of the unsafe requirements.

Figure 6 shows the outline of the tool composed of 4 components: text processor, property library, hazard analyzer and property library. When the user imports a scenario specification, the tool will send the input text file into the

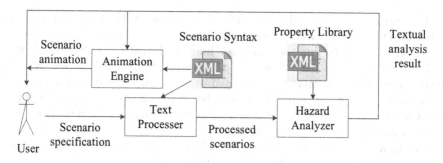

Fig. 6. The outline of the supporting tool

text processor. Based on the scenario syntax stored in a XML file, the *text proces-sor* analyzes the textual scenarios and represents them in a pre-defined format that can be recognized by the tool. Then the processed scenario information will be sent to *hazard analyzer* for safety analysis. By verifying the scenario require-ments against the safety properties in the *property library* stored as a XML file, the *hazard analyzer* can produce a textual analysis result which contains the identification of the implied hazards and the physical scenarios that cause the occurrence of the identified hazards. Such a textual analysis result will be sent to the user and the *animation engine*. For each identified hazard, the user can choose to look at the animation of the corresponding scenarios and the *anima-tion engine* will transform the selected textual information in the analysis result into an animation and display it to the user.

According to the above design, we implement the tool using C# and the main interface of the tool is shown in Fig. 7 where the left part displays the textual analysis result and the right part shows the animation of the selected scenarios.

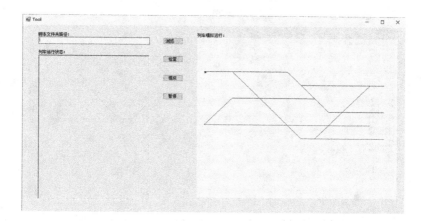

Fig. 7. The main interface of the safety anlaysis tool

A case study is conducted to show how the tool works. The imported scenario specification is shown in Fig. 8 (Only parts of the specification is given due to the sake of space). By pressing the "analyze" button, the safety analysis result will be displayed in the left part of the tool as shown in Fig. 9. Collision hazards are identified and the locations are highlighted in the map. To animate the physical scenarios that cause the collision hazards, button "animate" is pressed and the animation result is shown in Fig. 10. During the animation, button "pause" is provided for pausing and resuming the animation.

The result of the case study shows the effectiveness of our approach and tool in supporting safety analysis for train control system.

```
Map
  Line A
    Block b1(0, 0, 20, 0) Block b2(40, 0) Block b3(60, 0) Block b4(80, 0) Block b5(100, 0)

    Block b6(120, 0) Block b7(140, 20) Block b8(160, 20) ······
  Line B
    Block b14(140, 20, 160, 40) Block b15(180, 60) Block b16(200, 60) Block b17(220, 40)
    Block b18(240, 20) Block b19(220, 60) Block b20(240, 60) Block b21(260, 60)

  ······
Train t1(160, +)

    start(#(b1,0),360)   acc(1,20)     run(#(b44,0))     stop(#(b45,0))  ······
Train t2(160, +)

    start(#(b31,0),0)    acc(1,10)     acc(2,10)     run(#(36,0))  ······
Train t3(160, +)

    start(#(b23,0),300)  accTo(#(b24,0),20)   run(#(b26,0))     stop(#(b45,0))  ······
```

Fig. 8. The scenario specification for the case study

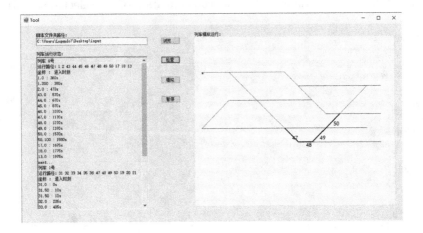

Fig. 9. The analysis result of the case study

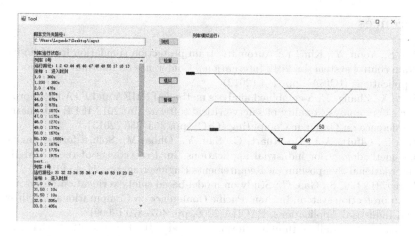

Fig. 10. The animation result of the case study

5   Conclusion

Safety analysis for train control system plays an important role in quality assurance of train-based transportation. In this paper, we present a scenario-based approach to safety analysis for train control system which carries out hazard identification on the scenario specification of the target system. A scenario language is provided in the approach for developers and domain experts to describe their expectations on the system. With the specified scenario requirements, the approach verifies the satisfaction of the given safety properties by the requirements. Then animation technique is adopted to animate the physical scenarios that lead to the violation of certain property. We also developed a tool for supporting the approach. By presenting a case study on the tool, we explain the main functions of the tool and demonstrate the effectiveness of the approach.

Writing textual specification using the given scenario language is still not intuitive enough for the practitioners. We plan to provide a visualized approach to support the drawing of the static map and the arrangement of the train movements. The tool support will also be enhanced in our future research.

Acknowledgments. This research is supported by the NSFC grants (No. 61402178, No. 61572306 and No. 91418203), STCS (No. 14YF1404300) and Shanghai Municipal Education Commission Training Program for University Young Teachers (No. ZZSD15071).

References

1. Oh, S., Yoon, Y., Kim, Y.: Automatic train protection simulation for radio-based train control system. In: 2012 International Conference on Information Science and Applications (ICISA), pp. 1–4 (2012)
2. Han, X., Zhang, J.: A combined analysis method of FMEA and FTA for improving the safety analysis quality of safety-critical software. In: 2013 IEEE International Conference on Granular Computing (GrC), pp. 353–356 (2013)
3. Liu, S., Offutt, A.J., Ho-Stuart, C., Sun, Y., Ohba, M.: Sofl: a formal engineering methodology for industrial applications. In: Proceedings of the Third IEEE International Symposium on Requirements Engineering, pp. 24–45 (1998)
4. Wang, H., Liu, S., Gao, C.: Study on model-based safety verification of automatic train protection system. In: Asia-Pacific Conference on Computational Intelligence and Industrial Applications, PACIIA 2009, pp. 467–470 (2009)
5. Parnas, D.L.: Really rethinking 'formal methods'. IEEE Softw. **43**, 28–34 (2010)
6. Chiappini, A., Cimatti, A., Macchi, L., Rebollo, O., Roveri, M., Susi, A., Tonetta, S., Vittorini, B.: Formalization and validation of a subset of the European train control system. In: 2010 ACM/IEEE 32nd International Conference on Software Engineering, vol. 2, pp. 109–118 (2010)
7. Cheng, R., Zhao, L., He, L.: Application of requirement analysis method based on UML and property in train control system requirement specification. Railway Signalling and Communication (2013)
8. Issad, M., Rauzy, A., Kloul, L.: A contribution to safety analysis of railway CBTC systems using scola. In: ESREL (2015)
9. Abo, R., Voisin, L.: Formal implementation of data validation for railway safety-related systems with OVADO. In: Counsell, S., Núñez, M. (eds.) SEFM 2013. LNCS, vol. 8368, pp. 221–236. Springer, Cham (2014). doi:10.1007/978-3-319-05032-4_17
10. Faber, J., Jacobs, S., Sofronie-Stokkermans, V.: Verifying CSP-OZ-DC specifications with complex data types and timing parameters. In: Davies, J., Gibbons, J. (eds.) IFM 2007. LNCS, vol. 4591, pp. 233–252. Springer, Heidelberg (2007). doi:10.1007/978-3-540-73210-5_13
11. Lee, Y.K., In, H.P., Kazman, R.: Customer requirements validation method based on mental models, vol. 1, pp. 199–206 (2014)
12. Aceituna, D., Do, H., Lee, S.W.: Sq$^{(2)}$e: an approach to requirements validation with scenario question. Proc. Royal Soc. London A Math. Phys. Eng. Sci. **161**, 367–381 (2010)
13. Aceituna, D., Do, H., Lee, S.W.: Interactive requirements validation for reactive systems through virtual requirements prototype. In: Model-Driven Requirements Engineering Workshop, pp. 1–10 (2011)
14. Liu, S.: Utilizing specification testing in review task trees for rigorous review of formal specifications. In: Tenth Asia-Pacific on Software Engineering Conference, p. 510 (2003)
15. Kurita, T., Chiba, M., Nakatsugawa, Y.: Application of a formal specification language in the development of the "Mobile FeliCa" IC chip firmware for embedding in mobile phone. In: Cuellar, J., Maibaum, T., Sere, K. (eds.) FM 2008. LNCS, vol. 5014, pp. 425–429. Springer, Heidelberg (2008). doi:10.1007/978-3-540-68237-0_31
16. Li, J.J., Horgan, J.R.: A tool suite for diagnosis and testing of software design specifications. In: International Conference on Dependable Systems and Networks, p. 295 (2000)

17. Li, M., Liu, S.: Integrating animation-based inspection into formal design specification construction for reliable software systems. IEEE Trans. Reliab. **65**, 88–106 (2013)
18. Gargantini, A., Riccobene, E.: Automatic model driven animation of SCR specifications. In: Pezzè, M. (ed.) FASE 2003. LNCS, vol. 2621, pp. 294–309. Springer, Heidelberg (2003). doi:10.1007/3-540-36578-8_21
19. Behrmann, G., David, A., Larsen, K.G.: A tutorial on UPPAAL. In: Bernardo, M., Corradini, F. (eds.) SFM-RT 2004. LNCS, vol. 3185, pp. 200–236. Springer, Heidelberg (2004). doi:10.1007/978-3-540-30080-9_7
20. Liu, J., Tang, T., Xu, T., Zhao, L.: Formal verification of CTCS-3 system requirements specification based UML model, pp. 93–99. China Railway Science (2011)
21. Haxthausen AE, P.J.: Formal development and verification of a distributed railway control system. IEEE Trans. Softw. Eng., 687–701 (2000)
22. Zou, L., Lv, J., Wang, S., Zhan, N., Tang, T., Yuan, L., Liu, Y.: Verifying Chinese train control system under a combined scenario by theorem proving. In: Cohen, E., Rybalchenko, A. (eds.) VSTTE 2013. LNCS, vol. 8164, pp. 262–280. Springer, Heidelberg (2014). doi:10.1007/978-3-642-54108-7_14

A Case Study of a GUI-Aided Approach to Constructing Formal Specifications

Fumiko Nagoya[1(✉)] and Shaoying Liu[2]

[1] College of Commerce, Nihon University, Tokyo, Japan
nagoya.fumiko@nihon-u.ac.jp
[2] Faculty of Computer and Information Sciences, Hosei University, Tokyo, Japan
sliu@hosei.ac.jp

Abstract. How to reduce the costs caused by changes made during and after writing a formal specification is a challenge in applying formal methods in practice. A GUI-Aided approach to constructing formal specifications has been proposed, but it has not been applied to a realistic development project. In this paper, we present an application of the approach to the construction of a formal specification for a medical dictionary system to demonstrate its usability and to explore potential issues in relation to the approach.

Keywords: Active GUI model · Rapid prototyping · Formal specification

1 Introduction

Recent years, formal methods receive remarkable attentions from many researchers in the field of robotics [1] and autonomous systems [2] as a correct-by-construction methodology required for safety-critical systems. They have a strong influence as rigorous techniques [3] to ensure the reliability or prevent safety-related errors in the rigorous mathematical specification, design, and verification of systems. Meanwhile, such formal techniques in practice still face some challenges in a cost-effectiveness perspective for eliminating ambiguity of functional requirements, and translating informal specifications into precise mathematical notations. To handle this problem, Liu proposed a GUI-aided approach for constructing formal specifications [4] for clearing up comprehension gaps between software developers and the clients. The GUI-aided approach is originated in rapid prototyping techniques, as an active GUI model derived from an informal specification clarifies required functions, input and output data items, and their constraints in the corresponding formal specification from the client's point of view. In order to facilitate the construction of a formal specification in a comprehensible manner, we use the Structured Object-Oriented Formal Language (SOFL) [5] as the specification language. SOFL is also an engineering method for software development in industry [6,7], and it contains effective guidelines for describing structured informal requirements and transforming them to formal specifications [8,9].

© Springer International Publishing AG 2017
S. Liu et al. (Eds.): SOFL+MSVL 2016, LNCS 10189, pp. 74–84, 2017.
DOI: 10.1007/978-3-319-57708-1_5

In this paper, we use the proposed GUI-aided approach to develop a medical dictionary system that supplies medical information to patients or non-professional people, by inputting a search-word, selecting a keyword from a category tree, using checklists. Although, numerous companies already supply medical information web pages [10] or symptom checking applications [11,12] for patients, still newcomers, such as Google [13] and IBM [14], are starting or planning to enter this market. We believe that safety-critical systems should be rigorously verified to ensure high reliability of software. Also, the systems related healthcare or medical information require to provide user friendly interfaces and smooth interactive operations for persons of middle or advanced age. However, it is extremely difficult for software developers to fulfill both high reliability and good usability under pressures of costs and schedules. We will explain how to combine the SOFL formal engineering method and a rapid prototyping using a case study for the development of a medical dictionary system, and discuss the effects on our proposed GUI-aided approach.

The remainder of this paper is organized as follows. Section 2 briefly introduces a structure of the GUI-aided approach. Section 3 explains our rapid prototyping based on an informal specification for our medical dictionary system. Then, Sect. 4 describes how to construct a formal specification in accordance with our GUI-aided approach. Section 5 discusses the lessons learned. Lastly, in Sect. 6, we give conclusions and point out future research.

2   A GUI-Aided Approach

Our GUI-aided approach aims to construct formal specifications systematically using its power of rapid prototyping techniques. A rapid prototyping enhances effective communications between software analysts and their clients, and reduces development costs and time [15].

As shown in Fig. 1, firstly, the developer or analyst needs to define the informal specification which is written in a natural language about required functions

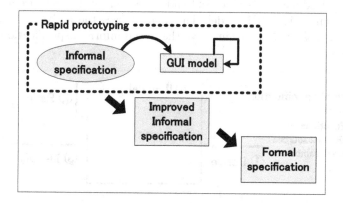

Fig. 1. A GUI-aided approach

based on communications with their clients. Then, the analyst derives a GUI model from the informal specification, and shows it to the clients. The clients examine the GUI model and provide their feedback. According to the feedback, the analyst revises and enhances the GUI model. The analyst and the clients continue to prototype until the analyst identifies all necessary required functions, input and output data items, and their constraints.

Secondly, the analyst improves the initial informal specification by using an active GUI model. The active GUI model does not need to implement all required functions, however, it plays an important role in building a consensus between the analyst and the clients to identify the corresponding input and output data items with a button-related function. As the result of observations and discussions with the analyst and the client through the active GUI model, the improved informal specification becomes sophisticated from the initial one.

Finally, a formal specification is constructed based on the improved informal specification, as following aspects: *keeping hierarchical structure, drawing conditional data flow diagram (CDFD)*, and *contracting module for each CDFD*. The hierarchical structure means a SOFL formal specification obeys in a hierarchical fashion for describing precisely the functionality of systems. SOFL formal specifications use formal notations based on set theory, logics, and algebra for improving the correctness of software by formal specification and formal verification based on mathematics.

3 Rapid Prototyping

A rapid prototyping includes user participation. Because users review whether a prototype matches their requirements and should be improved based on their feedback. Our GUI-aided approach uses a rapid prototyping to improve the initial informal specification from the user's point of view.

In this section, as illustrated in Fig. 2, we start an informal specification for a medical dictionary system as our target system, and then explain how a prototype can be derived from the informal specification. The prototype is refined by the user's feedback, and it revised and enhanced by the software analyst for changing to an active GUI model. The analyst uses the active GUI model to identify all necessary items to improve the initial informal specification.

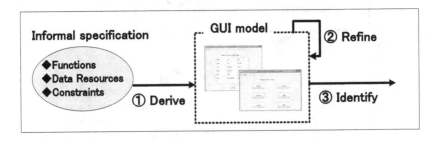

Fig. 2. The rapid prototyping in our GUI-aided approach

3.1   Informal Specification

Following the general style of the SOFL informal specification, the informal specification for the medical dictionary system also consists of three parts: functions, data resources, and constraints. The functions include:

- Required Functions:
  - Login
  - Search
  - Check
  - History
  - Edit
  - Logout
  - Exit
- Data Resources:
  - account: id, password, age, and gender
  - disease: name, common features, types or causes, and treatments
  - question: questions about symptom
  - history: historical log file for Check function
- Constraints:
  - A user ID should be unique.
  - A user ID and password within 13 characters maximum.
  - A question should be unique.
  - All items of one disease data should not be empty.

3.2   GUI Model

GUI models in our approach incorporate buttons, menu bar, or menu items to represent the corresponding required functions which are defined in the informal specification. According to the required functions described in the informal specification, the analyst developed a GUI model for our medical dictionary system as shown in Fig. 3.

We implemented look-and-feels on the GUI model under the Eclipse environment using Swing in Java. The analyst demonstrated it in front of the clients, discussed with the clients about desirable functions, and got their feedback for refining the model. The analyst revised and enhanced the model based on the clients' feedback. Then he extended the model to add event handlers in the current GUI model. Each event handler is not necessarily associated with any database; it is not a real program. However, it takes an important role as a springboard for discussions with analysts and clients, therefore it is enough to clarify of button-related functions on the current model.

Figure 4 represents a GUI model linked from the "Search" button in Fig. 3. In the same way, the Fig. 5 is a successor GUI model linked from Fig. 4. Playing a sequence of GUI models (Figs. 3, 4, and 5) in motion means an animation, which we call "active GUI model" in Sect. 2, for the clients to check functions

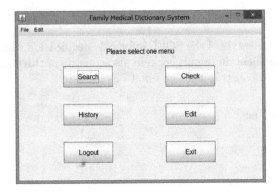

Fig. 3. A preliminary GUI model

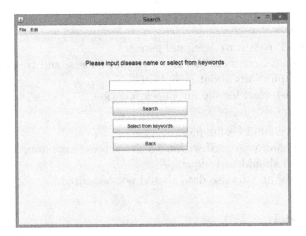

Fig. 4. The second level of button-related functions

and services of the product. At the same moment, it also provides a hierarchical structure (Fig. 3, for first level; Fig. 4, for second level; and Fig. 5, for third level) for the analyst to improve the required functions in the informal specification. Furthermore, the analyst and clients gradually recognized the corresponding input and output data items with a button-related function.

For instance, the GUI model depicted in Fig. 5 appears after inputting any search-word in the text box and pushing the "Search" button in Fig. 4. If the search-word has more than one disorder, the GUI model shows multiple possible disease names by list and encourages to select one item. In other word, in the GUI model depicted in Fig. 5, the corresponding input data item is one of disease names in the list, and the output data items are a set of disease name, diagnosis and department, common features, types or causes, and treatments.

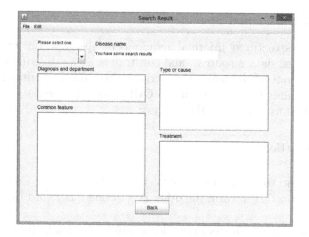

Fig. 5. The third level of button-related function

4   Construction of Formal Specifications

As mentioned above, the active GUI model indicates a hierarchical structure of the required functions and the corresponding input and output data items with a button-related function. Identifying both hierarchical structure and input and output data items becomes a basis for improving the informal specification and constructing formal specifications. In this section, we will explain the improved informal specification and formal specification in our development as illustrated in Fig. 6.

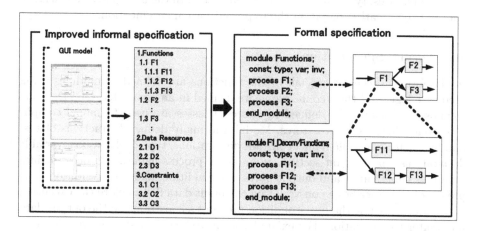

Fig. 6. The Construction of formal specifications

4.1 Improved Informal Specification

SOFL uses the structured informal requirement specification which includes required functions, data resources, and constraints as we described in Sect. 3.1. We already understood the required functions, the input and output data items, and their constraints through our active GUI model. The initial informal specification is revised as follows by the analyst:

1 Required Functions
  1.1 Login: ⋯
  1.2 Search: the tool supplies medical information by two search functions. One is inputting a word, the other is selecting a keyword from a category tree.
    1.2.1 Input a word: the tool provides a search function by inputting a search word. (**input data:** search word: *value 1*, **output data:** search result: *Compound value 2*)
    1.2.2 Select from keyword: the tool provides a category tree, and the user selects one keyword from the tree. (**input data:** search word: *value 3*, **output data:** search result: *Compound value 4*)
  1.3 Check: ⋯
2 Data Resources   ⋯
3 Constraints   ⋯

The improved specification denotes declarations of input data and output data, each parameter, and each value. The *Compound value* means a composite data type value, which is composed of disease name, diagnosis and department, common features, types or causes, and treatments. In the next part, we will show a formal specification based on the improved formal specification.

4.2 Formal Specification

In the formal specifications, all of the functions are defined in modules using predicate logic and their connections are defined in an associated CDFD. Some composite data are also defined in classes. Classes are used to model complicated data flows and data stores. Modules formally define abstractions of system functions: a module name, constant declarations, type declarations, variable declarations, an invariant section, and a list of process names. A process defines a process name, input and output ports, pre-condition, and post-condition. The pre-condition describes a constraint on the input data flows before the execution of the process, while the post-condition provides a constraint on the output data flows after the execution. For example, we introduce a module in our development as follows;

module *Search_Decom/ Family medical dictionary*
type
    Disease = **composed of**
                disease_name: string
                hospital_department: string
                symptoms: set of Symptom
                type_cause: string
                treatment: string
                end;

      . . . . . .

var
    disease_data: **seq of** Disease;
. . . . . .
process *Input_a_word* (search_word: string)
        search_result: Disease | err_message: string
ext rd   disease: **seq of** Disease
pre   search_word < > null
post   if **exists**[x: disease] | x.disease_name = search_word
        then search_result = disease(x)
          else err_message = "The word you've entered isn't in the dictionary."
end_process;
. . . . . .
end_module;

The module *Search_Decom* relates to the required functions: **1.2** Search in the improved informal specification. The process *Input_a_word* declares input parameter: search_word, output parameters: search_result or err_message, external variable: disease, and their types respectively. The pre-condition describes search_word is not empty. The post-condition denotes that if the search_word exists in the database of disease, then the output data equals the value, else err_message is displayed.

Our GUI-aided approach sets three rules for translation into formal specifications from improved informal specifications: (1) *keeping hierarchical structure*, (2) *drawing conditional data flow diagram (CDFD)*, and (3) *contracting module for each CDFD*. The rule of *keeping hierarchical structure* applies to names of modules and processes as illustrated in Fig. 6. For example, process name: "*Input_a_word* " in the module *Search_Decom* is derived from its corresponding function name: "Input a word" in the improved informal specification. The Fig. 7 shows the top level CDFD of the system.

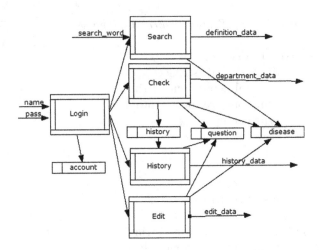

Fig. 7. The top level of CDFD

5   Lessons Learned

We have learned several lessons from our case study about the GUI-aided approach. Specifically, they include the following points:

- By adding event handlers, the prototype becomes a superior model for analyzing functional behaviors and the corresponding input and output data items.
  The understanding of them through our active GUI model not only supported
  to improve the informal specification, but also it had beneficial effects on type
  declarations in the formal specification.

- SOFL facilitates to transform from the improved informal specification into
  the formal specification. Especially, the rule of *keeping hierarchical structure*
  guides the analyst for constructing formal specifications.

- Formal specifications become available for verification techniques, such as
  specification based testing, rigorous inspection, formal proof. Our case study
  applied a specification based testing [16] to verify the correctness of program
  by generating test cases from the formal specification.

  We have also discovered a difficult to control development costs.

- The active GUI model is rather different from a product. In our case study,
  the active GUI model only shows button-related functions to create a visualization of potential behavior of the GUI, and do not connect any database.
  A development of a prototype should be simple to use any plain animation
  tool, or the analyst should decide a scope of the prototype before at the
  beginning of the development.

6 Conclusions

This paper presents a case study of applying the GUI-aided approach to the construction of a formal specification for a medical dictionary system. The approach can facilitate the construction of formal specifications accurately reflecting the client's requirements. The analyst required to understand about functional behaviors, the input and output data items, and their constraints corresponding with button-related functions based on discussions with their clients through an active GUI model. The challenge for the GUI-aided approach is how to effectively carry out a GUI-based animation to facilitate the communication between the analyst and the client. Our future research will focus on dealing the challenge and evaluate the GUI-aided approach with more empirical studies.

Acknowledgement. We would like to thank Kenshiro Takabe for developing a GUI model, including writing the informal specification and completing the implementation in Java. This work is supported by the Ministry of Education, Culture, Sports, Science and Technology of Japan under Grant-in-Aid for Scientific Research A (No. 26240008).

References

1. Lin, H.: Mission accomplished: an introduction to formal methods in mobile robot motion planning and control. Unmanned Syst. **2**(2), 201–216 (2014)
2. Seshia, S.A., Sadigh, D., Sastry, S.S.: Formal methods for semi-autonomous driving. In: Proceedings of the 52nd Annual Design Automation Conference, pp. 1–5. ACM (2015)
3. Almeida, J.B., Frade, M.J., Pinto, J.S., Melo de Sousa, S.: Rigorous Software Development: An Introduction to Program Verification. Undergraduate Topics in Computer Science. Springer, London (2011)
4. Liu, S.: A GUI-aided approach to formal specification construction. In: Liu, S., Duan, Z. (eds.) SOFL+MSVL 2015. LNCS, vol. 9559, pp. 44–56. Springer, Cham (2016). doi:10.1007/978-3-319-31220-0_4
5. Liu, S.: Formal Engineering for Industrial Software Development. Springer, Heidelberg (2004)
6. Liu, S., Hayashi, T., Takahashi, K., Kimura, K., Nakayama, T., Nakajima, S.: Automatic transformation from formal specifications to functional scenario forms for automatic test case generation. In: Proceedings of the 2010 Conference on New Trends in Software Methodologies, Tools and Techniques, pp. 383–397. IOS Press (2010)
7. Liu, S., Asuka, M., Komaya, K., Nakamura, Y.: An approach to specifying and verifying safety-critical systems with practical formal method SOFL. In: Proceedings. Fourth IEEE International Conference on Engineering of Complex Computer Systems (Cat. No. 98EX193), Monterey, CA, pp. 100–114. IEEE (1998)
8. Miao, W., Liu, S.: A formal engineering framework for service-based software modeling. IEEE Trans. Serv. Comput. **6**, 536–550 (2013)
9. Nagoya, F., Liu, S.: Development of a web-based conference management system using SOFL. In: Proceedings of the 2015 Conference on Research in Adaptive and Convergent Systems, RACS, pp. 337–342. ACM, New York (2015)
10. Merck: The merck manuals. http://www.merckmanuals.com/home

11. WebMD: Webmd symptom checker. http://www.symptoms.webmd.com/
12. Infermedica: Symptomate. https://symptomate.com/
13. Google: Google official blog. https://googleblog.blogspot.jp/2015/02/health-info-knowledge-graph.html
14. IBM: Ibm watson health. http://www.ibm.com/watson/health/
15. Gomaa, H.: The impact of rapid prototyping on specifying user requirements. SIG-SOFT Softw. Eng. Notes **8**, 17–27 (1983). ACM, New York
16. Liu, S., Nakajima, S.: A decompositional approach to automatic test case generation based on formal specifications. In: Fourth International Conference on Secure Software Integration and Reliability Improvement, Singapore, pp. 147–155. IEEE (2010)

Formal Development of Linear Structure Reusable Components in PAR Platform

Qimin Hu[1,2(⊠)], Jinyun Xue[1,2], and Zhen You[1,2]

[1] National Networked Supporting Software International
S&T Cooperation Base of China, Jiangxi Normal University,
Nanchang City, Jiangxi Province, People's Republic of China
qiminhu@163.com, youzhenjxnu@163.com,
jinyun@vip.sina.com
[2] Key Laboratory of High Performance Computing Technology,
Jiangxi Normal University, Nanchang City,
Jiangxi Province, People's Republic of China

Abstract. Formal method is key approach in developing safety critical systems. Set, Bag, List, Tree, Graph are important reusable components in PAR platform. The paper tries to formally develop Set, Bag, List components which have linear structure. The formal development of those components involves formalization of specification, the recurrence relation of problem solving sequence and loop invariant. Specification language Radl of PAR platform was used to describe the specification, recurrence relation and loop invariants; Software modelling language Apla was used to describe the abstract model of those components. The abstract model denoted by Apla was transformed to concrete model written by executable language; such as C++, Java, VB and C#, etc., based on the program generating systems in PAR platform.

Keywords: Reusable component · Formal development · Loop invariant · PAR platform

1 Introduction

Component-based software engineering (CBSE) emerged as an approach to software systems development based on reusing software components. A software component can be deployed independently and is subject to composition by third parties [2]. Reusing software component has now become the dominant development paradigm for web-based information systems and enterprise systems. Formal methods are mathematically-based approaches to software development where you define a formal model of the software. You may then formally analyze the model and use it as a basis for a formal system specification [11]. CBSE and formal methods are two important but largely independent approaches which have been visibly influential in recent years [6, 7].

PAR means PAR (Partition-and-Recur) method [14, 17–19] and its supporting platform, called PAR platform. PAR method and PAR platform consists of specification and algorithm describing language Radl, software modeling language Apla, a set

© Springer International Publishing AG 2017
S. Liu et al. (Eds.): SOFL+MSVL 2016, LNCS 10189, pp. 85–97, 2017.
DOI: 10.1007/978-3-319-57708-1_6

of rules for specification transformation, a set of reusable components and a set of automatic generating tools such as Radl to Apla generating system, Apla to Java, C++, C# executable program generating systems.

Set, Bag, List, Tree, Graph are reusable components defined in PAR platform. Set and Bag(an element may occur many times) have unordered linear structure. List has ordered linear structure. Tree and Graph have non-linear structure. With the support of those reusable components, the programs written by Apla are very short and easy to prove their correctness.

The reusable components are important for PAR platform. It is a challenge and urgent work to develop them formally and guarantee the correctness of those components.

In this paper, Set, Bag and List components were formally developed. Using formal specification language Radl to describe the specification of reusable components. Using the quantifier transformation rules to transform specification and construct the recurrence relation of problem. Using new strategies of developing loop invariants to develop loop invariants and construct the abstract programs written by Apla language. Using executable program generating system to generate the codes of reusable components.

The paper was organized as follows. The second section gave the related preliminary knowledge of PAR platform; the third section gave the formal development of Set component, the fourth section gave the formal development of Bag component, the fifth section gave formal development of List component; the sixth section gave an example of constructing program by composing the reusable components; Finally a short conclusion was presented.

2 Preliminary

PAR is a long-term research projects supported by a series of nature science research foundations of China. According to the methodology of MDD, PAR has been used in developing software with high reliability and safety, such as non-trivial algorithm programs [15, 20–22], traffic scheduling system [13], bank account management system and electric control system.

2.1 Specification Language Radl

Radl (Recur-based Algorithm Design Language) used the idiomatic mathematical symbols and style to describe the algorithm specification, specification transformation rules and the recurrence relation. Radl is the front language of the Apla language, with mathematical referential transparency. Using the unified format (Q i: r(i): f(i)) given by Dijkstra to denote quantifiers [3], where Q can be $\forall$ (all quantifier), $\exists$ (exists quantifier), MIN (minimum quantifier), MAX (maximum quantifier), Σ (summation quantifier), etc., and i is a bounded variable, r(i) is the variant range of i and f(i) is a function.

2.2 Software Modelling Language Apla

Apla (Abstract Programming Language) is the software modelling language and the target language of Radl to Apla program generating system, and the source language of Apla to Java, C++, C#, Dephi executable program generating system.

2.3 The Formal Development Steps with PAR

The formal development steps with PAR can be 6 steps:

Step 1. Construct the formal specification of problem using Radl;
Step 2. Partition the problem into a couple of subproblems each of that has the same structure with the original problem;
Step 3. Formally derive the algorithm from the formal specification. The algorithm is described using Radl and represented by recurrence relation.
Step 4. Develop loop invariant directly based on new strategy;
Step 5. Transformed the Radl program to the Apla program;
Step 6. Transforms the Apla program to an executable language program.

3 Formal Development of Set Component

3.1 Introduction of Set Reusable Component

A set is simply a collection of distinct(different) elements [5]. In PAR platform, the description of reusable component set's data and operations is given below:

Specify Set (sometype data, [size])
　//data denotes the data type of elements in set
　//size denotes the upper bound of set size
type set(sometype data, [size])
var
　n: integer;　　　　//n is the number of elements in set;
　A, B : set := {},{};　// A,B is empty set;
　e: data;　　　　　//e is element in set;
Operator:
　#A　　// the number of elements in set
　A∩B　// the intersection of set A and B
　A∪B　// the union of set A and B
　A - B　// the difference of set A and B
　x∈A　// judge whether x is a member of set A
　A⊂B　// judge whether set A is a proper subset of set B
　A = B　// judge whether set A is equal to set B
　A := B　// replace set A with set B
endspec;

3.2 Formal Development of Set Component

In order to guarantee the correctness of set component, we formally developed the body of operations of set component. Following is the formal development of the operation which can be used to judge whether set A is a proper subset of set B.

(1) **Problem and Its Specification**

Given a set A[1..m] containing m elements, a set B[1..n] containing n elements. Include(A[1..m], B[1..n]) means set A is a subset of set B.
The specification is following:

Q: Given set A[1..m] and set B[1..n], m < n
R: Include(A[1..m], B[1..n]) $\equiv$ ($\forall$i:1 $\leqslant$ i $\leqslant$ m:($\exists$j:1 $\leqslant$ j $\leqslant$ n:A[i] = B[j])

(2) **Partition**

We partition computing Include(A[1..m], B[1..n]) into computing Include (A[1..m − 1], B[1..n]) with A[m], then partition computing Include(A[1..m − 1], B[1..n]) into computing Include(A[1..m − 2], B[1..n]) with A[m − 1],..., until computing Include(A [1], B[1..n]). Let F be the partition function to be determined, we have

$$\text{Include}(A[1..m], B[1..n]) = F(\text{ Include}(A[1..m − 1], B[1..n]), A[m]) \quad m < n$$

So, the key of constructing recurrence relation is to determine function F.

(3) **Constructing Recurrence Relation**

Suppose Include(A[1..m − 1], B[1..n]) has been solved. We can derive the function F by using the properties of quantifiers. We have

Include(A[1..m], B[1..n])
$\equiv$ ($\forall$i:1 $\leqslant$ i $\leqslant$ m:($\exists$j:1 $\leqslant$ j $\leqslant$ n:A[i] = B[j]))
{Range Splitting}
$\equiv$ ($\forall$i:1 $\leqslant$ i $\leqslant$ m − 1:($\exists$j:1 $\leqslant$ j $\leqslant$ n:A[i] = B[j])) $\wedge$ ($\forall$i:1 $\leqslant$ i = m:($\exists$j:1 $\leqslant$ j n:A[i] = B[j]))
{Singleton Range with i = m}
$\equiv$ ($\forall$i:1 $\leqslant$ i $\leqslant$ m − 1:($\exists$j:1 $\leqslant$ j $\leqslant$ n:A[i] = B[j]) $\wedge$ ($\exists$j:1 $\leqslant$ j $\leqslant$ n:A[m] = B[j])
{The definition of Include}
$\equiv$ Include(A[1..m − 1], B[1..n]) $\wedge$ ($\exists$j:1 $\leqslant$ j $\leqslant$ n:A[m] = B[j])

Let is_a_member(A[m], B[1..n]) = ($\exists$j:1 $\leqslant$ j $\leqslant$ n:A[m] = B[j]), which denotes whether A[m] is a member of set B[1..n], We have the following recurrence:

Recurrence 1

$$\text{Include } (A[1..m], B[1..n]) = \begin{cases} \text{Include}(A[1..m − 1], B[1..n]) & \text{is\_a\_member}(A[m], B[1..n]) \text{ is true} \\ \text{False} & \text{is\_a\_member}(A[m], B[1..n]) \text{ is false} \end{cases}$$

To compute is_a_member(A[m], B[1..n]), we try to find the recurrence relation. Suppose is_a_member(A[m], B[1..n − 1]) has been computed, based on the properties of quantifiers, we have

is_a_member(A[m], B[1..n])
$\equiv (\exists j:1 \leqslant j \leqslant n:A[m] = B[j])$
{Range Splitting}
$\equiv (\exists j:1 \leqslant j < n:A[m] = B[j]) \vee (\exists j:1 \leqslant j = n:A[m] = B[j])$
{Singleton Range with j = n}
$\equiv (\exists j:1 \leqslant j < n:A[m] = B[j]) \vee (A[m] = B[n])$
{The definition of is_a_member}
$\equiv$ is_a_member(A[m], B[1..n − 1]) $\vee$ (A[m] = B[n])

Based on the above derivation, we have the following recurrence.

Recurrence 2

$$\text{is\_a\_member}(A[m], B[1..n]) = \begin{cases} \text{is\_a\_member}(A[m], B[1..n-1]) & A[m] \; ! = \; B[n] \\ \text{True} & A[m] \; == \; B[n] \end{cases}$$

(4) **Developing Loop Invariant and Program**

Based on the above recurrence relations, let variable In whose data type is boolean denotes the value of Include(A[1..i], B[1..n]), the loop invariant can be constructed mechanically as following:

$$\rho : \text{In} = \text{Include}(A[1..i], B[1..n]) \wedge 1 \leq i \leq m < n$$

Based on the recurrence relations and loop invariant, the abstract algorithmic program written by Apla language is following:

```
i:=m;
do i≥ 1→
    if ¬ is_a_member(A[i],B[1..n]) → In:=false; return;
          is_a_member(A[i],B[1..n]) → i:=i-1;
    fi
od
In:=true;
```

The above abstract program written by Apla can be translated into reusable component written by executable languages with our program generating systems automatically.

4 Formal Development of Bag Component

4.1 Introduction of Bag Reusable Component

A collection of elements in which an element may occur any(finite) number of times is called a bag [5]. In PAR platform, the description of reusable component bag's data and operations is similar to set component.

4.2 Formal Development of Bag Component

Following is the formal development of the operation which can be used to judge whether bag A is a proper subbag of bag B. Because an element may occur any number of times in bag, the formal development is different greatly from set.

(1) **Problem and Its Specification**

Given a bag $A[1..m]$ containing m elements, a bag $B[1..n]$ containing n elements. Include($A[1..m]$, $B[1..n]$) means bag A is a proper subbag of bag B. Let All($A[i]$, $A[1..m]$) denotes the number of elements in bag A whose value is equal to $A[i]$.

The specification is following:

Q: Given bag $A[1..m]$ and bag $B[1..n]$, $m < n$
R: Include($A[1..m]$, $B[1..n]$) $\equiv (\forall i:1 \leqslant i \leqslant m:($All($A[i]$, $A[1..m]$) $\leqslant$ All($A[i]$, $B[1..n]$)))

(2) **Partition**

We partition computing Include($A[1..m]$, $B[1..n]$) into computing Include($A[1..m-1]$, $B[1..n]$) with $A[m]$, then partition computing Include($A[1..m-1]$, $B[1..n]$) into computing Include($A[1..m-2]$, $B[1..n]$) with $A[m-1]$,..., until computing Include($A[1]$, $B[1..n]$). Let F be the partition function to be determined, we have

$$\text{Include}(A[1..m], B[1..n]) = F(\text{Include}(A[1..m-1], B[1..n]), A[m]) \quad m < n$$

So, the key of constructing recurrence relation is to determine function F.

(3) **Constructing Recurrence Relation**

Suppose Include($A[1..m-1]$, $B[1..n]$) has been solved. We can derive the function F by using the properties of quantifiers. We have

Include($A[1..m]$, $B[1..n]$)
$\equiv (\forall i:1 \leqslant i \leqslant m:($All($A[i]$, $A[1..m]$) $\leqslant$ All($A[i]$, $B[1..n]$)))
{Range Splitting}
$\equiv (\forall i:1 \leqslant i \leqslant m-1:($All($A[i]$, A) $\leqslant$ All($A[i]$, B)) $\wedge (\forall i:1 \leqslant i = m:($All($A[i]$, A) $\leqslant$All($A[i]$, B))
{Singleton Range with i = m}
$\equiv (\forall i:1 \leqslant i \leqslant m-1:$ (All($A[i]$, A) $\leqslant$ All($A[i]$, B)) $\wedge$ (All($A[m]$, A) $\leqslant$ All($A[m]$, B))

{The definition of Include}
$\equiv$ Include(A[1..m − 1], B[1..n]) $\wedge$ (All(A[m], A) $\leqslant$ All(A[m], B))

Then, we have the following recurrence:

Recurrence 1

$$\text{Include } (A[1..m], B[1..n]) = \begin{cases} \text{Include}(A[1..m-1], B[1..n]) & (A[m], A) \leq \text{All}(A[m], B) \text{ is true} \\ \text{False} & (A[m], A) \leq \text{All}(A[m], B) \text{ is false} \end{cases}$$

To compute All(A[m], B[1..n]), we try to find the recurrence relation. Suppose All (A[m], B[1..n − 1]) has been computed, based on the properties of quantifiers, we have

All(A[m], B[1..n])
$\equiv$ (Σ j:1 $\leqslant$ j $\leqslant$ n $\wedge$ A[m] = B[j]:1)
{Range Splitting}
$\equiv$ (Σ j:1 $\leqslant$ j <n $\wedge$ A[m] = B[j]) + (Σ j:1 $\leqslant$ j = n $\wedge$ A[m] = B[j]:1)
{Singleton Range with j = n}
$\equiv$ (Σ j:1 $\leqslant$ j < n $\wedge$ A[m] = B[j]) + (Σ j:j = n $\wedge$ A[m] = B[j]:1)
{The definition of All(A[m], B[1..n])}
$\equiv$ All(A[m], B[1..n − 1]) + (Σ j:j = n $\wedge$ A[m] = B[j]:1)

Based on the above derivation, we have the following recurrence.

Recurrence 2

$$\text{All}(A[m], B[1..n]) = \begin{cases} \text{All}(A[m], B[1..n-1]) + 1 & A[m] == B[n] \\ \text{All}(A[m], B[1..n-1]) & A[m] \,!= B[n] \end{cases}$$

(4) **Developing Loop Invariant and Program**

Based on the above recurrence relations, let variable In whose data type is boolean denotes the value of Include(A[1..i], B[1..n]), the loop invariant can be constructed mechanically as following:

$$\rho : \text{In} = \text{Include}(A[1..i], B[1..n]) \wedge 1 \leq i \leq m < n$$

Based on the recurrence relations and loop invariant, the abstract algorithmic program written by Apla language is following:

```
i:=m;
do i⩾ 1→
    if ¬ All(A[i],A[1..m]) ⩽ All(A[i],B[1..n]) → In:=false; return;
        All(A[i],A[1..m]) ⩽ All(A[i],B[1..n]) → i:=i-1;
    fi
od
In:=true;
```

5   Formal Development of List Component

5.1   Introduction of List Reusable Component

List has ordered linear structure. In PAR platform, the description of reusable component list's data and operations is given below:

> **Specify** list (sometype data, [size])
>   //data denotes the data type of list elements
>   //size denotes the upper bounds of list size
> **type** list(sometype data, [size])
>   **var**
>   h, t: integer;   //h and t denote the head and tail of List;
>   S, T: list := [], [];   //S and T is empty List
>   e: data; i,j: integer;   //e is element of List
>   **Operator:**
>   [e]   //List which contain just one element
>   []   //empty List
>   # S   //the number of elements in List S
>   S[i]   //the element in List S, S.h $\leqslant$ i $\leqslant$ S.t
>   S[i..j] //one sublist of List S, S.h $\leqslant$ i,j $\leqslant$ S.t
>   S $\uparrow$ T //construct a new List by concatenating List S and T. "$\uparrow$" operation
>   can conveniently express insert operations on the head, tail of List
>   S:=R   //replace list S with R
>   S[i..j]:=T[k..k+j-i] //replace S[i..j] with T[k..k+j-i]
>   **endspec;**

5.2   Formal Development of List Component

Following is the formal development of the operation $S[i..j] := T[k..k + j - i]$.

(1) **Problem and Its Specification**

Given a list s[1..m] containing m elements, a list T[1..n] containing n elements. S [i..j] := T[k..k + j − i] means sublist S[i..j] of list S be replaced by sublist T[k..k + j − i].

The specification is following:

> Q: Givenlist S[1..m] and list T[1..n], $1 \leqslant i < j \leqslant m, 1 \leqslant k \leqslant n - (j - i)$
> R: $S[i..j] := T[k..k + j - i] \equiv (\forall x : i \leqslant x \leqslant j : S[x] = T[k + x - i])$

(2) **Partition**

Suppose S[i..j − 1] := T[k..k + j − i − 1] has been solved. Let F be the partition function to be determined, we have

$$S[i..j] := T[k..k + j - i] \equiv F(S[i..j - 1] := T[k..k + j - i - 1])$$

So, the key of constructing recurrence relation is to determine function F.

(3) **Constructing Recurrence Relation**

We can derive the function F by using the properties of quantifiers.

$S[i..j] := T[k..k + j - i]$
$\equiv (\forall x : i \leqslant x \leqslant j : S[x] = T[k + x - i])$
{Range Splitting}
$\equiv (\forall x : i \leqslant x \leqslant j - 1 : S[x] = T[k + x - i]) \wedge (\forall x : i \leqslant x = j : S[x] = T[k + x - i])$
{Singleton Range with x = j}
$\equiv (\forall x : i \leqslant x \leqslant j - 1 : S[x] = T[k + x - i]) \wedge (S[j] = T[k + j - i])$
$\equiv (S[i..j - 1] := T[k..k + j - i - 1]) \wedge (S[j] = T[k + j - i])$

Then, we have the following recurrence:

$S[i..j] := T[k..k + j - i] \equiv (S[i..j - 1] := T[k..k + j - i - 1]) \wedge (S[j] = T[k + j - i])$

(4) **Developing Loop Invariant and Program**

Based on the above recurrence relations, the loop invariant can be constructed mechanically as following:

$$\rho : S[x] = T[k + x - i] \wedge i \leq x \leq j$$

Based on the recurrence relations and loop invariant, the abstract algorithmic program written by Apla language is following:

```
x := j;
do x >= i → S[x] := T[k + x − i]; x := x − 1;
od.
```

6   Construct Program by Composing Reusable Components

6.1   Simple and Accurate Apla Program Based on Reusable Components

With the support of reusable components, the apla program is simple and accurate. It gave a simplified way to prove correctness.

We formally derived the Dijkstra single-source shortest path Problem in [16]. With the support of set and graph (graph component included edge and vertex component in it. We will give the formal development of graph component which has non-linear structure in future work) reusable components, we can write the apla program as following:

```
program  Dijkstra;
var
  g:digraph((integer),(integer));
  e,e1: edge(integer,integer);     rr,source:vertex(integer);
  tt:set(edge(integer,integer));   S,other:set(vertex(integer));
 begin
    write("input vertex");i:=0;do i≤numv-1→read(rr);g,i:=g+rr,i+1;od;
    writeln("input edge");i:=0;do i≤nume-1→read(e1);g,i:=g+e1,i+1;od;
    write("choose the source vertex:"); read(source);
    tt,S,other:={ },{source},g.V-{source};
  tt,Left,M:=source,g.V,{ };
  Left,M:=Left-{tt},M∪{tt};dd[source.d]:=0;
  i:=0;
  do i≤#(Left)-1→dd[Left(i).d]:=g.arcvalue(tt,Left(i));i:=i+1;od;
  do ¬ (#(M)=#(g.V)) → choosemin(tt,Left,dd);
          M,Left:=M∪{tt},Left-{tt};
          i:=0;
          do i≤#(Left)-1→
                  dd[Left(i).d]:=min(dd[Left(i).d],dd[tt.d]+g.arcvalue(tt,Left(i)));
                  i:=i+1;
          od;
  od;
 end.
```

The core of the apla program is just 7 lines codes.

6.2 Generate Executable Program by Program Generating System

The executable program can be generated automatically from the Apla to C++, JAVA, C#, Vb.net generating system in PAR platform.

As shown in Fig. 1, we choose the "C# program generating system" to generate executable C# program.

- Firstly, we click "New Apla" button and input the Apla program in Sect. 6.1. The algorithm is very short, only 7 lines core codes, in the left side of Fig. 1.
- Secondly, we click "Generate" button, the corresponding C# program which has dozens of codes in the right side of Fig. 1 will be generated.
- Thirdly, we click "Run" button, the C# program can run immediately and the result is correct.

Fig. 1. The C# program generating system

7 Related Works

Abrial introduced the mechanism of abstract machine modeling and refinement in B-Method into structured program generation [9, 10]. Considering the generation of correct-by-construction programs, they suggested to integrate models, refinements and proofs into reusable proof-based patterns for alleviating the task of proof obligation and refinement checking. It was difficult for B-Method to derive formally logically intricate problems.

Smith implemented a number of algorithm design tactics in program generation systems such as KIDS and Designware developed by the Kestrel Institute [12]. The framework raises the level of automation, but the selection of appropriate algorithm design tactics is still difficult.

VDM [8], Z [1] could construct formal specification and proof. But they can't support the complete development steps from specification to executable programs.

Propositional Projection Temporal Logic (PPTL) is a useful logic in the specification and verification of concurrent systems [3, 23–25]. PPTL will be used to verificate the concurrent component in our future work.

8 Conclusion

We formally develop set, bag, list reusable components in PAR platform. Formal development gives us the formal specification, the recurrence relation of problem solving sequence, accurate loop invariant. Based on the recurrence relation, loop invariant, It is a simple task to verify the correctness of reusable components by standard proof techniques [4] or by proof assistant tools, such as Isabelle. The merits of this research can be summarized as following:

- The formal development can greatly improve reliability of reusable components. The recurrence relation of problem solving sequence and loop invariants were formally derived, the concrete executable codes of reusable components are generated with a series of program generating systems.
- The simple and accurate loop invariants would be very helpful for understanding the roles of every loop variables in the codes of reusable components.
- With the support of formally developed reusable components, the abstract programs described by software modelling language Apla are simple and accurate. It gave a simplified way to prove correctness.

We will do the research continuously and apply PAR method and PAR platform to develop more safety critical systems in industrial application.

Acknowledgments. The authors thank Professor David Gries for discussion about loop invariants in his tutorial lessons in FACS2013 hold in Jiangxi Normal University, Jiangxi Province, China.

This work was supported by the National Nature Science Foundation of China (Grant No. 61272075, No. 61462041, No. 61472167, No. 61662036), the Science and Technology Research Project of Jiangxi Province Educational Department (Grant No. 160329), and the Natural Science Foundation of Jiangxi Province.

References

1. Abrial, J.R., Hayes, I.J., Hoare, T.: The Z Notation: A Reference Manual, 2nd edn. Oriel College, Oxford (1998)
2. Szyperski, C.: Component software: Beyond Object-oriented Programming, 2nd edn. Addison-Wesley, Reading (2002)
3. Tian, C., Duan, Z., Zhang, N.: An efficient approach for abstraction-refinement in model checking. Theoret. Comput. Sci. **461**, 76–85 (2012)
4. Dijkstra, E.W.: A Discipline of Programming. Springer, New York (1994)
5. Gries, D., Schneider, F.B.: A Logical Approach to Discrete Math. Springer, New York (1981)
6. He, J., Liu, Z., Li, X.: Component calculus. In: Workshop on Formal Aspects of Component Software (FACS 2003), Satellite Workshop of FME 2003, Pisa, Italy (2003)
7. Jifeng, H., Li, X., Liu, Z.: Component-based software engineering-the need to link methods and their theories. In: Hung, D., Wirsing, M. (eds.) ICTAC 2005. LNCS, vol. 3722, pp. 70–95. Springer, Heidelberg (2005). doi:10.1007/11560647_5
8. Jones, C.B.: Systematic Software Development Using VDM, 2nd edn. Prentice Hall, Engelwood Cliffs (1990)
9. Morgan, C.C.: Programming from Specification. Prentice Hall, Upper Saddle River (1994)
10. Schneider, S.: B-Method. Palgrave, Basingstoke (2001)
11. Sommerville, I.: Software Engineering, 9th edn. Pearson Education, Upper Saddle River (2011)
12. Smith, D.R.: Designware: software development by refinement. In: Proceedings of the Eight International Conference on Category Theory and Computer Science, Edinburgh, September 1999

13. Wu, G., Xue, J.: PAR method and PAR platform used in development process of software outsourcing. Comput. Mod. 11.042 (2013)
14. Xue, J.: A unified approach for developing efficient algorithmic programs. J. Comput. Sci. Technol. **12**(4), 103–118 (1997)
15. Xue, J.: Two new strategies for developing loop invariants and their applications. J. Comput. Sci. Technol. **8**(2), 95–102 (1993)
16. Xue, J.: Formal derivation of graph algorithmic programs using Partition-and-Recur. J. Comput. Sci. Technol. **13**(6), 95–102 (1998)
17. Xue, J.: Methods of Programming. Higher Education Press, Beijing (2002)
18. Xue, J.: New concept of loop invariant and its application. In: Proceedings of the 3rd Colloquium on Logic in Engineering Dependable Software, Nanchang, China (2013)
19. Xue, J.: PAR method and its supporting platform. In: Proceedings of AWCVS 2006, Macao, 29–31 October 2006
20. Xue, J., Davis, R.: A simple program whose derivation and proof is also. In: Proceedings of The First IEEE International Conference on Formal Engineering Method (ICFEM 1997). IEEE CS Press, November 1997
21. Xue, J.: Implementation of model-driven development using PAR. In: Keynote Speech on the 6th International Workshop on Harnessing Theories for Tool Support in Software, Nanchang, China (2013)
22. Zuo, Z., You, Z., Xue, J.: Derivation and formal proof of non-recursive post-order binary tree traversal algorithm. Comput. Eng. Sci. **32**(3) (2013)
23. Duan, Z.: Temporal logic and temporal logic programming. Science Press, Beijing (2005)
24. Duan, Z., Tian, C., Zhang, L.: A decision procedure for propositional projection temporal logic with infinite models. Acta Informatica **45**(1), 43–78 (2008)
25. Duan, Z., Yang, X., Koutny, M.: Framed temporal logic programming. Sci. Comput. Program. **70**(1), 31–61 (2008)

Verification and Validation

E-SSL: An SSL Security-Enhanced Method for Bypassing MITM Attacks in Mobile Internet

Ren Zhao[1,3(✉)], Xiaohong Li[1,3(✉)], Guangquan Xu[1,3], Zhiyong Feng[2], and Jianye Hao[2]

[1] School of Computer Science and Technology, Tianjin University, Tianjin, China
{zh_r,xiaohongli,losin}@tju.edu.cn
[2] School of Computer Software, Tianjin University, Tianjin, China
{zyfeng,jianye.hao}@tju.edu.cn
[3] Tianjin Key Laboratory of Advanced Networking,
Tianjin University, Tianjin, China

Abstract. In mobile internet, the Secure Sockets Layer (SSL) validation vulnerabilities of applications can be easily exploited through SSL
Man-in-the-Middle (MITM) attacks, which are difficult to defeat. In this
paper, an SSL Security-Enhanced method (E-SSL) is proposed to detect
and defeat SSL MITM attacks, which improves the security of internet communication under malicious attacks. SSL proxy is used to find
SSL certificate validation vulnerabilities and detect SSL MITM attacks.
Based on randomness and hash theory, an SSL shared service with random port mapping is implemented to bypass SSL MITM attacks, the
spatio-temporal randomization will increase the difficulty of attacker's
correct guessing. We implement a prototype on Android platform, and
verify its effectiveness and reliability with 650 apps under realistic SSL
MITM attacks. Using the E-SSL approach, 185 apps out of 650 are
detected with SSL certificate validation vulnerabilities. Furthermore,
evaluation results show that the E-SSL approach enables these SSL certificate validation vulnerabilities apps to successfully bypass SSL MITM
attacks, thus significantly increases the security of user data privacy in
public mobile internet.

Keywords: Mobile internet · MIMT attack · SSL/TLS · Random port
mapping

1 Introduction

In recent years, public Wi-Fi has become the most popular social requirement
and common way of people connecting to the internet. The openness of Wi-
Fi network makes it vulnerable to a number of attacks such as eavesdropping
and jamming. One common attack is known as man in the middle (MITM)
attack, where an attacker usually can easily have access to the data flow within
a Wi-Fi network through setting up a Rogue Access Point (RAP), which can
be implemented by a simple equipment anytime and anywhere [1]. As a result,

© Springer International Publishing AG 2017
S. Liu et al. (Eds.): SOFL+MSVL 2016, LNCS 10189, pp. 101–120, 2017.
DOI: 10.1007/978-3-319-57708-1_7

the attacker can capture all the communication data between the two parties, then tamper with or remove the intercepted sensitive information, such as user information, passwords and bank accounts, etc. Usually, users are unconscious that they are deceived until an incident occurs.

Secure Sockets Layer (SSL) [2] and its successor Transport Layer Security (TLS) [3] are significant milestones in the path of improving the security of data communication. Unfortunately, if clients fail to properly validate SSL/TLS certificates, it may lead to SSL certificate validation vulnerabilities [4]. At all layers of the SSL protocol, certificate validation is confirmed to be inaccurate, from improper certificate handling in libraries, abuse of SSL APIs, to applications that are broken by design so that they are easier to use [5]. The crucial problem of causing SSL MITM attacks is incapability of clients to authenticate the server accurately in the face of public-key certificate [6,7]. In addition, the Android coarse-grained access control [8] and application permission escape behavior [9,10] severely damage the security of the Android system. There is no doubt that anyone of these lapses increases the threat of SSL MITM attacks, so when applications with SSL certificate validation vulnerabilities are executed in public Wi-Fi, it is more vulnerable to the SSL MITM attacks [11,12]. In this case, an attacker intercept and decrypt the supposedly-secure SSL traffic that be transited to or from a target server, and then read or modify it freely.

Until now, a number of works [4,12,13] have been proposed to address the problem of detection about SSL certificate validation vulnerabilities and SSL MITM attacks. However, detecting and notifying these vulnerabilities is not a good solution. Even if the developers are informed of confirmed SSL certificate validation vulnerabilities, Android SSL inappropriate use of vulnerabilities are still as high as 76% over a year [13]. Based on the above consideration, instead of detecting and making alarms, an alternatively important question is that how can we take effective measures to protect the users from SSL MITM attacks in the first place?

In this paper, we propose an SSL Security-Enhanced (E-SSL) method in mobile internet. This method consists of three steps: SSL proxy based SSL certificate validation vulnerabilities detection, SSL MITM attacks detection and random port mapping based SSL MITM attacks defense. It can detect whether there are SSL certificate validation vulnerabilities, including arbitrary self-signed certificates, inappropriate domain name certificates and expired certificates. Meanwhile, honeypot and dynamic analysis are applied to detect SSL MITM attacks. After identifying SSL MITM attacks, we employ the random port mapping method to allocate the applications' communication ports for bypassing the SSL MITM attacks. Random hash theory is applied to generate the ports allocation scheme, which increases the difficulty of speculation for the attackers. Therefore, the success rate of SSL MITM attacks can be significantly reduced, and thus the users' information privacy can be better protected.

Overall, this paper makes the following contributions:

- Our approach E-SSL can not only detect whether there are SSL certificate validation vulnerabilities in the applications, but also detect SSL MITM attacks at different stages in public Wi-Fi environments. After identifying SSL MITM attacks, the security defense service based on random port mapping is used to ensure security of the users' privacy under SSL MITM attacks.

- In order to strengthen the secure granularity, hierarchical protection mechanism is used to security defense service. Randomness and hash theory is applied to generate mapping ports. And load balance is implemented in these ports by multithreaded collaboration.
- An enhanced SSL security detection and defense prototype is implemented on Android platform. By simulating the real SSL MITM attacks in Wi-Fi, E-SSL can detect SSL MITM attacks at run time and ensure security of the users' privacy under SSL MITM attacks.

The rest of this paper is organized as follows. Section 2 discusses the related work, and the SSL MITM attack scenario is presented in Sect. 3. Section 4 elaborates the method and the model. Section 5 simulates SSL MITM attack scenarios to verify the effectiveness and reliability of E-SSL. We evaluate the E-SSL in Sect. 6 and discuss the limitations of E-SSL in Sect. 7. Finally, conclusion and future work are presented in Sect. 8.

2   Related Work

At present, the research team [14] studied the HTTPS deployment and the CA certificate ecosystem through large-scale data investigation, [15] researched trust relationship among root certificate, middle certificate and leaf certificate, and [16,17] summarized related causes of forged certificates. They proved the existence of vulnerabilities and bogus certificates in current SSL system. Georgiev et al. [18] analyzed the usages of SSL in various platforms, and found the SSL original security validation logics are completely broken in a lot of emphasis on security applications and libraries. Fahl et al. [4] analyzed the related implement of SSL validation functions in 13500 Android applications through the static analysis method, and found SSL certificate validation vulnerabilities in most of these applications. Sounthiraraj et al. [13] used static and dynamic analysis to automatically and large-scalely detect SSL certificate validation vulnerabilities of applications by simulating the UI triggering mechanism [19]. Guo et al. [20] mainly focused on the detection of SSL error handling in the hybrid web mobile applications. For the SSL certificate validation vulnerabilities [21,22], security researchers have proposed different technical solutions, but these techniques cannot be used to detect the SSL MITM attacks and protect existed applications.

The SSL MITM attack detection technologies have been considered in related literatures, but there are some limitations in these methods. Benton et al. [23] proposed an SSL MITM attacks detection method of desktop web browser, but it is not suitable for mobile applications studied in this paper. Conti et al. [24] extended sandroproxyLib open source library, which real-timely connected third-party server to provide additional information, so as to determine whether SSL MITM attacks exist in the current Wi-Fi. Liu et al. [12] proposed a detection method about SSL MITM attacks with the help of social network, online social network assists certificate validation to determine whether the accepted certificate is returned from real server. These methods used the third part server or social network do exist the uncertainties and deployment difficulties. However, E-SSL can detect SSL MITM attacks without the help of uncertain third part and ensure the security communication by security defense service under SSL MITM attacks.

In view of SSL certificate validation vulnerabilities, security researchers put forward different solutions to strengthen validation. Bates et al. [25] adjusted and changed call logics of the related SSL API from the angle of system, which can avoid SSL certificate validation vulnerabilities due to the developers' negligence. Fahl et al. [26] extended encapsulated SSL/TLS library interfaces, and provided the more abstract APIs into the system framework layer. Based on the same ideas, Tendulkar et al. [27] designed application configuration file during the process of developing application, and standardized the use of SSL in the development of debug and release. These methods cannot protect current existing applications, only alleviate the SSL inappropriate usage in the process of development. Random port mapping based E-SSL can guarantee the security of the existed applications under SSL MITM attacks, and also do not need to increase extra operations for the future development of applications.

3   Attack Scenario

Man-in-the-Middle attack is a kind of indirect invasion attacks. The attack occurs when a computer, completely controlled by an intruder, has been

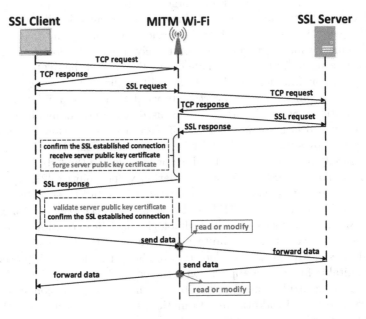

Fig. 1. Process of SSL MITM attacks

virtually deployed in the network connection between two communication computers through a variety of technical methods. In public Wi-Fi, there are different MITM scenarios, such as Address Resolution Protocol (ARP) deception, Rogue Access Point (AP), and Evil Twin AP. The process of MITM attacks based on SSL certificate validation vulnerabilities is illustrated in Fig. 1.

Usually, if the client correctly validates certificates, the network traffic can not be decrypted by the attacker. However, if the client accepts certificates without checking their signatures, domain names or deadline, the attacker can disguise as the server with a forged certificate. In this case, the attacker can decrypt the network flow with his own forged certificate, then they can read or modify it at will. There are many factors leading to SSL MITM attacks, such as the weak secure consciousness of developers and users, the polluted trust store, applications with SSL certificate validation vulnerabilities and negligence of secure warning.

4   Method and Design

This paper proposes an SSL Security-Enhanced method (E-SSL). The main features include: (1) potential SSL certificate validation vulnerabilities detection, (2) SSL MITM attacks detection and (3) random port mapping based security defense service. There are two goals of our work. One is to remedy and strengthen the security of applications with SSL certificate validation vulnerabilities, the other is to protect the security of users' privacy information under SSL MITM attacks. The main structure of E-SSL is as depicted in Fig. 2. We mainly introduce the E-SSL prototype, and describe its structure and key technologies from system level. The user interfaces of E-SSL and relevant configuration are ignored because of the space limitation.

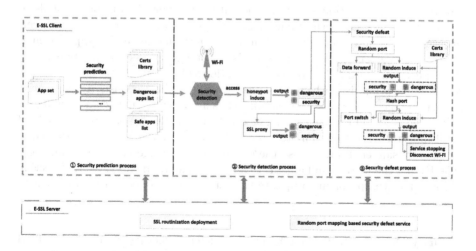

Fig. 2. Main structure of E-SSL

4.1   E-SSL Client

This prototype runs on mobile devices, which is responsible for the most works of the whole method. In order to complete the task more convenient and efficient, the prototype is divided into three main modules, including security prediction, security detection and security defense. Security prediction is used to find whether the application exists SSL certificate validation vulnerabilities. Security detection is adopted to detect the SSL MITM attacks in current Wi-Fi. And random port mapping based security defense service is launched to defeat the SSL MITM attacks after finding the attacks. We respectively describe the three modules as follows.

Security Prediction. Applications will be verified by security prediction at first. In order to find out SSL certificate validation vulnerabilities in applications, we defines a test certificate set Test_Certs. According to the different SSL certificate validation vulnerabilities caused by amending TrustManager and HostnameVerifier, we design the Test_Certs includes four types of tested certificates, Test_Certs = $\{C_1, C_2, C_3, C_4\}$. C_1 represent any certificate, which is different form real certificate in domain and signature. C_2 represent a certificate, which is same as real certificate besides signature. C_3 represent a certificate, which is same as real certificate besides domain. C_4 represent a certificate, which is same as real certificate besides expiry time.

In this module, the E-SSL acts as a middle application to communicate with remote server and intercept this communication between application and remote server. It will send test certificates, included in Test_Certs, back to the application. If security prediction module successfully establishes a connection with the application, it means that the application receives test certificates and exists SSL certificate validation vulnerabilities; if security prediction module fails or aborts the connection with application, the application does not exist SSL certificate validation vulnerabilities. But we do not guarantee the application is safe in other attack circumstances (it is beyond the scope of this paper). So the applications with SSL certificate validation vulnerabilities are added to dangerous application list, others are added to safe application list. After security prediction, the dangerous application list, safe application list and certificate knowledge base will be generated. The certificate knowledge base is composed of certificates returned from remote servers. The prediction process is conducted in a relatively safe environment, so the certificate knowledge base is safe and reliable. Even if the prediction happens to an unsafe environment, the lure detection will also find the problem to update the certificate knowledge base by security defense.

Security Detection. This module mainly detects whether there is SSL MITM attacks exist in the current Wi-Fi. In mobile internet, public Wi-Fi usually does not move or disappear in short time. And we also don't know when malicious attackers access to the current network and launch malicious attacks,

---

Algorithm 1. MITM Detect

Input: ssl_url, Test_Certs, Dangerous_List
Output: Detect Result
1: **function** MITM DETECTION(ssl_url)
2:      $result \leftarrow FALSE$
3:      $app \leftarrow FindAppByUid$(ssl_url)
4:      **if** $app \neq NULL$ **then**
5:          **if** $app \exists Dangerous\_List$ **then**
6:              $cert \leftarrow GetCert$(ssl_url)
7:              **if** $cert \exists Certs\_Library$ **then**
8:                  $result \leftarrow FALSE$
9:                  $LRU\_Sort(Certs\_Library)$
10:                  **return** $result$
11:              **else**
12:                  $result \leftarrow TRUE$
13:                  **return** $result$
14:              **end if**
15:          **else**
16:              $result \leftarrow FALSE$
17:              **return** $result$
18:          **end if**
19:      **end if**
20:      **return** $result$
21: **end function**

---

so we primarily focus on two key points to study and analyze as follows. One is the time of accessing to Wi-Fi to detect whether SSL MITM attacks already exist, the other one is the process of using Wi-Fi to real-timely detect SSL MITM attacks.

For the first point, we use the lure principle of honeypot to check the returned certificate by the remote server. Usually, malicious attackers want to achieve privacy information or other benefits. So we designedly request relevant privacy information, such as property, authentication. For the second point, E-SSL Client acts as benign MITM between applications and remote server, which is used to forward data and check whether the certificate is returned from the valid server. We think that the collected certificates are returned by the real server during the period of security prediction, and the server's certificates do not change in a short time. We match the returned certificate from the knowledge base in the detection process. If the match result is successful, there is no SSL MITM attacks; otherwise, there are SSL MITM attacks in the current Wi-Fi. The main idea of detection is presented in Algorithm 1. In order to reduce the search time and improve the detection efficiency, we sort the certificate knowledge base according to access frequency, which is based on the core idea of Least Recently Used (LRU).

Security Defense. After finding SSL MITM attacks, security defense service will achieve a safe and reliable communication port to forward data. This method implements the ports mapping service with fixed and dynamic ports. We also enhance the security granularity using hierarchical protection. So it is more difficult for the attacker's speculation owing to spatial randomization as well as temporal randomization. All of the first random port α_i are generated by (1), which are random ports between 50000 and 60000. Primary protection set Φ_1 consists of 20 first random ports by (2). 5 ports are randomly assigned to clients from primary protection set Φ_1, so number of combinations is $\binom{20}{5}$. $\binom{20}{x}$ is a symmetric convex function at the point of x = 10. But with the increase of x, the overlap becomes increasingly obvious among combination. So In order to make the ports dispersed as much as possible, we decide to choose the point of x = 5. And each client achieves the load balancing by status of distributed ports, which is used to accelerate the access speed.

$$\alpha_i = Random(50000, 60000); \{i \in [1, 20]\} \tag{1}$$

$$\Phi_1 = \cup_{i=1}^{20}\alpha_i; \{\alpha_i! = \alpha_j, i! = j; n = 20\} \tag{2}$$

For insurance purposes, once first random port is attacked, it will enable secondary random port to guarantee the security margin. The arbitrary length of input can be transformed into fixed length of the output through the hash algorithm. The output is a hash value, which also has the characteristics of randomness. Each first random port α_i acts as the seed to generate the corresponding hash value $H(x_i)$ by (3). In order to avoid conflict, we choose a linear function F(x) to make decisions, so secondary random port β_i is generated by (4), and the secondary protection set Φ_2 also includes 20 ports by (5).

$$H(x_i) = Hash(x_i); \{i \in [1, 20]\} \tag{3}$$

$$\beta_i = \begin{cases} H(x_i); H(x_i) \notin \Phi_1 \\ F(H(x_i)); others \end{cases} \tag{4}$$

$$\Phi_2 = \cup_{i=1}^{20}\beta_i; \{\beta_i! = \beta_j, i! = j; n = 20\} \tag{5}$$

The defense process is described in Algorithm 2. Data forwarding is implemented on mobile devices, no matter for the application or server, the visited result is seamless without any effect, and just transfer time is a bit long. But data forwarding is operated inside the equipment, the time can be neglected for the whole process. What's more, random ports from the same user are different in different attack scenarios, and random ports from different users may be different in the same attack scenarios. It is hard for malicious attackers to guess the HTTPS protocol shared random ports, thus E-SSL greatly improves the security of applications with SSL certificate validation vulnerabilities under SSL MITM attacks.

Algorithm 2. SSL Defense

Input: ssl_url, Test_Certs
Output: Defense Result
1: **function** MITM DETECTION(ssl_url)
2:     $result \leftarrow Success$
3:     $app \leftarrow FindAppByUid$(ssl_url)
4:     $port\_first \leftarrow RandomFirst(app)$
5:     **while** $Lure_Check(port\_first) \neq TRUE$ **do**
6:         $Data_Forward(port\_first)$
7:         $result \leftarrow Success$
8:     **end while**
9:     $port\_second \leftarrow HashSecond(app, port\_first)$
10:     **while** $Lure_Check(port\_second) \neq TRUE$ **do**
11:         $Data_Forward(port\_second)$
12:         $result \leftarrow Success$
13:     **end while**
14:     $result \leftarrow Failure$
15:     $Stop\_Protect()$
16:     $Stop\_WiFi()$
17: **end function**

4.2   E-SSL Server

This prototype, installed on https server, is mainly cooperated with E-SSL client to prevent from SSL MITM attacks, meanwhile it also guarantees the normal service. This paper proposes the idea of dynamic ports and fixed port mapping sharing service, the flow of dynamic port is forwarded to fixed port to make dynamic port enjoy corresponding service. It can not only ensure users communication under normal circumstances, but also guarantee some users enjoy the safe service by using dynamic ports under SSL MITM attacks.

As shown in Fig. 3, the working process of E-SSL Server is illustrated briefly. In normal internet environment, the user1 can transmit encrypt privacy communication data through the recognized port 443. But, in SSL MITM attacks, the user2 transmits encrypt privacy communication data by port 443, the communication can be intercepted easily by attackers. Whereas user3 and user4 will find SSL MITM attacks with help of the E-SSL in different times and different places. And due to the security guaranty in E-SSL, the port 443 is mapped to dynamic ports 50000 and 53202 respectively by security defense service. As a result, malicious attackers do not monitor corresponding ports traffic and they do not know dynamic ports' running services, so they cannot decrypt and temper with the corresponding communication.

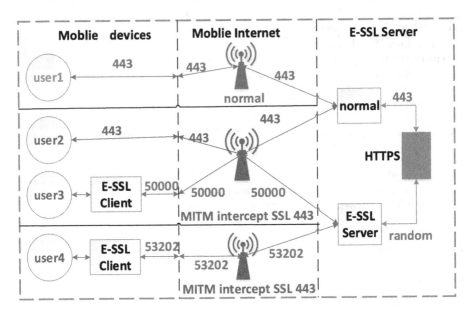

Fig. 3. The working process of E-SSL Server

5   Experiment and Result

Based on the proposed SSL security detection and defense method in mobile internet, we implement the E-SSL Client prototype on Android platform, and implement the E-SSL Server script file of security defense on the CentOS platform. The experiments are conducted on two DELL PC (2.7 GHz CPU, 4G memory) running Ubuntu 15.04 and CentOS 7, TP-Link and Huawei G660 mobile phone. We use 650 apps to test the security prediction module, which are collected from Android Market, and also include our developed application with SSL certificate validation vulnerabilities. Meanwhile, our developed application is mainly used to security defense module. Because we cannot add or modify the server's SSL service configurations of those apps from Android market. We deploy the security defense service on our own server, which is used to validate whether security defense service is reliable or not.

5.1   Security Prediction

Our experiment tests 650 apps and finds that there are as many as 185 apps with SSL certificate validation vulnerabilities, which continue to work without any exception or warning. In these 185 apps, 84 apps accept all certificates without validation, the 97 apps neglect the validation of domain name, and the others can communicate normally with expired certificates. These applications with SSL certificate validation vulnerabilities are still widely popular in Android market, since they have no malicious characteristics. The others 465 apps simply refuse

Table 1. SSL Pinning use situation

Application	SSL Pinning
Amazon MP3	✕
Chrome	✕
Expedia Bookings	✕
Facebook	✕
Gmail	✕
OfficeSuite Pro 6	✕
PayPal	✕
Twitter	✓
Voxer Walkie Talkie	✓
Yahoo! Messenger	✕
Yahoo! Mail	✕

to work, which mostly state that there are technical or connectivity problems and advise the user to try to reconnect later. SSL Pinning is a technique that allows developers to protect the application from MITM attacks resulting from fraudulently issued certificates or compromised CA credentials.

In order to investigate the usage of SSL Pinning, we analyze the most popular 11 apps form the 465 apps that are not prone to the previous attacks. SSL Pinning is a special SSL authentication method by implementing a TrustManager that only trusts specific certificate. So we install our own root certificate to test this case on the phone. Results are shown in Table 1, only two apps use SSL Pinning to assure the security of users' privacy in these apps. Others apps trust the root certificate, thus they are vulnerable to the attacks due to untrusted certificates installed in system truststore. What's more, the experiment result proves E-SSL can effectively detect SSL certificate validation vulnerabilities as well.

5.2   Security Detection

The test application with SSL certificate validation vulnerabilities is installed on the Android device, at the same time we also install E-SSL Client application. The test application hints none of exception, and normally shows visited results in the access process under normal environment and SSL MITM attacks. However, when we start the E-SSL Client security detection service, we find that the E-SSL Client receives two different certificates between normal environment and SSL MITM attacks, as shown in Fig. 4(a) and (b) respectively. This two certificates have different signatures. In the normal environment, E-SSL Client provides normal visits after certificate validation. Under the SSL MITM attacks, the E-SSL Client finds MITM attacks after strict certificate verification. Then the unsafe communication will be terminated, and the E-SSL Client security

(a) Normal certificate

(b) MITM certificate

Fig. 4. Result of detecting certificates

defense service will be launched to make sure user's normal access and ensure security of their privacy information.

5.3 Security Defense

This section introduces how applications with SSL certificate validation vulnerabilities bypass SSL MITM under SSL MITM attacks. Random port mapping based security defense service can ensure the safe communication between the application and the remote server. In order to depict the final comparison result, we install tcpdump [28], a packet capture tool, on the Android phone. Furthermore, we compare the communication data among different scenarios during the connected process. The experiment uses hostapd [29] and sslsplit [30] attack tools to simulate Wi-Fi, which hijacks users' data flow to implement SSL MITM attacks on Ubuntu15.04. We design four different Wi-Fi scenarios for validating our approach in Fig. 5. Figure 5(a) is the normal scenario, Fig. 5(b) is the SSL MITM attacks scenario where the attacker monitor the communication of port 443, Fig. 5(c) is security defense scenario using first random where port 443 is attacked, and Fig. 5(d) is security defense scenario using second hash where port 443 and 50000 are attacked.

We start tcpdump to capture packets between the test application and the corresponding server in the four different scenarios. As a result of the existence of SSL certificate validation vulnerabilities, the visited effect is the same for users. Therefore, in order to distinguish differences, we choose the middle packets as comparative objects with the Wireshark [31]. The Fig. 6(a) indicates the normal communication packets, The Fig. 6(b) indicates communication packets under the SSL MITM attacks, the Fig. 6(c) demonstrates the communication packets using first random after starting security defense service and the Fig. 6(d)

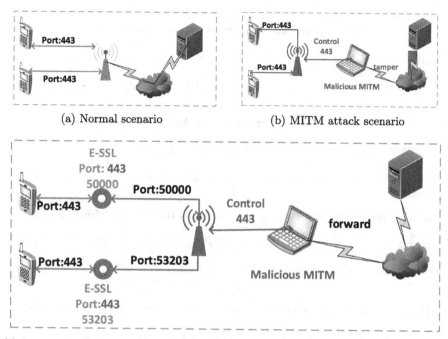

(a) Normal scenario   (b) MITM attack scenario

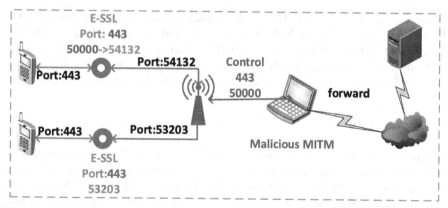

(c) Security defense scenario using first random, where the attacker monitor the port 443

(d) Security defense scenario using second hash, where the attacker monitor the port 443 and 50000

Fig. 5. Four different Wi-Fi scenarios

No.	Source	Destination	Protocol	Length Info
82	172.24.69.98	172.24.67.68	TCP	66 4655→443 [SYN] Seq=0 Win=8192 Len=0 MSS=1460 WS=4 SACK_PERM=1
83	172.24.67.68	172.24.69.98	TCP	66 443→4655 [SYN, ACK] Seq=0 Ack=1 Win=14600 Len=0 MSS=1460 SACK_PERM=1 WS=64
84	172.24.69.98	172.24.67.68	TCP	54 4655→443 [ACK] Seq=1 Ack=1 Win=65700 Len=0
85	172.24.69.98	172.24.67.68	TLSv1.2	571 Client Hello
86	172.24.67.68	172.24.69.98	TCP	60 443→4655 [ACK] Seq=1 Ack=518 Win=15680 Len=0
87	172.24.67.68	172.24.69.98	TLSv1.2	1368 Server Hello, Certificate, Server Key Exchange, Server Hello Done
88	172.24.69.98	172.24.67.68	TLSv1.2	180 Client Key Exchange, Change Cipher Spec, Hello Request, Hello Request
89	172.24.67.68	172.24.69.98	TLSv1.2	328 New Session Ticket, Change Cipher Spec, Encrypted Handshake Message
90	172.24.67.68	172.24.69.98	TLSv1.2	482 Application Data
91	172.24.67.68	172.24.69.98	TLSv1.2	414 Application Data, Application Data

(a) Communication packets in the normal scenario

No.	Source	Destination	Protocol	Length Info
36	172.24.69.98	172.24.67.68	TCP	66 4215→443 [SYN] Seq=0 Win=8192 Len=0 MSS=1460 WS=4 SACK_PERM=1
37	172.24.67.68	172.24.69.98	TCP	66 443→4215 [SYN, ACK] Seq=0 Ack=1 Win=14600 Len=0 MSS=1460 SACK_PERM=1 WS=64
38	172.24.69.98	172.24.67.68	TCP	54 4215→443 [ACK] Seq=1 Ack=1 Win=65700 Len=0
39	172.24.69.98	172.24.67.68	TLSv1.2	571 Client Hello
40	172.24.67.68	172.24.69.98	TCP	60 443→4215 [ACK] Seq=1 Ack=518 Win=15680 Len=0
41	172.24.67.68	172.24.69.98	TLSv1.2	1328 Server Hello, Certificate, Server Key Exchange, Server Hello Done
42	172.24.69.98	172.24.67.68	TLSv1.2	180 Client Key Exchange, Change Cipher Spec, Hello Request, Hello Request
43	172.24.67.68	172.24.69.98	TLSv1.2	328 New Session Ticket, Change Cipher Spec, Encrypted Handshake Message
44	172.24.69.98	172.24.67.68	TLSv1.2	482 Application Data
45	172.24.67.68	172.24.69.98	TLSv1.2	414 Application Data, Application Data

(b) Communication packets in the SSL MITM attacks scenario

No.	Source	Destination	Protocol	Length Info
38	172.24.69.98	172.24.67.68	TCP	66 4733→50000 [SYN] Seq=0 Win=8192 Len=0 MSS=1460 WS=4 SACK_PERM=1
39	172.24.67.68	172.24.69.98	TCP	66 50000→4733 [SYN, ACK] Seq=0 Ack=1 Win=14600 Len=0 MSS=1460 SACK_PERM=1 WS=64
40	172.24.69.98	172.24.67.68	TCP	54 4733→50000 [ACK] Seq=1 Ack=1 Win=65700 Len=0
41	172.24.69.98	172.24.67.68	TCP	571 4733→50000 [PSH, ACK] Seq=1 Ack=1 Win=65700 Len=517
42	172.24.67.68	172.24.69.98	TCP	60 50000→4733 [ACK] Seq=1 Ack=518 Win=15680 Len=0
43	172.24.67.68	172.24.69.98	TCP	1368 50000→4733 [PSH, ACK] Seq=1 Ack=518 Win=15680 Len=1314
44	172.24.69.98	172.24.67.68	TCP	180 4733→50000 [PSH, ACK] Seq=518 Ack=1315 Win=64384 Len=126
45	172.24.69.98	172.24.67.68	TCP	328 50000→4733 [PSH, ACK] Seq=1315 Ack=644 Win=15680 Len=274
46	172.24.69.98	172.24.67.68	TCP	488 4733→50000 [PSH, ACK] Seq=644 Ack=1589 Win=65700 Len=434
47	172.24.67.68	172.24.69.98	TCP	414 50000→4733 [PSH, ACK] Seq=1589 Ack=1078 Win=16768 Len=360

(c) Communication packets using first random in the security defense scenario

No.	Source	Destination	Protocol	Length Info
37	172.24.69.98	172.24.67.68	TCP	66 4768→54132 [SYN] Seq=0 Win=8192 Len=0 MSS=1460 WS=4 SACK_PERM=1
38	172.24.67.68	172.24.69.98	TCP	66 54132→4768 [SYN, ACK] Seq=0 Ack=1 Win=14600 Len=0 MSS=1460 SACK_PERM=1 WS=64
39	172.24.69.98	172.24.67.68	TCP	54 4768→54132 [ACK] Seq=1 Ack=1 Win=65700 Len=0
40	172.24.69.98	172.24.67.68	TCP	571 4768→54132 [PSH, ACK] Seq=1 Ack=1 Win=65700 Len=517
41	172.24.67.68	172.24.69.98	TCP	60 54132→4768 [ACK] Seq=1 Ack=518 Win=15680 Len=0
42	172.24.67.68	172.24.69.98	TCP	1368 54132→4768 [PSH, ACK] Seq=1 Ack=518 Win=15680 Len=1314
43	172.24.69.98	172.24.67.68	TCP	180 54132→4768 [PSH, ACK] Seq=518 Ack=1315 Win=64384 Len=126
44	172.24.67.68	172.24.69.98	TCP	328 54132→4768 [PSH, ACK] Seq=1315 Ack=644 Win=15680 Len=274
45	172.24.69.98	172.24.67.68	TCP	488 54132→4768 [PSH, ACK] Seq=644 Ack=1589 Win=65700 Len=434
46	172.24.67.68	172.24.69.98	TCP	414 54132→4768 [PSH, ACK] Seq=1589 Ack=1078 Win=16768 Len=360

(d) Communication packets using second hash in the security defense scenario

Fig. 6. Communication packets in the four different scenarios

demonstrates the communication packets using second hash after starting security defense service. Through data contrastive analysis, we find the certificates are different between the Fig. 6(a) and (b), because the size of certificates are 1368 and 1328, respectively. We also pay attention to the certificates are the same in Fig. 6(a), (c) and (d), besides the transmitted ports are changed.

6   Evaluation

In order to further prove the effectiveness of E-SSL, we make a correlation analysis from the perspective of theory. The smaller the attack's hitting rate is given to illustrate the effectiveness of the E-SSL is higher. The attack hitting rate depends on a variety of factors, such as the port pool size, number of probes, number of users, and the varying frequency. The influences of these factors will be analyzed under certain conditions. Now, in order to give a quantitative analysis, some basic parameters should be predefined. At the same time, we make some assumptions in ideal conditions, which does not consider the situations, including the attacker's hacking capabilities and the E-SSL's defense abilities.

- A: the set of varying ports;
- m: the number of A, $m = |A| < 10000$;
- n_i: the i port of A, $n_i \in A$;
- P(x): the probability of hitting the port x to attacker;
- P_i: the probability of hitting at the i times;
- T_i: the probability of hitting at the varying frequency i;
- The attacker has certain statistical learning ability;
- The attacker is aware of the range of port pool (m ports).

Considering the scenario where attacker knew the range of port pool, and every user uses the different varying port. In this case, the probability of hitting port n_i is $\frac{1}{m}$, in others words, the attack hitting rate P(X) is $\frac{1}{m}$. The relation of attack hitting rate and port pool size is shown in Fig. 7. From the visual display, the greater the range of port pool is, the more difficult attack is. But due to number restrictions of port on the device, it is impossible to unlimitedly expand the range of port pool. The ports are be classified to three categories, including Well Known Ports (0-1024), Registered Ports (1025-49151), and Dynamic and/or Private Ports (49152-65535). In order to avoid ports' collision, we set the range of port form 50000 to 60000.

The number of probes is another factor, which has an effect on the attack hitting rate. We assume the scenario that the attacker has certain statistical learning ability. Study results will be added to monitoring set at a time, and the port of monitoring set will be ruled out in the learning process, which will narrow the scope of the guess. So the probability P_i of guessing at i times is $\frac{1}{m-i}$. Obviously, in Fig. 8, the attack hitting rate increases as the number of probes increases, and the attack hitting rate is close to 1 when the number of probes $c \geqslant m$. At i times, the probability P_i decreases as the number of varying port pool. So we need to simultaneously control the port pool size and number of probes.

The previous assumption where the varying frequency is not considered. In this case, we will analyze the relation of the varying frequency and attack hitting rate.

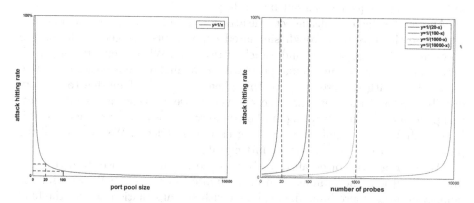

Fig. 7. The relation of attack hitting rate and port pool size

Fig. 8. The relation of attack hitting rate and number of probes

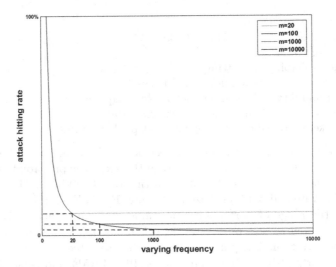

Fig. 9. The relation of attack hitting rate and varying frequency

In this scenario, the varying frequency is equivalent to the times of varying in total learning process. Under the precondition that the port is different by varying mechanism at every time, and the number of probes is equal to the port pool size, so the attack hitting rate defines by (6).

$$T_i = \begin{cases} 1/(i-1); i \leqslant m \\ 1/m; others \end{cases} \qquad (6)$$

The relation of the varying frequency and attack hitting rate is clearly presented in Fig. 9. Looking from the Fig. 9, we can know that the attack hitting rate decreases as the varying frequency increases when the number of probes is fixed. But the varying time is very long due to the authentication feature of SSL, so the varying frequency can not be too large.

Another key factor which affects the attack hitting rate is the number of users, which use the E-SSL. Through simulated experiments, we get a relationship between the number of users and attack hitting rate. When users are very small in the current network, individual ports will be highlighted in attacker's learning data. Along with the user to join, this phenomenon will fade due to random distribution of ports. But when the number of users reaches a extreme point, this phenomenon will appear again. Fortunately, the processing capacity of Wi-Fi is limited, so the number of accessing users is restricted. We can control the port pool size to reduce the attack hitting rate.

We make a series of detailed analysis based on the influence from the four different factors. The number of users is limited in the same Wi-Fi, and the number of ports is also limited. Combined with actual situation, we get the final result that the range of port form 50000 to 60000 and hierarchical protection mechanism. Through theoretical analysis and the experimental results, E-SSL

Table 2. Method comparison

Method	Characters		
	SSL certificate validation vulnerabilities detect	SSL MITM attack detect	SSL MITM attack defense
Fahl [4]	✓	✗	✗
Liu [12]	✓	✓	✗
Sounthiraraj [13]	✓	✗	✗
Georgiev [18]	✓	✗	✗
Guo S [20]	✓	✗	✗
Conti [24]	✓	✓	✗
E-SSL	✓	✓	✓

can not only find the SSL certificate validation vulnerabilities of applications and the existence of SSL MITM attacks, but also be able to defeat SSL MITM attacks.

To prove the effectiveness and find drawbacks of this method, we compare the experiment result with the previous approaches and analyze advantages and drawbacks of each one in related work. Method comparison result is shown in Table 2. E-SSL acts as vital roles in public Wi-Fi environment. E-SSL guarantees the security of the mobile terminal user's privacy information, and also meets the requirement of using Wi-Fi under SSL MITM attacks.

7   Discussion

7.1   Communication Overhead

Without considering the overhead of port varying, the E-SSL can be a very good defense mechanism. In order to implement port varying, E-SSL exists some interception behaviors, which need to monitor the user's SSL request operations for real-timely detecting and analyzing. The overhead of port varying grows exponentially as the hopping frequency increases. Therefore, the system overhead caused by varying events must be considered. Meanwhile they may introduce risks into the environments they're meant to protect. But the monitor activity focuses on the terminal equipment, no one can access the monitoring information, so this behavior is relative safety and controllable.

7.2   Latency

Due to the port varying event, the connection between two communication parties will be interrupted, which will cause communication latency. So we evaluate the average time of accessing to HTTPS URLs in security detection, security defense and normal access. Then we compare the latency relative to normal

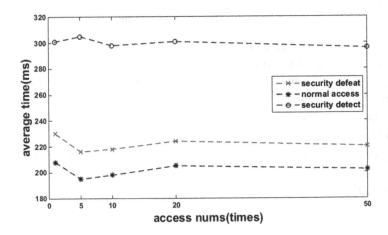

Fig. 10. Statistical result of average time about security detection, security defense and normal access

access. Because the HTTPS has SSL session reuse function, the completed SSL handshake process will not be built in the continuity of access.

Consequently, we use intermittent access to calculate the average time with the help of E-SSL and no help of E-SSL. We set 1, 5, 10, 20, 50 times to calculate the average time respectively. The statistical result of average time is shown in Fig. 10. There are two opinions in the result. On the one hand, security detection time is longer than the normal access, which reason is security detection conducts an additional SSL handshake in the middle process. On the other hand, security defense service expends almost the same time with normal access cost because of its forwarding process. In order to improve the security, delays are inevitable, but it is in the range of tolerance.

8   Conclusion

In this paper, we design and implement the prototype of an SSL Security-Enhanced method (E-SSL) on Android platform, which mainly aims to the secure communication. In Wi-Fi environment, E-SSL can not only detect SSL MITM attacks, but also defeat SSL MITM attacks with security defense service based on random port mapping. This method will ensure the users' online requirement of surfing internet, and guarantee the security of sensitive information under SSL MITM attacks. We analyze 650 apps under the realistic SSL MITM attacks, and find 185 apps that have SSL certificate validation vulnerabilities. Meanwhile, by comparing the communicated packets among different Wi-Fi scenarios in the WireShark, we come to the conclusion that the visited effects are same besides the transmitted ports are changed. A series of experimental results prove the effectiveness and reliability of E-SSL.

In future work, we will further improve this method to compatible with the different system platforms. Although our method solves the security problems of SSL MITM attacks, there are still several limitations of our prototype. We need to seek for a better approach to improve the real-timely detection efficiency of SSL MITM attacks. And more detailed coordination works need to be strengthened between the application and the server.

Acknowledgement. This work has partially been sponsored by the National Science Foundation of China (No. 61572349, 61272106, 61572355), Tianjin Research Program of Application Foundation and Advanced Technology under grant No. 15JCYBJC15700, and Tianjin Key Laboratory of Advanced Networking.

References

1. Song, Y., Yang, C., Gu, G.: Who is peeping at your passwords at Starbucks? To catch an evil twin access point. In: IEEE/IFIP International Conference on Dependable Systems and Networks (DSN), pp. 323–332. IEEE (2010)
2. Freier, A., Karlton, P., Kocher, P.: The secure sockets layer (SSL) protocol version 3.0 (2011)
3. Dierks, T., Rescorla, E.: The transport layer security (TLS) protocol version 1.2 (2008)
4. Fahl, S., Harbach, M., Muders, T.: Why eve and mallory love android: an analysis of android SSL (in) security. In: Proceedings of the 2012 ACM Conference on Computer and Communications Security, pp. 50–61. ACM (2012)
5. Clark, J., van Oorschot, P.C.: SoK: SSL and HTTPS: revisiting past challenges and evaluating certificate trust model enhancements. In: Security and Privacy (SP), pp. 511–525. IEEE (2013)
6. Duan, Z.: Temporal Logic and Temporal Logic Programming. Science Press, Beijing (2005)
7. Duan, Z., Tian, C., Zhang, L.: A decision procedure for propositional projection temporal logic with infinite models. Acta Informatica $45(1)$, 43–78 (2008)
8. Egners, A., Marschollek, B., Meyer, U.: Messing with Android's permission model. In: Proceedings of the IEEE TrustCom, pp. 1–22 (2012)
9. Bugiel, S., Davi, L., Dmitrienko, A., Fischer, T., Sadeghi, A.-R., Shastry, B.: Towards taming privilege-escalation attacks on android. In: Proceedings of NDSS (2012)
10. Becher, M., Freiling, F., Hoffmann, J., Holz, T., Uellenbeck, S., Wolf, C.: Mobile security catching up? revealing the nuts and bolts of the security of mobile devices. In: IEEE Security and Privacy (SP), pp. 96–111 (2011)
11. Marlinspike, M.: New tricks for defeating SSL in practice. In: BlackHat DC, February 2009
12. Liu, H., Zhang, Y., Wang, H., Yang, W., Li, J., Gu, D.: TagDroid: hybrid SSL certificate verification in android. In: Hui, L.C.K., Qing, S.H., Shi, E., Yiu, S.M. (eds.) ICICS 2014. LNCS, vol. 8958, pp. 120–131. Springer, Cham (2015). doi:10.1007/978-3-319-21966-0_9. 16th International Conference, ICICS 2014, Hong Kong, China, December 16-17, 2014
13. Sounthiraraj, D., Sahs, J., Greenwood, G.: Smv-hunter: large scale, automated detection of SSL/TLS man-in-the-middle vulnerabilities in android apps. In: Proceedings of the 21st Annual Network and Distributed System Security Symposium (2014)

14. Durumeric, Z., Kasten, J., Bailey, M.: Analysis of the HTTPS certificate ecosystem. In: Proceedings of the 2013 Conference on Internet Measurement Conference, pp. 291–304. ACM (2013)
15. Holz, R., Braun, L., Kammenhuber, N.: The SSL landscape: a thorough analysis of the x.509 PKI using active and passive measurements. In: Proceedings of the 2011 ACM SIGCOMM Conference on Internet Measurement Conference, pp. 427–444. ACM (2011)
16. Akhawe, D., Amann, B., Vallentin, M.: Here's my cert, so trust me, maybe? understanding TLS errors on the web. In: Proceedings of the 22nd International Conference on World Wide Web, pp. 59–70. International World Wide Web Conferences Steering Committee (2013)
17. Huang, L.S., Rice, A., Ellingsen, E.: Analyzing forged SSL certificates in the wild. In: Security and Privacy (SP), pp. 83–97. IEEE (2014)
18. Georgiev, M., Iyengar, S., Jana, S.: The most dangerous code in the world: validating SSL certificates in non-browser software. In: Proceedings of the 2012 ACM Conference on Computer and Communications Security, pp. 38–49. ACM (2012)
19. Zheng, C., Zhu, S., Dai, S.: Smartdroid: an automatic system for revealing ui-based trigger conditions in android applications. In: Proceedings of the Second ACM Workshop on Security and Privacy in Smartphones and Mobile Devices, pp. 93–104. ACM (2012)
20. Zuo, C., Wu, J., Guo, S.: Automatically detecting SSL error-handling vulnerabilities in hybrid mobile web apps. In: Proceedings of the 10th ACM Symposium on Information, Computer and Communications Security, pp. 591–596. ACM (2015)
21. Duan, Z., Yang, X., Koutny, M.: Framed temporal logic programming. Sci. Comput. Program. **70**(1), 31–61 (2008)
22. Tian, C., Duan, Z., Zhang, N.: An efficient approach for abstraction-refinement in model checking. Theoret. Comput. Sci. **461**, 76–85 (2012)
23. Benton, K., Jo, J., Kim, Y.: Signaturecheck: a protocol to detect man-in-the-middle attack in SSL. In: Proceedings of the Seventh Annual Workshop on Cyber Security and Information Intelligence Research, p. 60. ACM (2011)
24. Conti, M., Dragoni, N., Gottardo, S.: MITHYS: mind the hand you shake - protecting mobile devices from SSL usage vulnerabilities. In: Accorsi, R., Ranise, S. (eds.) STM 2013. LNCS, vol. 8203, pp. 65–81. Springer, Heidelberg (2013). doi:10.1007/978-3-642-41098-7_5. 9th International Workshop, STM 2013, Egham, UK, September 12-13, 2013
25. Bates, A., Pletcher, J., Nichols, T.: Securing SSL certificate verification through dynamic linking. In: Proceedings of the 2014 ACM SIGSAC Conference on Computer and Communications Security, pp. 394–405. ACM (2014)
26. Fahl, S., Harbach, M., Perl, H.: Rethinking SSL development in an appified world. In: Proceedings of the 2013 ACM SIGSAC Conference on Computer & Communications Security, pp. 49–60. ACM (2013)
27. Tendulkar, V., Enck, W.: An application package configuration approach to mitigating android SSL vulnerabilities (2014)
28. tcpdump. http://www.tcpdump.org
29. hostapd. http://w1.fi/hostapd
30. SSLsplit. http://www.roe.ch/SSLsplit
31. wireshark, https://www.wireshark.org

A Proof System for MSVL Programs in Coq

Lin Qian, Zhenhua Duan$^{(\boxtimes)}$, Nan Zhang, and Cong Tian

Institute of Computing Theory and Technology,
Xidian University, Xi'an 710071, China
zhhduan@mail.xidian.edu.cn

Abstract. In this paper, we propose a semi-automatic proof approach for programs written in Modeling, Simulation and Verification Language (MSVL) based on the interactive theorem prover Coq. To this end, first, the syntax and semantics of MSVL are briefly introduced, and the specification and proof tactics of Coq are described. Further, an axiomatic system of MSVL programs is specified in Coq. Based on these, MSVL programs and related properties can be recognized in Coq so that theorems to be proved can be formalised and the verification can be conducted when proof tactics are provided in the Coq prover. Finally, an example is given to illustrate how our proposed approach works.

Keywords: MSVL · Semi-automatic proof · Interactive theorem prover · Coq

1 Introduction

Theorem proving [1] and model checking [2] are two kinds of modern mainstream formal verification technologies. Compared with model checking, theorem proving can deal with a program or system with infinite state space and does not suffer from the "state explosion problem" [4]. However, users need to guide the proving process and intervene directly in the intermediate steps. Thus the subjectivity of users is introduced in the proof. At present, there are many theorem provers such as Coq [6], PVS [9], ACL2 [10], HOL [11], Isabelle [12], Nuprl [13] and so on.

As a proof development system, Coq provides a formal language Gallina to write mathematical definitions, algorithms and theorems together with an environment for semi-interactive development of machine-checked proofs. In fact, it provides interactive proof methods, decision and semi-decision algorithms, and a tactic language to allow users to define their own proof methods. It also allows users to use external algebra systems or theorem provers. As a platform for the formalization of mathematics or the development of programs, Coq also provides support for high-level notations, implicit contents and other useful kinds of macros. At present, Coq is widely used in the verification area [15,16].

The research is supported by the National Natural Science Foundation of China under Grant Nos. 61133001, 61572386, 61420106004 and 91418201.

S. Liu et al. (Eds.): SOFL+MSVL 2016, LNCS 10189, pp. 121–143, 2017.
DOI: 10.1007/978-3-319-57708-1_8

In this paper, we investigate a verification technique based on theorem proving using Coq for verifying programs of Modelling, Simulation and Verification language (MSVL) [3].

MSVL is a temporal logic programming language with types. It is a useful formalism for specification and verification of concurrent [18,19,22] and real time systems [14]. MSVL contains common statements used in most of imperative programming languages (e.g. C, Java) such as assignment, sequential $(p; q)$, branch (if b then p else q) and iteration (while b do p) statements as well as parallel and concurrent statements such as conjunct $(p$ and $q)$, parallel $(p\|q)$ and projection $((p_1, \ldots, p_m)$ prj $q)$ statements. Further, a Cylinder Computation Model (CCM) is proposed and included in MSVL [20,21], which can be used to describe and reason about multi-core parallel programs. To make MSVL more practical and useful, multi-types such as (unsigned) int, float, (unsigned) char, string, list, array, pointer, struct and union have been formalized and implemented [5]. Therefore, multi-typed values, functions and predicates concerning the extended data domain can be defined. To support modeling, simulation and verification of a system using MSVL, a tool kit called MSV [23] has been developed.

Currently, the available verification tools for MSVL are mostly based on model checking, however, theorem proving of MSVL programs are not yet well supported by tools. Therefore, in this paper, we are motivated to formalise a proof system [17] for MSVL programs so that property verification can be carried out semi-automatically. Further, Coq strongly supports a rich type system and logical inference as well as interactive proof methods, we choose it as the implementation environment of the proof system.

To realize the theorem prover, we describe the variables, expressions and functions of MSVL in terms of the specification language Gallina; then we define MSVL statements and derived statements as well as abbreviations using Gallina; finally we formalize the axioms and inference rules of MSVL proof system in Coq.

The contribution of this paper is two-fold: (1) we propose a theorem proving method for MSVL programs based on axiomatic semantics; (2) we develop a theorem prover for MSVL programs based on Coq.

The rest of the paper is organized as follows: MSVL and its axiom semantics are briefly introduced in Sect. 2. An MSVL proof system in Coq is developed in Sect. 3, including the coding of expressions, statements of MSVL, axioms and inference rules of operational semantics of programs. In Sect. 4, a verification example is given. Finally, conclusions are drawn in Sect. 5.

2   Preliminaries

2.1   MSVL

In MSVL, arithmetic expression e and boolean expression b are defined by the following grammar:

$$e::= c \mid x \mid \bigcirc x \mid \ominus x \mid f(e_1, ..., e_m)$$

Table 1. MSVL statements

Statement	Syntax	Definition in PTL (model semantics)
Termination:	$empty$	$\overset{\text{def}}{=} \varepsilon$
Positive immediate assignment:	$x \Leftarrow e$	$\overset{\text{def}}{=} x = e \wedge p_x$
Assignment:	$x := e$	$\overset{\text{def}}{=} \bigcirc x \Leftarrow e$
State frame:	$lbf(x)$	$\overset{\text{def}}{=} (\neg p_x \rightarrow \exists b(\ominus x = b \wedge x = b))$
Interval frame:	$frame(x)$	$\overset{\text{def}}{=} \square(more \rightarrow \bigcirc lbf(x))$
Conjunction:	p and q	$\overset{\text{def}}{=} p \wedge q$
Selection:	p or q	$\overset{\text{def}}{=} p$ or q
Next:	next p	$\overset{\text{def}}{=} \bigcirc p$
Always:	alw p	$\overset{\text{def}}{=} \square p$
Conditional:	$if\ b\ then\ p\ else\ q$	$\overset{\text{def}}{=} (b \rightarrow p) \wedge (\neg b \rightarrow q)$
Existential quantification:	$local\ x\ p(x)$	$\overset{\text{def}}{=} \exists x\ p(x)$
Sequential:	$p; q$	$\overset{\text{def}}{=} p; q$
While:	$while\ b\ do\ p$	$\overset{\text{def}}{=} (b \wedge p)^* \wedge \square(\varepsilon \rightarrow \neg b)$
Parallel:	$p \parallel q$	$\overset{\text{def}}{=} p \wedge (q; true)$ or $q \wedge (p; true)$
Projection:	$(p_1, ..., p_m)$ prj q	$\overset{\text{def}}{=} (p_1, ..., p_m)$ prj q
Synchronised communication:	$await(c)$	$\overset{\text{def}}{=} frame(V_c) \wedge halt(c)$

$$b:: = true \mid false \mid p \mid \neg b \mid b_1 \wedge b_2 \mid e_1 = e_2 \mid e_1 < e_2$$

where c is a typed constant, x a variable; $\bigcirc x$ and $\ominus x$ denote variable x at the next and previous states respectively; f is an m arity function; in particular, $e_1\ op\ e_2$ ($op:: = + \mid - \mid * \mid mod$) is treated as $f(e_1, e_2)$. In boolean expressions, p is an atomic proposition, and e_i ($i = 1, 2$) arithmetic expression.

MSVL [7,8] statements can be defined inductively as shown in Table 1, where x denotes a variable, e an arithmetic expression, and b a boolean expression, and $p, p_1, ..., p_m$ and q MSVL programs.

The assignment $x := e$, positive immediate assignment $x \Leftarrow e$, state frame $lbf(x)$ and $empty$ can be thought of as basic statements and others can be treated as composite statements. The explanation of these statements can be found in [3].

2.2 MSVL Axiomatic System

The axiomatic semantics of MSVL [17] is studied in terms of axioms and inference rules: state axioms and state inference rules deduce an MSVL program to its normal form while a set of interval axioms and inference rules deduce a program over an interval. These rules enable us to transform a program from the current state to the next one, and simultaneously verify properties over intervals.

As a result, we establish an axiomatic system for MSVL based on its axiomatic semantics, denoted by Π_{MSVL}.

Note that, in our axiomatic system, we are only concerned with the verification of a satisfiable program, and do not consider the case of $p \equiv false$. Hence, we claim that all of the programs appearing in the following context are satisfiable.

Axioms and Inference Rules within a State

For convenience, we use $p \cong^{\bullet} q$ to denote $\vdash \Box(p \leftrightarrow q)$. Appendix A lists the set of state axioms and state inference rules, respectively, for the purpose of deducing a program to its normal form. In axiom A8, q is a lec-formula; in axioms A7, A9 and A19, p is required to be a terminable program; in axiom A9, A14, A15 and A16, w is a present component. Axioms A1 and A2 deal with the assignment statement $x = e$ and $x \Leftarrow e$. When they are conjuncted with the state frame $lbf(x)$, they are deduced to $x \Leftarrow e$. In A1, e is a new value different from the previous value x. Axioms A3 and A4 deal with $\Box p$, and axioms A5 and A6 deal with the interval frame $frame(x)$. These are described in terms of the interval length: ε(that is,$len(0)$) or more (that is, $len(n)$, $n > 0$). Axioms A7-A9 deal with the sequential statement $p; q$. Axioms A10 deals with the parallel statement $p \parallel q$ in terms of its definition. Axiom A11 deals with $\bigcirc p$. Axioms A12-A17 deal with the projection statement $(p_1, ..., p_m)$ prj q. Axioms A18 and A19 deal with the conditional and while statements, respectively. Axiom A20 is a basic axiom that describes the substitution instances of all valid classical first-order formulas into temporal contexts.

Rule R1 is a substitution rule, where $prog[p]$ is a program in MSVL involving a subprogram p, and $prog[q/p]$ denotes the program given by replacing some occurrences of p in prog by q. Rule R2 deals with the existential quantifier. Provided $p(x)$ has a normal form, $\exists x : p(x)$ can be reduced to normal form. Rule R3 says that if $\vdash P$, then P always holds over intervals, that is, $\vdash \Box P$.

Axioms and Inference Rules over Intervals

This subsection is devoted to interval deduction. To this end, we define a modification of the Hoare triple [24] as a correctness assertion, and formalise a set of axioms and inference rules over intervals to transform a program in normal form from the current state to the next one, and simultaneously verify the properties over intervals. The correctness assertion can be defined as

$$\{\sigma_k, A\} \, p \, \{\sigma_h, B\}$$

where p is an MSVL program, σ_k and σ_h are intervals, with σ_k a prefix of $\sigma_h(k, h \in N_\omega, 0 \le k \le h)$, and A and B are PPTL formulas [25, 26].

In Appendix B, axioms AEM and APC are concerned with the terminal and assignment statements, respectively (that is, present components). Rule ISR tells us that in the triple $\{\sigma_k, A\}prog[p]\{\sigma_h, B\}$, if $p \cong q$ can be deduced by state axioms and state inference rules, then we can replace sub-program p by q in program $prog$.

For convenience, we will now define state components, $ps(x)$, by

$$ps(x) :: = x = e \mid x \Leftarrow e \mid b$$

So $ps(x)$ consists of the assignment statement $x = e$, the positive immediate assignment $x \Leftarrow e$ and boolean expressions b. A state program is a conjunction of state components such as $ps(x_1) \wedge ps(x2) \wedge ... \wedge ps(x_n)$.

We write $e[x \mapsto e_0]$ for the arithmetic (or boolean) expression obtained by replacing each occurrence of a variable x in an arithmetic expression e (or boolean expression b) with another expression e_0 (or b_0). This is called substitution.

Rules AAS and LBF are concerned with evaluating the state component $ps(x)$ and the state frame $lbf(x)$. In rule AAS, we apply substitution to state components to evaluate arithmetic and boolean expressions. Note that we do not allow $lbf(x)$ (or $lbf(y)$) to occur in p because $lbf(x) \wedge x = m \cong x \Leftarrow m$ by axiom A1. In rule LBF, the condition $x = e$ and $x \Leftarrow e$ does not occur in p, ensures that the value of variable x at state s_k is equivalent to the previous value of x.

Further, the normal form of A is denoted by $A \equiv (A_e \wedge \varepsilon) \wedge (A_c \wedge \bigcirc A_f)$, where p_c, p_e, A_c and A_e are present components. For rule ANext, If $p_c \rightarrow A_c$, by axiom APC, we have $\vdash \{\sigma_k, A_c\} p_c \{\sigma_k, A_c\}$. This means that the state program p_c satisfies the property A_c, which is a present component decomposed by A at state s_k. We then further transform the "next" program p_f to state s_{k+1}, and replace the assertion A by its next formula A_f. Thus, we can obtain the triple $\{\sigma_{k+1}, A_f\} p_f \{\sigma_h, B\}$ to continue to deduce program p_f over the remaining interval $\sigma_{(k+1...h)} = <s_{k+1}, ..., s_h>$. If a state program at each state $s_k (0 \leq k \leq h)$ satisfies a present component property, we say that the program satisfies property A over the whole interval over which the program is deduced. If $p_c \rightarrow A_c$ is not true, we say that the program does not satisfy the given property, which is denoted by $false$, and the program stops with an error.

Rule AEmpty is concerned with the terminal statement ε, which means that program p terminates at state s_k. Note that we have assumed that $p \equiv p_c \wedge \bigcirc p_f$ is satisfiable. Therefore, when $p_c \rightarrow A_c$ is $false$, we can affirm that p cannot satisfy A. However, this is not the case for an unsatisfiable program since program p always satisfies A for $p \equiv false$.

Rule SSR is for selection statement q_1 or q_2 and rules EQR1 and EQR2 for local statement $local\ x : p(x)$. In SSR, if the correctness assertion $\{\sigma_k, A\} q_i \{\sigma_h, B\}$ holds for $q_i (i = 1\ or\ 2)$, then it is obvious that $\{\sigma_k, A\} q_1 \vee q_2 \{\sigma_h, B\}$ holds. Rules EQR1 and EQR2 enable us to eliminate quantifiers in programs, where p(y) is a renamed formula, and pe(y) and pc(y) are present components (that is, state programs).

We have now formalised the whole axiom system of MSVL programs, including the state axioms, the state inference rules, the interval axioms and the interval inference rules.

3   An MSVL Proof System in Coq

In this section, we present the key part of the coding in Coq used in setting up of our MSVL proof system. The code presented here is fragmentary and merely for illustrative purposes.

3.1   Principle

The theorem proving method we proposed involves three main parts:

(1) we describe the variables, expressions and functions of MSVL in terms of the specification language Gallina;
(2) we define MSVL statements and derived statements using specification language Gallina;
(3) we formalize the axioms and inference rules of the MSVL axiomatic system in Coq.

This enables MSVL programs to be correctly recognized by Coq and we can compile them to check the correctness of syntax.

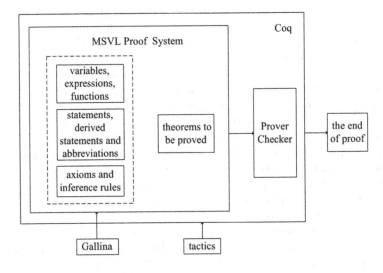

Fig. 1. Proof principle

As shown in Fig. 1, the details of the proof principle are described as follows. In the first part, we mainly define variables, expressions and functions using Gallina. For doing so, we adopt the inductive type of Gallina in the definitions. An inductive definition is specified by giving the names and types of the inductive sets (or families) and the constructors of the inductive predicates to be defined. The Coq type-checker verifies that all parameters are applied in the correct manner for the type of each constructor. For the definition of functions, we can directly use the recursive types if needed. A definition can be seen as a way to give meaning to a name or term. After the definition, the name can be replaced at any time by its definition. In addition, a definition is accepted by the Coq system if and only if the defined name or term is well-typed in the current context of the definition. A recursive type is commonly used for defining recursive functions, in particular, for defining primitive recursive functions. In that case the recursion enjoys a special syntactic restriction, namely each parameter involving recursion belongs to an inductive type. The implementation details are given later on in this section.

In the second part, we define statements, derived statements as well as abbreviations using Gallina. We still use the inductive type to define statements and derived statements. In fact, all constructors make up the body of the inductive definitions and must in complete manner to ensure the soundness of the inductive definitions. As for abbreviations, we use the notation structure of the Coq system. A notation is a symbolic abbreviation denoting some expressions or formulas and always surrounded by double quotes. A notation is composed of identifiers and symbols separated by spaces starting without digits and single quote('). The parameters of notations are identifiers consisting of letters, digits, under score(_), and single quote. Each parameter must occur at least once in the denoted expression or formula, and the other symbols are user-defined. An identifier can be used as a symbol but it must be surrounded by single quotes to avoid confusions.

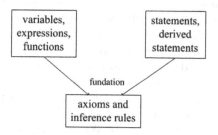

Fig. 2. The relationship of three parts

Based on the first two parts, we formalize the axioms and inference rules of MSVL axiomatic system with the assumption structure of Coq. An assumption links a type to a name as its specification and is accepted by Coq if and only if this type is a correct type in the environment. These axioms and inference rules will be guided to act on proof by tactics which is a manual input in the proving process.

In fact, three parts are closely related. The relationship of three parts is shown in Fig. 2. Before defining the second part, we need to import the first part to the current environment. Similarly, before defining the third part, we need to import the first two parts.

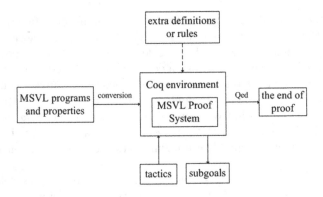

Fig. 3. Proving process

As shown in Fig. 3, for a specific proof instance, we first model the problem with an MSVL program and extract related properties to be proved. Then we need Coq to verify whether the MSVL program satisfies the properties or not. Obviously, we can express the program and properties in the proof development system of Coq through importing the definitions we have written in the former three parts to the current environment so as to obtain theorems to be proved. Sometimes, extra definitions or rules may be needed for different examples. The proof editing mode is entered by asserting a statement, which typically is the assertion of a theorem. In the proving process, we choose reasonable tactics to act on the current proof in each step. The tactics implement backward reasoning. When applied to a goal, a tactic replaces the current goal with subgoals it generates. Namely, a tactic deduces a goal to its subgoals. However, neither each rule we defined applies to a given statement, nor each tactic can be used to deduce a goal. In other words, before applying a tactic to a given goal, the system checks whether preconditions are satisfied. If it is not the case, the tactic raises an error message. Hence, which tactics and laws to be adopted is important in the proving process. The Coq system provides us rich tactics, and each choice depends largely on the current subgoals. When all the subgoals are solved, the proof is completed. Finally, the Qed command is used to finish the proof process formally and thus, in the meantime, extracts a proof from the proof script and attaches the extracted proof to the declared name of the original goal. At this point, we draw a conclusion that the program satisfies related properties.

3.2 Implementation

In this subsection, we focus on the implementation of the proof system.

(1) Describing variables, expressions and functions in Coq

First we define MSVL variables and atomic propositions which are denoted by Var and Ap respectively.

```
Inductive Var : Set := var : Z -> Var.
Inductive Ap : Set := prop : nat -> Ap.
```

Since Var and Ap are now defined as an ordinary Coq type, we can declare variables with type Var or Ap. For example, variable A and atomic proposition P can be defined as follows:

```
Variable A : Var        (*A is a MSVL variable*)
Variable P : Ap     (*P is a MSVL atomic proposition*)
```

The Arithmetic expressions are inductively defined as shown below:

```
Inductive Aexp : Set :=
    AInt : Z -> Aexp
  | AId : Var -> Aexp
  | ANext : Aexp -> Aexp
  | APre : Aexp -> Aexp
  | APlus : Aexp -> Aexp -> Aexp
  | AMinus : Aexp -> Aexp -> Aexp
  | AMult : Aexp -> Aexp -> Aexp
  | AMod : Aexp -> Aexp -> Aexp.
```

The type of arithmetic expression is called *Aexp*. Other constructors such as AInt are actually functions over a certain set. For example, AInt indicates a function over integer numbers. If x is an integer, then (AInt x) is an arithmetic expression with Aexp type. APlus indicates a function over two arithmetic expressions. Hence, (APlus $e1$ $e2$) is also an arithmetic expression with type Aexp if $e1$ and $e2$ are both arithmetic expressions.

The Boolean expressions are inductively defined as follows:

```
Inductive Bexp : Set :=
  | BTrue : Bexp
  | BFalse : Bexp
  | BNot : Bexp -> Bexp
  | BAnd : Bexp -> Bexp -> Bexp
  | BEq : Aexp -> Aexp -> Bexp
  | BLe : Aexp -> Aexp -> Bexp.
```

The type of boolean expression is represented by *Bexp*. We use *record* construction to denote a state over Var and Ap, so there are two fields in the record. Constructor Ivar defines a mapping from Var to Z, and Iprop defines a mapping from Ap to {true,false}.

```
Record state : Set := {Ivar : Var -> Z; Iprop : Ap -> bool}.
CoInductive Stream : Type := Cons : state -> Stream -> Stream.
Inductive Interval : Set :=
  | IL : list state -> Interval
  | IS : Stream -> Interval.
```

An interval is a non-empty sequence of states. *Co-inductive* type is used to denote infinite interval called *Stream*. Interval with constructors IL and IS is the complete definition of interval. Finite interval adopts the list construction which is an embedded type of Coq. We have also defined a set of operations about intervals. Here as examples we just show two functions: the connection function *Concatenation* and the sub-interval function *sub-Interval* of intervals.

```
Fixpoint list_stream(l : list state)(s : Stream) : Stream :=
  match l with
    | nil => s
    | x :: l' => Cons x (list_stream l' s)
```

```
     end.
 Definition Concatenation(seq1 seq2 : Interval) : Interval :=
   match seq1 with
     | IL l1 => match l1 with
                    | nil => seq2
                    | _ => match seq2 with
                              | IS s => IS (list_stream l1 s)
                              | IL l2 => match l2 with
                                            | nil => seq1
                                            | _ => IL (l1 ++ l2)
                                         end
                           end
                 end
     | IS s => seq1
   end.
 Fixpoint SfirstN (n:nat)(s:Stream) : list state :=
   match n with
     | 0 => nil
     | S n => match s with
                 | Cons a s' => a :: (SfirstN n s')
              end
   end.
 Fixpoint skipN (n:nat)(s:Stream) : Stream:=
   match n with
     | 0 => s
     | S n => match s with
                 | Cons a s' => skipN n s'
              end
   end.
 Definition sub(start termi :nat)(sigma:Interval) : Interval :=
   match sigma with
     | IL l => IL (firstn (termi-start+1) (skipn start l))
     | IS s => IL (SfirstN (termi-start+1) (skipN start s))
   end.
```

The *list_stream*, *SfirstN* and *skipN* are some auxiliary functions. The *firstn* and *skipn* are two functions of package *List* of the library.

(2) Defining MSVL statements and derived statements
The basic MSVL statements are defined inductively as follows:

```
Inductive st : Set :=
   | Emp : st
   | Ass : Var -> Aexp -> st
   | Pass : Var -> Aexp -> st
   | SF : Var -> st
   | IFr : Var -> st
   | Coj : st -> st -> st
   | Sec : st -> st -> st
   | Nex: st -> st
   | Alw : st -> st
   | Cond : Bexp -> st -> st -> st
   | Exqu : Var -> Ap ->st
   | Sequ : st -> st -> st
   | Whi : Bexp -> st -> st
   | Para : st -> st -> st
   | Pro : list st -> st -> st
   | Syn : Bexp -> st.
```

The type of basic statements is denoted by *st*. The definition above describes the following grammar: $st:: = empty \mid x = e \mid x \Leftarrow e \mid lbf(x) \mid frame(x) \mid p \text{ and } q \mid p \text{ or } q \mid next\ p \mid alw\ p \mid if\ b\ then\ p\ else\ q \mid local\ x, p(x) \mid p; q \mid while\ b\ do\ p \mid p \parallel q \mid (p_1, ..., p_m)\ prj\ q \mid await(c).$
Some composite MSVL statements are defined as follows:

```
Notation "'empty'" := Emp.
Notation "x =. e" := (Ass x e).
Notation "x <<= e" := (Pass x e).
Notation "'lbf' x" := (SF x).
Notation "'frame' x" := (IFr x).
Notation "p /\. q" := (Coj p q).
Notation "p \/. q" := (Sec p q).
Notation "'O' s" := (Nex s).
Notation "'[]' s" := (Alw s).
Notation "'If' b'Then' f1'Else' f2" := (Cond b f1 f2).
Notation "s1 ; s2" := (Sequ s1 s2).
Notation "'While' b'Do' f" := (Whi b f).
Notation "f1 ** f2" := (Para f1 f2).
Parameter not : st -> st.
Definition Imp(p q : st) : st := Sec (not p) q.
Definition fin(p : st) : st := Alw (Imp Emp p).
Definition keep(p : st) : st := Alw (Imp (not Emp) p).
Definition halt(p : st) : st := Alw (Coj (Imp Emp p) (Imp p Emp)).
Definition nexEq(x : Var)(e : Aexp) : st := Nex (Ass x e).
Notation "x'O=' e" := (nexEq x e).
Definition Som(p : st) := not (Alw p).
Notation "'<>' f" := (Som f).
Definition M_add(e1 e2 : Aexp) : Aexp := APlus e1 e2.
Infix "+." := M_add.
Definition M_minus(e1 e2 : Aexp) : Aexp := AMinus e1 e2.
Infix "-." := M_minus.
Definition M_mult(e1 e2 : Aexp) : Aexp := AMult e1 e2.
Infix "*." := M_mult.
Definition M_mod(e1 e2 : Aexp) : Aexp := AMod e1 e2.
Infix "/." := M_mod.
```

A derived intermediate statement called *Fin* is defined as alw(if empty then p else false)($\Box(\varepsilon \to p)$) and the notation *fin* tells us how it is symbolically written. Other notations can be explained in the same way. The frequently used derived statements are shown as follows:

$$if\ b\ then\ p \stackrel{def}{=} if\ b\ then\ p\ else\ false$$
$$fin(p) \stackrel{def}{=} alw(if\ empty\ then\ p)$$
$$keep(p) \stackrel{def}{=} alw(if\ more\ then\ p)$$
$$halt(p) \stackrel{def}{=} alw(if\ empty\ then\ p\ and\ if\ p\ then\ empty)$$

(3) Formalizing axioms and inference rules of MSVL axiomatic system
As we mentioned in the second part, the axiomatic system of MSVL has state axioms and inference rules as well as interval axioms and inference rules. In this subsection, the implementation of the axiomatic system is described in Coq. To this end, the deductive relation and correctness assertion are first defined in Coq. Notation $\vdash p$ gives an abbreviation of the predicate *DeduceRelation* over a statement p. *Htriple* shows the definition of correctness assertion $\{\sigma_k, A\}\, p\, \{\sigma_h, B\}$.

```
Parameter DeduceRelation : st -> Prop.
Notation "|- p" := (DeduceRelation p).
Parameter Htriple : Interval -> nat -> st -> st
                            -> nat -> st -> Prop.
```

In the following, we only describe four axioms and two inference rules. The others can be done in the similar way.

Descriptions of axioms:

(1) $\Box p \wedge \varepsilon \cong p \wedge \varepsilon$ can be expressed as Axiom A4

```
Axiom A4 : forall p : st,
           |-(Alw((Çoj (Alw p) Emp)<=>(Coj p Emp))).
```

(2) $\bigcirc p; q \cong \bigcirc(p; q)$ can be expressed as Axiom A7

```
Axiom A7 : forall p q : st,
           |-(Alw ((Sequ (Nex p) q)<=>Nex(Sequ p q))).
```

(3) *if p1 $\cong$ p2 then $\bigcirc$p1 $\cong \bigcirc$p2* can be expressed as Axiom R1

```
Axiom R1 :forall p1 p2 : st,
          (|-(Alw(p1<=>p2))) -> |-(Alw((Nex p1)<=>(Nex p2))).
```

(4) *tautology $p \rightarrow p$* can be expressed as Axiom implies_reflexive

```
Axiom implies_reflexive : forall p : st,|-(Alw(Imp p p)).
```

Descriptions of inference rules:

(5) $\{\sigma_k, \varepsilon\} \varepsilon \{\sigma_k, \varepsilon\}$ can be expressed as Axiom AEM

```
Axiom AEM : forall (sigma : Interval)(k : nat),
               (Htriple sigma k Emp Emp k Emp).
```

(6) Axiom ISR

```
Axiom ISR :
   forall (p q A B : st)(sigma : Interval)(k h : nat),
      (|-(Alw(p<=>q))) ->
      (Htriple sigma k A p h B <-> Htriple sigma k A q h B).
```

4   Example

In order to show how the proposed approach works for verifying properties of MSVL programs, in this section, an example for verifying the feasibility of frog routing problem is given.

4.1   Problem Description

There are six frogs, each of which is on a lotus leaf on a lake, and three yellow ones are on the left hand side whereas three green ones are on the right hand side. The two groups of frogs are separated by one empty lotus leaf. The moving rules are as follows: each frog can move one step to an empty lotus leaf or jump over another frog as long as an empty lotus leaf as its neighbor is available. Now a question arises: whether or not there is a sequence of legal moves such that the two groups of frogs can be swapped according to the moving rules.

4.2   Proving Process

We model the above problem with MSVL, and extract the relevant property to be proved. Then we verify whether or not the property is valid with the program in Coq.

(1) Modeling

Since frogs jump in a fixed direction, there is always a moment where all the frogs are unable to move. As the moving steps are carried out, this moment is bound to come. According to the nature of the problem, the solution space can be viewed as a subset tree. Each parent node contains up to four nodes as its children which are likely to jump in the current step.

We use an array named *stone* with seven elements initialized to 0 denoting empty, 1 denoting yellow or 2 denoting green, to describe the initial case. Then we can swap two elements of the array in the following way: (1) swapping the element zero with its neighbors, or (2) swapping the element zero with its next neighbors if any. (3) The swapping process stops when two groups elements with 1 and 2 has all been swapped. We model the above process in MSVL as follows:

```
frame(stone,path,des,step) and
(
  int stone[7]<==[1,1,1,0,2,2,2] and skip;
  int path[20] and skip;        //location before jump
  int des[20] and skip;         //location after jump
  int step<==1 and skip;        //steps
  function change(int i)
  {
    if(i-1>=0 and stone[i-1]=1 and stone[i-1]!=0) then
    {
      path[step-1]:=i;
      des[step-1]:=i+1;
      step:=step+1;
      stone[i]:=stone[i-1] and stone[i-1]:=0;
      change(i-1);
      stone[i-1]:=stone[i] and stone[i]:=0;
      step:=step-1
    }
    else
    {
        skip
    };
    if(i-2>=0 and stone[i-2]=1 and stone[i-2]!=0) then
    {
        path[step-1]:=i-1;
        des[step-1]:=i+1;
        step:=step+1;
        stone[i]:=stone[i-2] and stone[i-2]:=0;
        change(i-2);
        stone[i-2]:=stone[i] and stone[i]:=0;
        step:=step-1
    }
    else
    {
        skip
    };
    if(i+1<7 and stone[i+1]=2 and stone[i+1]!=0) then
    {
        path[step-1]:=i+2;
        des[step-1]:=i+1;
        step:=step+1;
        stone[i]:=stone[i+1] and stone[i+1]:=0;
```

```
        change(i+1);
        stone[i+1]:=stone[i] and stone[i]:=0;
        step:=step-1
    }
    else
    {
        skip
    };
    if(i+2<7 and stone[i+2]=2 and stone[i+2]!=0) then
    {
        path[step-1]:=i+3;
        des[step-1]:=i+1;
        step:=step+1;
        stone[i]:=stone[i+2] and stone[i+2]:=0;
            change(i+2);
            stone[i+2]:=stone[i] and stone[i]:=0;
            step:=step-1
    }
    else
    {
        skip
    }
};
function main(int RValue)
{
    frame(return) and
    (
        int return<==0 and skip;
        change(3);
        return<==1 and RValue:=0;
        skip
    )
};
main(RValue)
)
```

(2) Property

As you can see, the initial state can be denoted by the array *stone* as $s_0 = [1, 1, 1, 0, 2, 2, 2]$, and the final state can be denoted as $s_1 = [2, 2, 2, 0, 1, 1, 1]$. Then the property we want to prove is $\Box(s_0 \rightarrow \Diamond s_1)$. That is,

$$
\begin{aligned}
\Box((stone[0] = 1 \land stone[1] = 1 \land stone[2] = 1 \land stone[3] = 0 \land \\
stone[4] = 2 \land stone[5] = 2 \land stone[6] = 2) \rightarrow \\
\Diamond(stone[0] = 2 \land stone[1] = 2 \land stone[2] = 2 \land stone[3] = 0 \land \\
stone[4] = 1 \land stone[5] = 1 \land stone[6] = 1))
\end{aligned}
$$

The property means that we can always find a state path which begins with state s_0 and ends with state s_1.

(3) Verification

We define four auxiliary functions: *remove, insert, nth, where_empty*. The correctness of these functions has been checked by Coq. Actually, these functions are used for the definition of jumping rules.

(1) Function **remove**: deleting an element

```
Require Import ZArith.
Open Scope Z_scope.
Require Import List.
```

```
Fixpoint remove(l : list Z)(i : Z) : list Z :=
    let pos:=Z.to_nat i in
    match pos with
        | 0 => match l with
                | nil => nil
                | x  ::  l' => l'
               end
        | S n => match l with
                   | nil => nil
                   | x  ::  l' => x  ::  remove l' (Z.of_nat n)
                  end
    end.
```

(2) Function **insert**: inserting an element

```
Fixpoint insert(l : list Z)(i : Z)(value : Z) : list Z :=
    let pos:=Z.to_nat i in
    match l with
    | nil => value  ::  nil
    | x  ::  l' => match pos with
                    | 0 => cons value l
                    | S n => x  ::  insert l' (Z.of_nat n) value
                   end
    end.
```

(3) Function **nth**: getting the value with index n

```
Fixpoint nth (n:Z) (l:list Z) : Z := let pos:=Z.to_nat n in
    match pos, l with
    | 0, nil => -1
    | 0, x  ::  l' => x
    | S m, nil => -1
    | S m, x  ::  l' => nth (Z.of_nat m) l'
    end.
```

(4) Function **where_empty**: getting the index with value 0

```
Fixpoint where_empty(arr : list Z)(script : Z) : Z :=
    match arr with
    | nil => -1
    | x  ::  l' => if Zeq_bool x 0 then script
                   else where_empty l' (script+1)
    end.
```

Now we import the definitions which we have defined in the previous part and declare variables we need to use. Then we formalize the moving rules in Coq. As an example, in the following, a jumping rule is given.

```
Require Import msvl.
Require Import laws.
Require Import notation.
Parameter stone0 stone1 stone2 stone3 : Var.
Parameter stone4 stone5 stone6 empty_pos : Var.
```

Jumping Rules: If we want to make a state transition, some subgoals need to be proved so as to ensure the correct conversion among states. The following rule named *JumpRule0_2* is one of the jumping rules.

```
Axiom JumpRule0_2 : forall n0 n1 n2 n3 n4 n5 n6 : Z,
  let l1 := cons n0 (cons n1 (cons n2 (cons n3
            (cons n4 (cons n5 (cons n6 nil)))))) in
  let l2 := insert (remove l1 2) 0 n2 in
  let l3 := insert (remove l2 1) 2 n0 in
```

```
0 = where_empty 11 0 /\ 2 = where_empty 13 0 /\
nth 0 13 = n2 /\ nth 1 13 = n1 /\ nth 2 13 = n0
/\ nth 3 13 = n3 /\ nth 4 13 = n4 /\ nth 5 13 = n5
/\ nth 6 13 = n6 ->
|-(Alw(Imp
    (Coj (Coj (Coj (Coj (Coj (Coj (Coj (Ass empty_pos (AInt 0))
    (Ass stone0 (AInt n0))) (Ass stone1 (AInt n1)))
    (Ass stone2 (AInt n2))) (Ass stone3 (AInt n3)))
    (Ass stone4 (AInt n4))) (Ass stone5 (AInt n5)))
    (Ass stone6 (AInt n6)))
    (Coj (Coj (Coj (Coj (Coj (Coj (Coj (Ass empty_pos (AInt 2))
    (Ass stone0 (AInt n2))) (Ass stone1 (AInt n1)))
    (Ass stone2 (AInt n0))) (Ass stone3 (AInt n3)))
    (Ass stone4 (AInt n4))) (Ass stone5 (AInt n5)))
    (Ass stone6 (AInt n6))))).
```

The Lemma *Jump* is what we need to prove. Knowing the initial state, we can adopt different jumping rules to change states. In this process as shown in Fig. 4 and Fig. 5, a state satisfies the given property at a certain time, which indicates the program satisfies the property. Most parts of the proof are omitted here, but a rough description of the verification using the proof assistant is shown in Appendix C.

```
Axiom implies_transitive : forall p1 p2 p3 : st,
  (|-(Alw(Imp p1 p2))) /\ (|-(Alw(Imp p2 p3))) -> |-(Alw(Imp p1 p3)).

Axiom implies_reflexive : forall p : st,|-(Alw(Imp p p)).

Lemma Jump :
    |-(Alw(Imp
        (Coj (Coj (Coj (Coj (Coj (Coj (Coj (Ass empty_pos (AInt 3))
        (Ass stone0 (AInt 1))) (Ass stone1 (AInt 1)))
        (Ass stone2 (AInt 1))) (Ass stone3 (AInt 0)))
        (Ass stone4 (AInt 2))) (Ass stone5 (AInt 2)))
        (Ass stone6 (AInt 2)))
        (Coj (Coj (Coj (Coj (Coj (Coj (Coj (Ass empty_pos (AInt 3))
        (Ass stone0 (AInt 2))) (Ass stone1 (AInt 2)))
        (Ass stone2 (AInt 2))) (Ass stone3 (AInt 0)))
        (Ass stone4 (AInt 1))) (Ass stone5 (AInt 1)))
        (Ass stone6 (AInt 1))))).
Proof.
(*The tactic apply ... with is adopted in order to use the axiom
  implies_transitive*)
apply implies_transitive with (p2:=
    (Coj (Coj (Coj (Coj (Coj (Coj (Coj (Ass empty_pos (AInt 2))
    (Ass stone0 (AInt 1))) (Ass stone1 (AInt 1)))
    (Ass stone2 (AInt 0))) (Ass stone3 (AInt 1)))
    (Ass stone4 (AInt 2))) (Ass stone5 (AInt 2)))
    (Ass stone6 (AInt 2)))).
(*The tactic split is used to separate subgoals that are generated*)
split.
apply JumpRule3_2.
(*The tactic repeat takes another tactic and keeps applying this
 tactic until the tactic fails *)
repeat split.

...

apply JumpRule4_3.
repeat split.
apply implies_reflexive.
Qed.
```

As all subgoals are resolved, we can conclude that the property holds.

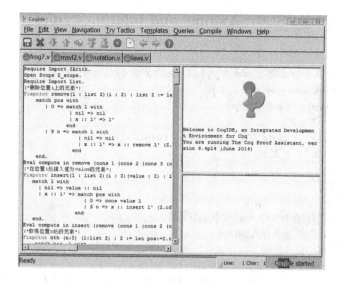

Fig. 4. Proving process

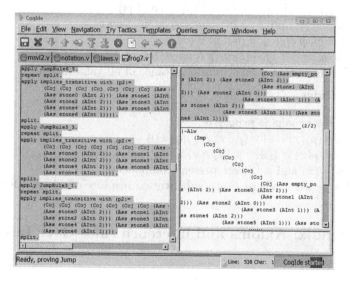

Fig. 5. Proving process

5   Conclusion

In this paper, we present an approach for encoding of MSVL axiomatic system with the Coq proof assistant and give a verification example using Coq. We demonstrate the feasibility of using Coq as a proof assistant for building an MSVL proof system. However, the encoding itself still needs to be further improved. In addition, we will focus on improving the degree of automation in theorem proving using our proof system in the future.

A Appendix: State Axioms and inference rules

Axioms

A1 $lbf(x) \wedge x = e \cong x = e \wedge p_x$ (where $\ominus x \neq e$)
A2 $lbf(x) \wedge x \Leftarrow e \cong x = e \wedge p_x$
A3 $\Box p \wedge more \cong p \wedge \bigcirc \Box p$
A4 $\Box p \wedge \varepsilon \cong p \wedge \varepsilon$
A5 $frame(x) \wedge more \cong \bigcirc(lbf(x) \wedge frame(x))$
A6 $frame(x) \wedge \varepsilon \cong \varepsilon$
A7 $\bigcirc p; q \cong \bigcirc(p; q)$
A8 $\varepsilon; q \cong q$
A9 $(w \wedge p); q \cong w \wedge (p; q)$
A10 $p \parallel q \cong (((p; true) \wedge q) \vee ((q; true) \wedge p))$
A11 $\bigcirc p \wedge q \cong \bigcirc p \wedge q \wedge more$
A12 $\varepsilon \; \mathsf{prj} \; q \cong q$
A13 $(p_1, ..., p_m) \; \mathsf{prj} \; \varepsilon \cong p_1; ...; p_m$
A14 $(p_1, ..., p_{i-1}, w \wedge \varepsilon, p_{i+1}, ..., p_m) \; \mathsf{prj} \; q \cong (p_1, ..., p_{i-1}, w \wedge p_{i+1}, ..., p_m) \; \mathsf{prj} \; q$
A15 $(w \wedge p_1, p_2, ..., p_m) \; \mathsf{prj} \; q \cong w \wedge (p_1, ..., p_m) \; \mathsf{prj} \; q$
A16 $(p_1, ..., p_m) \; \mathsf{prj} \; (w \wedge q) \cong w \wedge (p_1, ..., p_m) \; \mathsf{prj} \; q$
A17 $(\bigcirc p_1, ..., p_m) \; \mathsf{prj} \; \bigcirc q \cong \bigcirc(p_1; (p_2, ..., p_m) \; \mathsf{prj} \; q)$
A18 $if \; b \; then \; p \; else \; q \cong (b \wedge p) \vee (\neg b \wedge q)$
A19 $while \; b \; do \; p \cong if \; b \; then \; (p \wedge more; while \; b \; do \; p) \; else \; \varepsilon$
A20 $\vdash P$, where P is a substitution instance of all valid formulas.

Inference Rules

R1 $p \cong q \Longrightarrow prog[p] \cong prog[q/p]$
R2 $p(x) \cong ((p_e(x) \wedge \varepsilon) \vee (p_c(x) \wedge \bigcirc p_f(x)))$
      $\Longrightarrow \exists x : p(x) \cong ((\exists x : p_e(x) \wedge \varepsilon) \vee (\exists x : p_c(x) \wedge \bigcirc \exists x : p_f(x)))$
      where $p_e(x)$ and $p_c(x)$ are present components.
R3 $\vdash P \Longrightarrow \vdash \Box P$, where P is a substitution instance of all valid formulas.

B Appendix: Axioms and inference rules Over Intervals

Axioms

AEM $\{\sigma_k, \varepsilon\} \varepsilon \{\sigma_k, \varepsilon\}$
APC $\{\sigma_k, A\} p \{\sigma_k, A\} \quad if \; p \to A$
      where A and p are present components

Inference Rules

ISR
$\{\sigma_k, A\}\, prog[p]\, \{\sigma_h, B\}\, and\, p \cong q$
$\Longleftrightarrow \{\sigma_k, A\}\, prog[q/p]\, \{\sigma_h, B\}\, and\, p \cong q$

AAS
$\{\sigma_k, A\}\, x = m \wedge ps(y) \wedge p\, \{\sigma_h, B\}$
$\{\sigma_k, A\}\, x = m \wedge ps(y)[x \mapsto m] \wedge p\, \{\sigma_h, B\}$
where lbf(y) and lbf(x) does not occur in p.

LBF
$\{\sigma_k, A\}\, lbf(x) \wedge p\, \{\sigma_h, B\}$
$\{\sigma_k, A\}\, x = \sigma_{k-1}(x) \wedge p\, \{\sigma_h, B\}(k \geq 1)$
where $x = e$ and $x \Leftarrow e$ does not occur in p.

ANext
$\{\sigma_k, A\}\, p_c \wedge \bigcirc p_f\, \{\sigma_h, B\}$
$$\Longleftrightarrow \begin{cases} \{\sigma_k[p_c]\cdot < s_{k+1} >, A_f\}\, p_f\, \{\sigma_h, B\} \\ \text{and } \{\sigma_k, A_c\}\, p_c\, \{\sigma_k, A_c\} & \text{if } p_c \to A_c \\ \{\sigma_k, false\}\, p_c \wedge \bigcirc p_f\, \{\sigma_h, B\} & \text{otherwise} \end{cases}$$
where $A \equiv (A_c \wedge \bigcirc A_f) \vee (A_e \wedge \varepsilon)$.

AEmpty
$\{\sigma_k, A\}\, p_e \wedge \varepsilon\, \{\sigma_h, B\}$
$$\Longleftrightarrow \begin{cases} \{\sigma_k[p_e], \varepsilon\}\, \varepsilon\, \{\sigma_k[p_e], \varepsilon\} \\ \text{and } \{\sigma_k, A_e \wedge B\}\, p_e\, \{\sigma_k, A_e \wedge B\} & \text{if } p_e \to A_e \wedge B \\ \{\sigma_k, false\}\, p_e \wedge \varepsilon\, \{\sigma_k, false\} & \text{otherwise} \end{cases}$$
where $A \equiv (A_c \wedge \bigcirc A_f) \vee (A_e \wedge \varepsilon)$.

SSR
$\{\sigma_k, A\}\, q_i\, \{\sigma_h, B\}$
$\Longrightarrow \{\sigma_k, A\}\, q_1 \vee q_2\, \{\sigma_h, B\}(i = 1, 2)$

EQR1
$\{\sigma_k, A\}\, p_c(y) \wedge \bigcirc p\, \{\sigma_h, B\}$
$\Longrightarrow \{\sigma_k, A\}\, \exists x : p_c(x) \wedge \bigcirc p\, \{\sigma_h, B\}$

EQR2
$\{\sigma_k, A\}\, p_e(y) \wedge \varepsilon\, \{\sigma_h, B\}$
$\Longrightarrow \{\sigma_k, A\}\, \exists x : p_e(x) \wedge \varepsilon\, \{\sigma_h, B\}$

C   Appendix: Deducting Frog Routing Problem in Coq

```
Lemma Jump1 :  |-([]((empty_pos=.AInt 3/\.stone0=.AInt 1/\.
    stone1=.AInt 1/\.stone2=.AInt 1/\.stone3=.AInt 0/\
    .stone4=.AInt 2/\.stone5=.AInt 2/\.stone6=.AInt 2)-->
    (empty_pos=.AInt 3/\.stone0=.AInt 2/\.
    stone1=.AInt 2/\.stone2=.AInt 2/\.stone3=.AInt 0
    /\.stone4=.AInt 1/\.stone5=.AInt 1/\.stone6=.AInt 1))).
Proof.
apply implies_transitive with (p2:=
    (Coj (Coj (Coj (Coj (Coj (Coj (Ass empty_pos (AInt 2))
    (Ass stone0 (AInt 1))) (Ass stone1 (AInt 1)))
    (Ass stone2 (AInt 0))) (Ass stone3 (AInt 1)))
    (Ass stone4 (AInt 2))) (Ass stone5 (AInt 2)))
    (Ass stone6 (AInt 2)))).
split.
apply JumpRule3_2.
repeat split.
apply implies_transitive with (p2:=
    (Coj (Coj (Coj (Coj (Coj (Coj (Coj (Ass empty_pos (AInt 4))
    (Ass stone0 (AInt 1))) (Ass stone1 (AInt 1)))
    (Ass stone2 (AInt 2))) (Ass stone3 (AInt 1)))
    (Ass stone4 (AInt 0))) (Ass stone5 (AInt 2)))
    (Ass stone6 (AInt 2)))).
split.
apply JumpRule2_4.
```

```
repeat split.
apply implies_transitive with (p2:=
        (Coj (Coj (Coj (Coj (Coj (Coj (Coj (Ass empty_pos (AInt 5))
        (Ass stone0 (AInt 1))) (Ass stone1 (AInt 1)))
        (Ass stone2 (AInt 2))) (Ass stone3 (AInt 1)))
        (Ass stone4 (AInt 2))) (Ass stone5 (AInt 0)))
        (Ass stone6 (AInt 2)))).
split.
apply JumpRule4_5.
repeat split.
apply implies_transitive with (p2:=
        (Coj (Coj (Coj (Coj (Coj (Coj (Coj (Ass empty_pos (AInt 3))
        (Ass stone0 (AInt 1))) (Ass stone1 (AInt 1)))
        (Ass stone2 (AInt 2))) (Ass stone3 (AInt 0)))
        (Ass stone4 (AInt 2))) (Ass stone5 (AInt 1)))
        (Ass stone6 (AInt 2)))).
split.
apply JumpRule5_3.
repeat split.
apply implies_transitive with (p2:=
        (Coj (Coj (Coj (Coj (Coj (Coj (Coj (Ass empty_pos (AInt 1))
        (Ass stone0 (AInt 1))) (Ass stone1 (AInt 0)))
        (Ass stone2 (AInt 2))) (Ass stone3 (AInt 1)))
        (Ass stone4 (AInt 2))) (Ass stone5 (AInt 1)))
        (Ass stone6 (AInt 2)))).
split.
apply JumpRule3_1.
repeat split.
apply implies_transitive with (p2:=
        (Coj (Coj (Coj (Coj (Coj (Coj (Coj (Ass empty_pos (AInt 0))
        (Ass stone0 (AInt 0))) (Ass stone1 (AInt 1)))
        (Ass stone2 (AInt 2))) (Ass stone3 (AInt 1)))
        (Ass stone4 (AInt 2))) (Ass stone5 (AInt 1)))
        (Ass stone6 (AInt 2)))).
split.
apply JumpRule1_0.
repeat split.
apply implies_transitive with (p2:=
        (Coj (Coj (Coj (Coj (Coj (Coj (Coj (Ass empty_pos (AInt 2))
        (Ass stone0 (AInt 2))) (Ass stone1 (AInt 1)))
        (Ass stone2 (AInt 0))) (Ass stone3 (AInt 1)))
        (Ass stone4 (AInt 2))) (Ass stone5 (AInt 1)))
        (Ass stone6 (AInt 2)))).
split.
apply JumpRule0_2.
repeat split.
apply implies_transitive with (p2:=
        (Coj (Coj (Coj (Coj (Coj (Coj (Coj (Ass empty_pos (AInt 4))
        (Ass stone0 (AInt 2))) (Ass stone1 (AInt 1)))
        (Ass stone2 (AInt 2))) (Ass stone3 (AInt 1)))
        (Ass stone4 (AInt 0))) (Ass stone5 (AInt 1)))
        (Ass stone6 (AInt 2)))).

split.
apply JumpRule2_4.
repeat split.
apply implies_transitive with (p2:=
        (Coj (Coj (Coj (Coj (Coj (Coj (Coj (Ass empty_pos (AInt 6))
        (Ass stone0 (AInt 2))) (Ass stone1 (AInt 1)))
        (Ass stone2 (AInt 2))) (Ass stone3 (AInt 1)))
        (Ass stone4 (AInt 2))) (Ass stone5 (AInt 1)))
        (Ass stone6 (AInt 0)))).
split.
apply JumpRule4_6.
repeat split.
apply implies_transitive with (p2:=
        (Coj (Coj (Coj (Coj (Coj (Coj (Coj (Ass empty_pos (AInt 5))
        (Ass stone0 (AInt 2))) (Ass stone1 (AInt 1)))
```

```
              (Ass stone2 (AInt 2))) (Ass stone3 (AInt 1)))
              (Ass stone4 (AInt 2))) (Ass stone5 (AInt 0)))
              (Ass stone6 (AInt 1)))).
split.
apply JumpRule6_5.
repeat split.
apply implies_transitive with (p2:=
              (Coj (Coj (Coj (Coj (Coj (Coj (Coj (Ass empty_pos (AInt 3))
              (Ass stone0 (AInt 2))) (Ass stone1 (AInt 1)))
              (Ass stone2 (AInt 2))) (Ass stone3 (AInt 0)))
              (Ass stone4 (AInt 2))) (Ass stone5 (AInt 1)))
              (Ass stone6 (AInt 1)))).
split.
apply JumpRule5_3.
repeat split.
apply implies_transitive with (p2:=
              (Coj (Coj (Coj (Coj (Coj (Coj (Coj (Ass empty_pos (AInt 1))
              (Ass stone0 (AInt 2))) (Ass stone1 (AInt 0)))
              (Ass stone2 (AInt 2))) (Ass stone3 (AInt 1)))
              (Ass stone4 (AInt 2))) (Ass stone5 (AInt 1)))
              (Ass stone6 (AInt 1)))).
split.
apply JumpRule3_1.
repeat split.
apply implies_transitive with (p2:=
              (Coj (Coj (Coj (Coj (Coj (Coj (Coj (Ass empty_pos (AInt 2))
              (Ass stone0 (AInt 2))) (Ass stone1 (AInt 2)))
              (Ass stone2 (AInt 0))) (Ass stone3 (AInt 1)))
              (Ass stone4 (AInt 2))) (Ass stone5 (AInt 1)))
              (Ass stone6 (AInt 1)))).
split.
apply JumpRule1_2.
repeat split.
apply implies_transitive with (p2:=
              (Coj (Coj (Coj (Coj (Coj (Coj (Coj (Ass empty_pos (AInt 4))
              (Ass stone0 (AInt 2))) (Ass stone1 (AInt 2)))
              (Ass stone2 (AInt 2))) (Ass stone3 (AInt 1)))
              (Ass stone4 (AInt 0))) (Ass stone5 (AInt 1)))
              (Ass stone6 (AInt 1)))).
split.
apply JumpRule2_4.
repeat split.
apply implies_transitive with (p2:=
              (Coj (Coj (Coj (Coj (Coj (Coj (Coj (Ass empty_pos (AInt 3))
              (Ass stone0 (AInt 2))) (Ass stone1 (AInt 2)))
              (Ass stone2 (AInt 2))) (Ass stone3 (AInt 0)))
              (Ass stone4 (AInt 1))) (Ass stone5 (AInt 1)))
              (Ass stone6 (AInt 1)))).
split.
apply JumpRule4_3.
repeat split.
apply implies_reflexive.
Qed.
```

References

1. Bledsoe, W., Loveland, D.: Interactive Theorem Proving and Program Development. Contemporary Mathematics Series, vol. 29. American Mathematical Society, Providence (1984)
2. Clarke, E.M., Grumberg, O., Peled, D.: Model Checking, pp. 54–56. MIT Press, Cambridge (2000)
3. Duan, Z., Tian, C.: A unified model checking approach with projection temporal logic. In: Liu, S., Maibaum, T., Araki, K. (eds.) ICFEM 2008. LNCS, vol. 5256, pp. 167–186. Springer, Heidelberg (2008). doi:10.1007/978-3-540-88194-0_12

4. Comert, F., Ovatman, T.: Attacking state space explosion problem in model checking embedded TV software. IEEE Trans. Consum. Electron. **61**(4), 572–579 (2015)
5. Duan, Z., Yang, X., Koutny, M.: Frammed temporal logic programming. Sci. Comput. Program. **70**(1), 31–61 (2008)
6. Barras, B., Boutin, S., Cornes, C., et al.: The Coq proof assistant: reference manual. Rapport technique - INRIA (2000), https://coq.inria.fr
7. Wang, X., Duan, Z., Zhao, L.: Formalizing and implementing types in MSVL. In: Liu, S., Duan, Z. (eds.) SOFL+MSVL 2013. LNCS, vol. 8332, pp. 62–75. Springer, Cham (2014). doi:10.1007/978-3-319-04915-1_5
8. Duan, Z.: An Extended Interval Temporal Logic and A Framing Technique for Temporal Logic Programming. Ph.D Thesis (Technical Report No. 556). University of Newcastle upon Tyne (1996)
9. Owre, S., Rushby, J.M., Shankar, N.: PVS: a prototype verification system. In: Kapur, D. (ed.) CADE 1992. LNCS, vol. 607, pp. 748–752. Springer, Heidelberg (1992). doi:10.1007/3-540-55602-8_217
10. Brock, B., Kaufmann, M., Moore, J.S.: ACL2 theorems about commercial microprocessors. In: Srivas, M., Camilleri, A. (eds.) FMCAD 1996. LNCS, vol. 1166, pp. 275–293. Springer, Heidelberg (1996). doi:10.1007/BFb0031816
11. Gordon, M., Melham, T.: Introduction to HOL: A Theorem Proving Environment for Higher Order Logic. Cambridge University Press, Cambridge (1993)
12. Kalvala, S.: Using isabelle to prove simple theorems. In: Joyce, J.J., Seger, C.-J.H. (eds.) HUG 1993. LNCS, vol. 780, pp. 514–517. Springer, Heidelberg (1994). doi:10.1007/3-540-57826-9_160
13. Howe, D.J.: Importing mathematics from HOL into Nuprl. In: Goos, G., Hartmanis, J., Leeuwen, J., Wright, J., Grundy, J., Harrison, J. (eds.) TPHOLs 1996. LNCS, vol. 1125, pp. 267–281. Springer, Heidelberg (1996). doi:10.1007/BFb0105410
14. Ma, Q., Duan, Z., Zhang, N., Wang, X.: Verification of distributed systems with the axiomatic system of MSVL. Formal Aspects Comput. **27**(1), 103–131 (2015)
15. Appel, A.W., Blazy, S.: Separation logic for small-step CMINOR. In: Schneider, K., Brandt, J. (eds.) TPHOLs 2007. LNCS, vol. 4732, pp. 5–21. Springer, Heidelberg (2007). doi:10.1007/978-3-540-74591-4_3
16. Chlipala, A.: Mostly-automated verification of low-level programs in computational separation logic. In: Proceedings of the ACM SIGPLAN 2011 Conference on Programming Language Design and Implementation, vol. 47(6), pp. 234–245 (2011)
17. Yang, X., Duan, Z., Ma, Q.: Axiomatic semantics of projection temporal logic programs. Math. Struct. Comput. Sci. **20**(5), 865–914 (2010)
18. Valmari, A.: A stubborn attack on state explosion. In: Clarke, E.M., Kurshan, R.P. (eds.) CAV 1990. LNCS, vol. 531, pp. 156–165. Springer, Heidelberg (1991). doi:10.1007/BFb0023729
19. Godefroid, P., Wolper, P.: A partial approach to model checking. Inf. Comput. **110**(2), 305–326 (1994)
20. Zhang, N., Duan, Z., Tian, C.: An axiomatization for cylinder computation model. In: Cai, Z., Zelikovsky, A., Bourgeois, A. (eds.) COCOON 2014. LNCS, vol. 8591, pp. 71–83. Springer, Cham (2014). doi:10.1007/978-3-319-08783-2_7
21. Zhang, N., Duan, Z.: A semantic model for many-core parallel computing. In: Wang, W., Zhu, X., Du, D.-Z. (eds.) COCOA 2011. LNCS, vol. 6831, pp. 464–479. Springer, Heidelberg (2011). doi:10.1007/978-3-642-22616-8_36
22. Esparza, J.: Model checking using net unfoldings. Sci. Comput. Program. **23**, 151–195 (1994)

23. Ma, Y., Duan, Z., Wang, X.: An interpreter for framed tempura and its application. In: Proceedings of First Joint IEEE/IFIP Symposium on Theoretical Aspects of Software Engineering, pp. 251–260. IEEE Press (2007)
24. Borgstrom, J., Gordon, A., Pucella, R.: Roles, stacks, histories: a triple for hoare. In: Reflections on the Work of C.A.R. Hoare, pp. 71–99 (2010)
25. Duan, Z., Zhang, N., Koutny, M.: A complete proof system for propositional projection temporal logic. Theoret. Comput. Sci. **497**(5), 84–107 (2013)
26. Tian, C., Duan, Z., Zhang, L.: A decision procedure for propositional projection temporal logic with infinite models. Acta Informatica **45**, 43–78 (2008)

Runtime Verification Monitor Construction for Three-valued PPTL

Xiaobing Wang$^{(\boxtimes)}$, Dongmiao Liu, Liang Zhao$^{(\boxtimes)}$, and Yina Xue

Institute of Computing Theory and Technology,
Xidian University, Xi'an 710071, People's Republic of China
xbwang@mail.xidian.edu.cn, 734956629@qq.com,
lzhao@xidian.edu.cn, xyn0118@126.com

Abstract. Runtime Verification is a lightweight verification technique, which estimates whether a system satisfies a desired property by monitoring the system. An algorithm is proposed for constructing a runtime verification monitor for three-valued Propositional Projection Temporal Logic. A given property P and its negation $\neg P$ are first translated into normal forms, and further Normal Form Graphs. Then, the Büchi automata and finite automata are obtained by changing the accepting sets. Finally, the monitor is built up by making the product of the two automata. An example is illustrated to show how this algorithm works.

Keywords: Runtime verification · Monitor · Projection temporal logic · Three-valued logic · Automata

1 Introduction

Runtime Verification (RV) [1] is a lightweight verification technology, which monitors a system at the runtime instead of constructing the model of the system. Usually, an RV monitor is generated from the requirements of a system, and it can judge whether the system satisfies a given property by checking the trace generated at runtime. RV is a formal verification technology complementing model checking [2], for it does not need to construct the whole model of the system. Specifically, it only considers runtime behaviors of the system, thus reducing the state explosion for large systems. Another feature it owns is that it deals with finite traces instead of infinite traces, which can reduce the complexity and get the verification result as early as possible. RV has already been used in various areas, such as formal verification [3], Web Services [4], malicious attack detection [5] and train control system [6].

Projection Temporal Logic (PTL) is a state-based temporal logic with a projection construct $(P_1, \ldots, P_m)$ prj Q [7,8]. Propositional PTL (PPTL) is a propositional subset of PTL which has full regular expressive power and is

X. Wang—This research is supported by the NSFC Grant Nos. 61672403, 61272118, 61272117, 61133001, 61402347, and the Fundamental Research Funds for the Central Universities No. JBG160306.

S. Liu et al. (Eds.): SOFL+MSVL 2016, LNCS 10189, pp. 144–159, 2017.
DOI: 10.1007/978-3-319-57708-1_9

decidable [9], and it has a support platform Modeling, Simulation and Verification platform, which has already been used in the verification of scheduling systems [10], C programs [11], parallel computing [12], etc. PPTL is more suitable for RV for it owns more powerful expressiveness. For example, it can describe the periodic property such as

a proposition holds at all even states

which cannot be described by Linear Temporal Logic (LTL). But until now there is no RV technology for PPTL yet.

This paper extends PPTL for runtime verification, and the main contributions are as follows. (1) A three-valued $PPTL_3$ is defined based on PPTL. (2) An algorithm for constructing a RV monitor for $PPTL_3$. (3) A social network application is illustrated to show how this method works. With these contributions, PPTL can be used to check traces of a system at runtime and get verification results.

The rest of the paper is organized as follows. The syntax and semantics of PPTL are briefly introduced in the following section. Section 3 describes how to construct the RV monitor based on $PPTL_3$. Section 4 is devoted to a case study to illustrate the monitor construction. Section 5 reviews related work. Conclusions are drawn in Sect. 6.

2   Propositional Projection Temporal Logic

Let *Prop* be a countable set of atomic propositions and $B = \{true, false\}$ the Boolean domain. Usually, we use small letters, possibly with subscripts, like p, q, r to denote atomic propositions and capital letters, possibly with subscripts, like P, Q, R to denote general PPTL formulas. Then, the formulas of PPTL are defined by the following grammar:

$$P ::= p \mid \neg P \mid P_1 \wedge P_2 \mid \bigcirc P \mid (P_1, \ldots, P_m)\, prj\ P$$

where $p \in Prop$, $P, P_1, \ldots, P_m$ are well-formed PPTL formulas, and $\bigcirc$ (next), prj (projection) are temporal operators.

The state s that we defined over *Prop* is a mapping $s : Prop \rightarrow B$. We write $s[p]$ to denote the valuation of p at state s. An interval $\sigma = <s_0, s_1, \ldots>$ is a non-empty state sequence which can be finite or infinite. We use $|\sigma|$ to denote the length of σ. It is the number of states in σ minus one if σ is finite, otherwise it is ω. Let N_0 denote the set of non-negative integers. To have a uniform notation for both finite and infinite intervals, we will express that by a new symbol, that is $N_\omega = N_0 \cup \{\omega\}$, and extend the comparison operators $=, <, \leq$ to N_ω by considering $\omega = \omega$ and for all $i \in N_0, i < \omega$. Moreover, we write $\preceq$ as $\leq -\{(\omega, \omega)\}$. To simplify definitions, we use $<s_0, \ldots, s_{|\sigma|}>$ to denote the interval σ, where $s_{|\sigma|}$ is undefined if σ is infinite. Under this notation, $\sigma_{(i,\ldots,j)}(0 \leq i \preceq j \leq |\sigma|)$ denote the sub-interval $<s_i, \ldots, s_j>$.

To formalize the semantics of the projection construct, we need an auxiliary operator $\downarrow$. Let $\sigma = <s_0, s_1, \ldots>$ be an interval and $r_1, \ldots r_h(h \geq 1)$ an integer sequence such that $0 \leq r_1 \leq \ldots \leq r_h \preceq |\sigma|$. The projection of σ onto $r_1, \ldots, r_h$ is the projected interval

$$\sigma \downarrow (r_1, \ldots, r_h) = <s_{t_1}, s_{t_2}, \ldots, s_{t_l}>$$

Where $t_1, t_2, \ldots, t_l$ are obtained form $r_1, \ldots r_h$ by deleting all duplicates. In other words, $t_1, t_2, \ldots, t_l$ is the longest strictly increasing subsequence of $r_1, \ldots r_h$. For instance, $<s_0, s_1, s_2, s_3, s_4> \downarrow (0, 0, 2, 2, 2, 3) = <s_0, s_2, s_3>$. The concatenation ($\cdot$) of a finite interval $\sigma = <s_0, s_1, \ldots, s_{|\sigma|}>$ with another interval $\sigma' = <s_0', s_1', \ldots, s_{|\sigma|}'>$ is represented by $\sigma \cdot \sigma' = <s_0, s_1, \ldots, s_{|\sigma|}, s_0', s_1', \ldots, s_{|\sigma|}'>$ (no state is shared).

An interpretation is a tuple $\mathcal{I} = (\sigma, k, j)$, where $\sigma = <s_0, s_1, \ldots>$ is an interval, k is a non-negative integer and j is an integer or ω, such that $0 \leq k \preceq j \leq |\sigma|$. We write (σ, k, j) to denote that a formula is interpreted over a subinterval $\sigma_{(k, \ldots, j)}$ with the current state being s_k. We use $\mathcal{I}_{prop}^k$ to state the state interpretation at state s_k. The satisfaction relation $\models$ for formulas is inductively defined as follows:

1. $\mathcal{I} \models p$ iff $s_k[p] = \mathcal{I}_{prop}^k[p] = true$.
2. $\mathcal{I} \models \neg p$ iff $\mathcal{I} \nvDash p$.
3. $\mathcal{I} \models P_1 \wedge P_2$ iff $\mathcal{I} \models P_1$ and $\mathcal{I} \models P_2$.
4. $\mathcal{I} \models \bigcirc P$ iff $k < j$ and $(\sigma, k+1, j) \models P$.
5. $\mathcal{I} \models (P_1, \ldots, P_m)$ prj P iff there exist integers $r_0, \ldots r_m$ and $k = r_0 \leq \ldots \leq r_{m-1} \preceq r_m \leq j$ such that $(\sigma, r_{l-1}, r_l) \models P_l$ for all $1 \leq l \leq m$ and $(\sigma', 0, |\sigma'|) \models P$ for σ' given by:
   (a) $r_m < j$ and $\sigma' = \sigma \downarrow (r_0, \ldots, r_m) \cdot \sigma_{(r_m+1 .. j)}$
   (b) $r_m = j$ and $\sigma' = \sigma \downarrow (r_0, \ldots, r_h)$ for some $0 \leq h \leq m$.

For convenience, some derived formulas from elementary PPTL formulas are shown as follow. The abbreviations $true$, $false$, $\vee$, $\rightarrow$ and $\leftrightarrow$ are defined as usual.

$$\varepsilon \overset{def}{=} \neg \bigcirc true \qquad more \overset{def}{=} \neg \varepsilon$$
$$P; Q \overset{def}{=} (P, Q) \, prj \, \varepsilon \qquad \Diamond P \overset{def}{=} true; P$$
$$len(0) \overset{def}{=} \varepsilon \qquad len(n) \overset{def}{=} \bigcirc len(n-1)(n > 0)$$
$$skip \overset{def}{=} len(1) \qquad \Box P \overset{def}{=} \neg \Diamond \neg P$$
$$fin(P) \overset{def}{=} \Box(\varepsilon \rightarrow P) \quad halt(P) \overset{def}{=} \Box(\varepsilon \leftrightarrow P)$$

If there is no temporal operator in a PPTL formula, we call the formula a state formula. Usually, $\models \Box(P \leftrightarrow Q)$ is represented by $P \equiv Q$ (strong equivalence), meaning that P and Q have the same truth value at all states of any models while $\models \Box(P \rightarrow Q)$ is denote by $P \supset Q$ (strong implication), showing that $P \rightarrow Q$ is true at all states of any models. The following is some useful logic laws, where w is a state formula.

$$(L1)\Diamond P \qquad\qquad\qquad \equiv P \vee \bigcirc \Diamond P$$
$$(L2)\Box P \qquad\qquad\qquad \equiv P \wedge \varepsilon \vee P \wedge \bigcirc \Box P$$
$$(L3)\Box(P \wedge Q) \qquad\qquad \equiv \Box P \wedge \Box Q$$
$$(L4)\Diamond(P \vee Q) \qquad\qquad \equiv \Diamond P \vee \Diamond Q$$
$$(L5)\bigcirc(P \wedge Q) \qquad\qquad \equiv \bigcirc P \wedge \bigcirc Q$$
$$(L6)\bigcirc(P \vee Q) \qquad\qquad \equiv \bigcirc P \vee \bigcirc Q$$
$$(L7)Q;(P_1 \vee P_2) \qquad\quad \equiv (Q;P_1) \vee (Q;P_2)$$
$$(L8)P_1;(P_2;P_3) \qquad\quad \equiv (P_1;P_2);P_3$$
$$(L9)w \wedge (P;Q) \qquad\qquad \equiv (w \wedge P);Q$$
$$(L10)true \qquad\qquad\qquad \equiv \varepsilon \vee \bigcirc true$$
$$(L11)(P_1,\ldots P_m)\,prj\,\varepsilon \qquad \equiv P_1;P_2;\ldots;P_m$$
$$(L12)(w \wedge P_1,\ldots,P_m)\,prj\,Q \equiv w \wedge ((P_1,\ldots,P_m)\,prj\,Q)$$
$$(L13)(P_1,\ldots,P_m)\,prj\,(w \wedge Q) \equiv w \wedge ((P_1,\ldots,P_m)\,prj\,Q)$$

3   The Monitor Based on PPTL$_3$

3.1   Three-valued Semantics

The syntax and semantics of the traditional PPTL have been introduced in the previous section. However, the traditional two-valued logic is incompetent to give correct results at some cases in RV [13,14]. We give a simple example to explain this. A C program cannot write data to a file until it opens the file. It means the C program should satisfy the property that a file cannot be written before it is opened, which can be described by a PPTL formula $\Box \neg write; open$. Then, we monitor the execution trace to verify whether the property is satisfied. If the monitor detects an open operation in the current trace and $\neg write$ holds in the whole detected trace, the property is valid. If a write operation is detected and no open operation occurs before in the trace, the property is invalid. In addition to these, while the monitor only detects $\neg write$ in the trace, the verification result is inconclusive and the monitor needs to continue monitoring the current execution trace to get more information to ensure the verification result.

By studying this example, we know the necessity to extend PPTL with a three-valued semantics for RV. The reason is that we can only obtain a finite prefix when we monitor a system in a runtime application, and we need to evaluate whether the system satisfies the given property by monitoring the finite prefix. Hence a three-valued logic is more useful than the classical binary logic. For a property φ and a finite prefix u, if all extensions of u satisfy the property, we are sure that u satisfies φ; if all extensions of u violate the property, we are sure that u violates φ; otherwise it cannot illustrate whether u satisfies or violates the property φ.

$$[u \models \varphi] = \begin{cases} true, & \forall \omega \in \Sigma^\omega : u\omega \models \varphi; \\ false, & \forall \omega \in \Sigma^\omega : u\omega \nvDash \varphi; \\ inconclusive, & otherwise \end{cases}$$

3.2   Constructing the Monitor

The process of constructing the monitor is shown in Fig. 1:

Step 1: Describe the property φ and its negation $\neg\varphi$
In Runtime Verification, a monitor can only obtain a finite prefix of the current
execution trace at runtime, which means we need to use the prefix to express
the same meaning as the whole trace. This is the reason why both the property
φ and its negation $\neg\varphi$ should be described: if the current prefix has already
violated the property, it means that there is no succeed leading it to satisfy the
property φ, so the output is *false*, and vice versa. If the current prefix satisfies
both φ and $\neg\varphi$, different succeeds will cause different results, and we cannot give
a correct verdict, so the output is *inconclusive*. For a language, a prefix is called
good (bad) if connected with all of its succeeds it still belongs (not belong) to
the language. And, a good (bad) prefix is called minimal, if each of its strict
prefix is not good (bad) anymore. In RV, the prefix is called minimal bad (good)
while it first violates the property φ ($\neg\varphi$).

Step 2: Translate every PPTL$_3$ formula into a Büchi Automaton (BA)
The reason of doing this is that an automaton is more suitable for constructing
the monitor than a logic formula. The procedure is shown in Fig. 2.

First, we need to use the concept of Normal Form (NF) and NF Graph
(NFG), the details can be found in [15], so we only give a brief introduction.

Definition 3.1 (Normal Form). Let Q_p be the set of atomic propositions
appearing in a PPTL formula Q. The normal form of Q can be defined as follows:

$$Q \equiv \bigvee_{j=0}^{n_0}(Q_{ej} \wedge \varepsilon) \vee \bigvee_{i=0}^{n_1}(Q_{ci} \wedge \bigcirc Q_i')$$

where $Q_{ej} \equiv \wedge_{k=1}^{m_0}\dot{q}_{jk}$, $Q_{ci} \equiv \wedge_{h=1}^{m}\dot{q}_{ih}$, $q_{jk}, q_{ih} \in Q_p$, for any $r \in Q_p$, $\dot{r}$ denotes r
or $\neg r$, Q_i' is a PPTL formula that the main operator is not "$\vee$". If $\vee_i Q_{ci} \equiv true$
and $\vee_{i \neq j}(Q_{ci} \wedge Q_{cj}) \equiv false$, and Q_i' is an arbitrary PPTL formula, we call the
NF complete normal form (CNF).

For a PPTL formula P, the NFG of P is a directed graph, $G = (CL(P),$
$EL(P), V_0)$, where $CL(P)$ denotes the set of nodes, which is specified by a

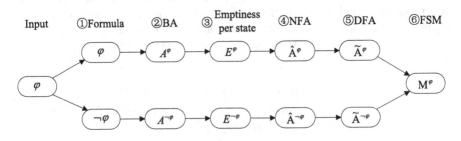

Fig. 1. Process of constructing the monitor

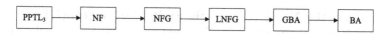

Fig. 2. Procedure about translating $PPTL_3$ formula into BA

formula, $EL(P)$ the set of edges, that is a directed arc from a node to another node and labeled with a state formula, and V_0 the set of root nodes that belong $CL(P)$. The NFG of a PPTL formula is inductively defined.

Definition 3.2 (Normal Form Graph). For a PPTL formula P, the set $CL(P)$ of nodes and the set $EL(P)$ of edges connecting nodes in $CL(P)$ are inductively constructed as follows.

1. Initially, let $V_0 = CL(P) = EL(P) = \emptyset$.
2. Let $P \equiv \vee_i P_i$. For each i, $P_i \in V_0, P_i \in CL(P)$.
3. For all $Q \in CL(P) \backslash \{\varepsilon, false\}$, if Q is rewritten into its normal form $\bigvee_{j=0}^{h}(Q_{ej} \wedge \varepsilon) \vee \bigvee_{i=0}^{k}(Q_{ci} \wedge \bigcirc Q_i')$, then $\varepsilon \in CL(P), (Q, Q_{ej}, \varepsilon) \in EL(P)$ for each j, $1 \le j \le h$; $Q_i' \in CL(P), (Q, Q_{ci}, Q_i') \in EL(P)$ for all i, $1 \le i \le k$.

The NFG of a PPTL formula describes its models according to the normal form, but it may contain some errors if there are chop operators in the PPTL formula. The reason is that PPTL may have infinite models, and for a PPTL formula like $P;Q$, if P has only infinite models, the formula has no model because the above method can only construct the model of P. If P has both finite and infinite models, we should eliminate all infinite models of P. Labeled NFG (LNFG) [15] is defined based on the above analysis to solve the problem. The main idea is adding a label l_i to indicate that a node in a cycle can only repeat for finite many times. An LNFG is a tetrad $G = \{CL(P), EL(P), V_0, L = \{L_1, \ldots, L_m\}\}$, where $CL(P), EL(P)$ and V_0 are identical to the ones in the NFG, while each $L_i \subseteq CL(P), 1 \le i \le m$, is the set of nodes with $fin(l_i)$ labels. For a property φ, if we get its LNFG, we can construct the corresponding BA, $A^\varphi = \{Q^\varphi, \Sigma, Q_0^\varphi, \delta^\varphi, F^\varphi\}$. Notice that if there is no finite labels in LNFG which means $L = \emptyset$, the LNFG can be transformed to a BA directly. Otherwise, it should be transformed to a generalized BA (GBA) first, and then to a BA. A trace ending with ε cannot be recognized by BA, so we extend it with an infinite suffix consisting of null-labels [16] which are always executable but with no effect.

Step 3: Define an emptiness function $E^\varphi(q)$
We define a function $E^\varphi : Q^\varphi \to B(B = \{true, false\})$ to detect whether there exists an accepted path starting from a state in Q^φ. If the automaton starts at state q and can arrive at the accepting states, we say the language recognized is nonempty and the value of $E^\varphi(q)$ is $true$. Otherwise, $E^\varphi(q)$ is $false$. To get the values of $E^\varphi(q)$, we identify the strongly connected components (SCC) in A^φ which can be solved by Tarjan's algorithm in linear time. Hence, the value of $E^\varphi(q)$ is $true$ if the automaton starts at state q and it can arrive at the SCC which include the accepting states.

Step 4: Define the Nondeterministic Finite Automaton(NFA)

We define a Nondeterministic Finite Automaton (NFA) $\hat{A}^\varphi$ using the function $E^\varphi(q)$. The elements of an NFA are the same as the elements of a BA except the accepting states, which is defined as $\hat{F}^\varphi = \{q \in Q^\varphi | E^\varphi(q) = true\}$. For instance, a system is expected to satisfy a given property P which can be translated into a BA. During the process of verification, if the current execution trace passes the accepting states infinite times, the property P is satisfied. Nevertheless, a trace is always finite in RV, so we cannot prove the satisfiability directly, but we can prove the system violates the property once the current trace cannot arrive at the accepting states. So, we define the NFA with accepting-state set F including all states q that the value of $E^\varphi(q)$ is $true$. Hence, if the system possibly satisfies the property starting from state q, the state q must be in the set of accepting states in NFA. On the contrary, if the current trace leads the NFA to move into a state not in the accepting set, it confirms that the property is violated.

Step 5: Transform to Deterministic Finite Automaton(DFA)

Every NFA has an equivalent DFA which can be obtained by the standard subset method. It starts at an initial state. Then, it can go to a state set when fed with a character, and the set is seen as a state in the DFA. This process is repeated until the whole DFA is constructed. The accepting states of the DFA are the state sets which include accepting states in NFA.

Step 6: Make the product of the automata

Two DFA $\tilde{A}^\varphi$ and $\tilde{A}^{\neg\varphi}$ can be obtained by the method mentioned above. Then, we make the product of them obtaining $\bar{A}^\varphi = \{\Sigma, \bar{Q}, \bar{Q}_0, \bar{\delta}, \bar{\lambda}\}$, where:

- $\bar{Q} = Q^\varphi \times Q^{\neg\varphi}$,
- $\bar{Q}_0 = (Q_0^\varphi, Q_0^{\neg\varphi})$,
- $\bar{\delta}((q, q'), a) = (\delta^\varphi(q, a), \delta^{\neg\varphi}(q', a))$, and
- $\bar{\lambda} : \bar{Q} \to B_3$ $(B_3 = \{true, false, inconclusive\})$ is a mapping from states to truth values, defined as

$$\bar{\lambda}(q, q') = \begin{cases} true & iff \quad q' \notin \tilde{F}^{\neg\varphi} \\ false & iff \quad q \notin \tilde{F}^\varphi \\ inconclusive & iff \quad q \in \tilde{F}^\varphi \wedge q' \in \tilde{F}^{\neg\varphi}. \end{cases}$$

We use the Hopcroft's algorithm to get the final monitor $M^\varphi = \{\Sigma, Q, q, \delta, \lambda\}$ which is minimal in the number of states by reducing the states of the above automaton $\bar{A}^\varphi$. With the monitor M^φ, we can verify whether the system satisfies the property by using the prefix in the current trace: $[u \models \varphi] = \lambda(\delta(q_0, u))$.

4   Example

In this section, we present an example to illustrate the RV monitor construction of PPTL$_3$.

This example describes a property in social network. Thinking about the situation that once a person opens his social network software, for example

WeChat, and finds there are many junk messages from strangers, which is an annoying experience. So, it is very important to ensure a property that a message can only be delivered from a person to his friends in most social network systems, in another word, if a person wants to send a message to another one at some point in the future, he must make friends with the person in the future and before the time. We describe the strategy by using formal notations:

- s means sending a message, and
- f means two users are friends.

According to the symbols above we can describe the property P in $PPTL_3$ that the system should satisfy: $\Diamond(\Diamond s \rightarrow f) \equiv true; (\Box \neg s \vee f)$. This is a chop formula and we should add a label $fin(l_i)$ ($i \in N_0$) to states that the node can only repeat finite times to solve the problem of chop operator as mentioned in Sect. 3. The property is finally described by the formula $fin(l_1); (\Box \neg s \vee f)$.

Having the property, the first thing we should do in the procedure of building the monitor is getting the normal form of the formula.

$$NF(fin(l_1); (\Box \neg s \vee f))$$
$$\equiv CHOP(fin(l_1); (\Box \neg s \vee f))$$
$$\equiv CHOP(NF(fin(l_1)); (\Box \neg s \vee f))$$
$$\equiv CHOP((l_1 \wedge \varepsilon \vee \bigcirc fin(l_1)); (\Box \neg s \vee f))$$
$$\equiv CHOP(l_1 \wedge \varepsilon; (\Box \neg s \vee f)) \vee CHOP(\bigcirc fin(l_1); (\Box \neg s \vee f))$$
$$\equiv NF(l_1 \wedge NF(\Box \neg s \vee f)) \vee \bigcirc fin(l_1); (\Box \neg s \vee f)$$
$$\equiv (f \vee \neg s) \wedge l_1 \wedge \varepsilon \vee f \wedge l_1 \wedge \bigcirc true \vee \neg s \wedge l_1 \wedge \bigcirc \Box \neg s \vee \bigcirc fin(l_1); f \vee$$
$$\bigcirc fin(l_1); \Box \neg s$$

Then we can get the LNFG according to the normal form above.
Initial: $V_0 = CL(P) = EL(P) = L = \emptyset$.
Then we add nodes and edges through the normal form.

First, add the root node into $CL(P)$ and V_0, $V_0 = CL(P) = L_1 = \{fin(l_1); (\Box \neg s \vee f)\}$;

For $(f \vee \neg s) \wedge l_1 \wedge \varepsilon$, add node $\{\varepsilon\}$ and edge($fin(l_1); (\Box \neg s \vee f), (f \vee \neg s) \wedge l_1, \varepsilon$);

For $f \wedge l_1 \wedge \bigcirc true$, add node $\{true\}$ and edge $(fin(l_1); (\Box \neg s \vee f), f \wedge l_1, true)$, and the normal form of $\{true\}$ is $\varepsilon \vee \bigcirc true$, so we can add the edges $(true, true, true)$ and $(true, true, \varepsilon)$;

For $\neg s \wedge l_1 \wedge \bigcirc \Box \neg s$, add node $\{\Box \neg s\}$ and edge $(fin(l_1); (\Box \neg s \vee f), \neg s \wedge l_1, \Box \neg s)$, and the normal form of $\{\Box \neg s\}$ is $\neg s \wedge \varepsilon \vee \neg s \wedge \bigcirc \Box \neg s$, so we can add edges $(\Box \neg s, \neg s, \Box \neg s)$ and $(\Box \neg s, \neg s, \varepsilon)$.

For $\bigcirc fin(l_1); f$, add node $\{fin(l_1); f\}$ and edge $(fin(l_1); (\Box \neg s \vee f), true, fin(l_1); f)$, and the normal form of $\{fin(l_1); f\}$ is $l_1 \wedge f \wedge \varepsilon \vee l_1 \wedge f \wedge \bigcirc true \vee \bigcirc fin(l_1); f$, so we can add edges $(fin(l_1); f, l_1 \wedge f, \varepsilon)$, $(fin(l_1); f, l_1 \wedge f, true)$ and $(fin(l_1); f, true, fin(l_1); f)$.

For $\bigcirc fin(l_1); \Box \neg s$, add node $\{fin(l_1); \Box \neg s\}$ and edge $(fin(l_1); (\Box \neg s \vee f), true, fin(l_1); \Box \neg s)$, and the normal form of $\{fin(l_1); \Box \neg s\}$ is $l_1 \wedge \neg s \wedge \varepsilon \vee l_1 \wedge$

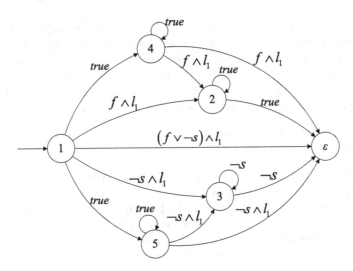

Fig. 3. LNFG of the property P

$\neg s \wedge \bigcirc\square\neg s \vee \bigcirc fin(l_1); \square\neg s$, so we can add edges $(fin(l_1); \square\neg s, l_1 \wedge \neg s, \varepsilon)$, $(fin(f_1); \square\neg s, l_1 \wedge \neg s, \square\neg s)$ and $(fin(l_1); \square\neg s, true, fin(l_1); \square\neg s)$.

Now, we can get the LNFG(we number the node for drawing the automaton easily).

$V_0 = \{fin(l_1); (\square\neg s \vee f)\}$;

$CL(P) = \{fin(l_1); (\square\neg s\vee f)\ 1, true\ 2, \square\neg s\ 3, fin(l_1); f\ 4, fin(l_1); \square\neg s5, \varepsilon\}$;

$EL(P) = \{(1, (f \vee \neg s) \wedge l_1, \varepsilon), (1, f \wedge l_1, 2), (2, true, 2), (2, true, \varepsilon), (1, \neg s\wedge l_1, 3), (3, \neg s, 3), (3, \neg s, \varepsilon), (1, true, 4), (4, l_1 \wedge f, \varepsilon), (4, l_1\wedge f, 2), (4, true, 4), (1, true, 5), (5, l_1 \wedge \neg s, \varepsilon), (5, l_1 \wedge \neg s, 3), (5, true, 5)\}$;

$L = \{L_1\}$ and $L_1 = \{1, 4, 5\}$. See as Fig. 3.

The responding BA can be constructed according to the information above, and it is important to note that we need to transform the LNFG to a GBA first for it contains a fin label. The accepting states set F of BA include ε nodes and nodes which repeat infinite times and have no fin labels: $I = \{fin(l_1); (\square\neg s\vee f)\ 1\}$, $Q = \{1, true\ 2, \square\neg s\ 3, fin(l_1); f\ 4, fin(l_1); \square\neg s\ 5, true\ 6, \square\neg s\ 7, \varepsilon\}$, $F = \{6, 7, \varepsilon\}$. See as Fig. 4.

The definitions of NFA and BA are very similar. All states can reach accepting states in BA which be deemed to accepting states in NFA (the problem about reachability can be solved by using Tarjan algorithm). The self-loop is reduced from the BA, with the NFA shown in Fig. 5.

The equivalent DFA can be constructed by using the subset method, and the states can be minimised as shown in the Fig. 6.

After solving the property P, we deal with the negative P by the same method.

$\neg P : \neg(\lozenge(\lozenge s \rightarrow f)) \equiv \square(\lozenge s \wedge \neg f) \equiv \square((true; s) \wedge \neg f)$

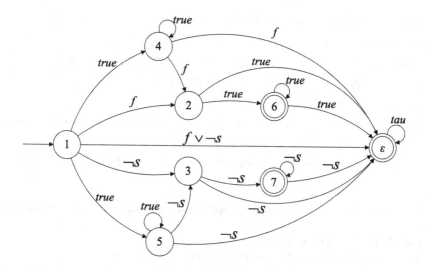

Fig. 4. BA of the property P

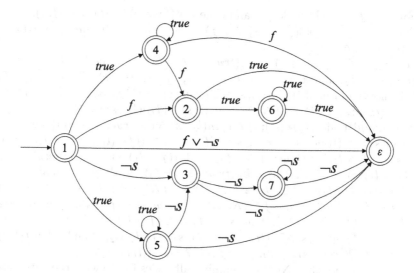

Fig. 5. NFA

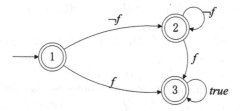

Fig. 6. Equivalent DFA

The normal form should be obtained at first.

$NF(\Box((true; s) \wedge \neg f))$

$\equiv NF((true; s) \wedge \neg f \wedge \varepsilon) \vee NF((true; s) \wedge \neg f \wedge \bigcirc\Box((true; s) \wedge \neg f))$

$\equiv AND(NF(true; s), NF(\neg f \wedge \varepsilon)) \vee AND(NF(true; s), NF(\neg f \wedge$
$\bigcirc\Box((true; s) \wedge \neg f)))$

$\equiv AND((s \wedge \varepsilon \vee s \wedge \bigcirc true \vee \bigcirc true; s), \neg f \wedge \varepsilon) \vee AND((s \wedge \varepsilon \vee s \wedge \bigcirc true$
$\vee (\bigcirc fin(l_1); s)), \neg f \wedge \bigcirc\Box((true; s) \wedge \neg f))$

$\equiv s \wedge \neg f \wedge \varepsilon \vee s \wedge \neg f \wedge \bigcirc\Box((true; s) \wedge \neg f) \vee \neg f \wedge \bigcirc((fin(l_1); s) \wedge \Box((true; s)$
$\wedge \neg f))$

The responding LNFG can be constructed according to the normal form above.

Initial: $V_0 = CL(P) = EL(P) = L = \emptyset$.

Then we add nodes and edges through the normal form.

First, add the root node into $CL(P)$ and V_0, $V_0 = CL(P) = \{\Box((true; s) \wedge \neg f)\}$;

For $s \wedge \neg f \wedge \varepsilon$, add node $\{\varepsilon\}$ and edge $(\Box((true; s) \wedge \neg f), s \wedge \neg f, \varepsilon)$;

For $s \wedge \neg f \wedge \bigcirc\Box((true; s) \wedge \neg f)$, add edge $(\Box((true; s) \wedge \neg f), s \wedge \neg f, \Box((true; s) \wedge \neg f))$.

For $\neg f \wedge \bigcirc((fin(l_1); s) \wedge \Box((true; s) \wedge \neg f))$, add node $\{(fin(l_1); s) \wedge \Box((true; s) \wedge \neg f)\}$ and edge $(\Box((true; s) \wedge \neg f), \neg f, (fin(l_1); s) \wedge \Box((true; s) \wedge \neg f))$, and the normal form of $\{(fin(l_1); s) \wedge \Box((true; s) \wedge \neg f)\}$ is $s \wedge \neg f \wedge l_1 \wedge \varepsilon \vee s \wedge \neg f \wedge l_1 \wedge \bigcirc\Box((true; s) \wedge \neg f) \vee \neg f \wedge \bigcirc((fin(l_1); s) \wedge (fin(l_2); s) \wedge \Box((true; s) \wedge \neg f))$, so we can add node $\{(fin(l_1); s) \wedge (fin(l_2); s) \wedge \Box((true; s) \wedge \neg f)\}$ and edges $((fin(l_1); s) \wedge \Box((true; s) \wedge \neg f), s \wedge \neg f \wedge l_1, \varepsilon)$, $((fin(l_1); s) \wedge \Box((true; s) \wedge \neg f), s \wedge \neg f \wedge l_1, \Box((true; s) \wedge \neg f))$ and $((fin(l_1); s) \wedge \Box((true; s) \wedge \neg f), \neg f, (fin(l_1); s) \wedge (fin(l_2); s) \wedge \Box((true; s) \wedge \neg f))$, and the normal form of $(fin(l_1); s) \wedge (fin(l_2); s) \wedge \Box((true; s) \wedge \neg f)$ is $\neg f \wedge \bigcirc((fin(l_1); s) \wedge \Box((true; s) \wedge \neg f)) \vee s \wedge \neg f \wedge l_1 \wedge l_2 \wedge \varepsilon \vee s \wedge \neg f \wedge l_1 \wedge l_2 \wedge \bigcirc\Box((true; s) \wedge \neg f)$, so we can add edges $((fin(l_1); s) \wedge (fin(l_2); s) \wedge \Box((true; s) \wedge \neg f), \neg f, (fin(l_1); s) \wedge \Box((true; s) \wedge \neg f))$, $((fin(l_1); s) \wedge (fin(l_2); s) \wedge \Box((true; s) \wedge \neg f), s \wedge \neg f \wedge l_1 \wedge l_2, \varepsilon)$ and $((fin(l_1); s) \wedge (fin(l_2); s) \wedge \Box((true; s) \wedge \neg f), s \wedge \neg f \wedge l_1 \wedge l_2, \Box((true; s) \wedge \neg f))$.

Now, we can get the LNFG (we number all nodes for drawing the automaton easily).

$V_0 = \{\Box((true; s) \wedge \neg f)\}$;

$CL(P) = \{\Box((true; s) \wedge \neg f) \, 1, (fin(l_1); s) \wedge \Box((true; s) \wedge \neg f) \, 2, (fin(l_1); s) \wedge (fin(l_2); s) \wedge \Box((true; s) \wedge \neg f) \, 3, \varepsilon\}$;

$EL(P) = \{(1, s \wedge \neg f, 1), (1, \neg f, 2), (1, s \wedge \neg f, \varepsilon), (2, \neg f, 3), (2, s \wedge \neg f \wedge l_1, \varepsilon), (2, s \wedge \neg f \wedge l_1, 1), (3, \neg f, 2), (3, s \wedge \neg f \wedge l_1 \wedge l_2, 1), (3, s \wedge \neg f \wedge l_1 \wedge l_2, \varepsilon)\}$;

$L = \{L_1, L_2\}$, $L_1 = \{2, 3\}$, $L_2 = \{3\}$. See as Fig. 7.

According to the information mentioned above, we can get the corresponding BA that $I = \{\Box((true; s) \wedge \neg f) \, 1\}$, $Q = \{\Box((true; s) \wedge \neg f) \, 1, (fin(l_1); s) \wedge \Box((true; s) \wedge \neg f) \, 2, (fin(l_1); s) \wedge (fin(l_2); s) \wedge \Box((true; s) \wedge \neg f) \, 3, \Box((true; s) \wedge \neg f) \, 4, \varepsilon\}$, $F = \{4, \varepsilon\}$. See as Fig. 8.

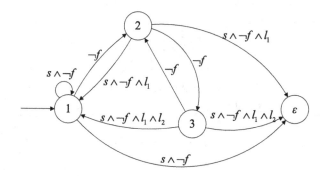

Fig. 7. LNFG of $\neg P$

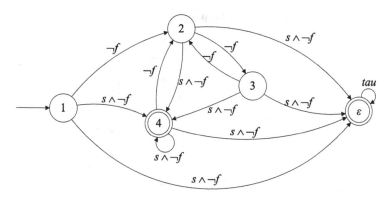

Fig. 8. BA of $\neg P$

We can define the NFA just like what we do before, which is shown in the Fig. 9.

Then we use the subset method to get the equivalent DFA shown in the Fig. 10 as we do before.

We construct the monitor by getting the production of two DFA shown in Fig. 11, and each state has a corresponding truth value according to the function $\bar{\lambda}$. With the monitor, we can give a correct verdict according to the current execution trace, for example, if we can get information that two person become friends from the trace, the DFA of $\neg P$ is violated, which states that the current execution satisfies the property P.

Finally, we will give a simple system model described by *Büchi* Automaton shown in Fig. 12 to contrast runtime verification with model checking.

(1) In runtime verification, only the current execution trace, for example, $\{f, \neg s, \neg s, s, s...\}$ is monitored, and the monitor will ensure whether the current execution satisfies the property or not as early as possible, and in this case, the verification result is valid while the monitor detects f in the trace. In contrast, model checking will make the product of the BA of the system and the BA

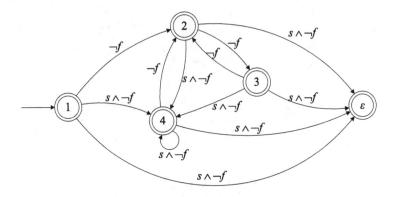

Fig. 9. NFA

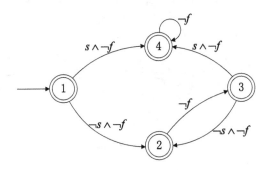

Fig. 10. Equivalent DFA

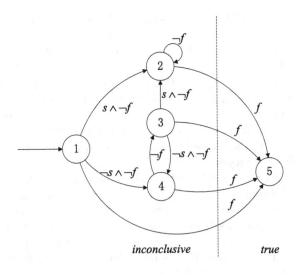

Fig. 11. Monitor

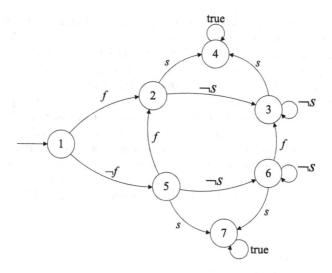

Fig. 12. BA of the system

of the negative property shown in Fig. 8, and then give the verification results according to the emptiness of the product of two BAs.

(2) Almost all software will be updated over a period of time to provide a better user experience, in model checking, this will cause the BA of the system will be constructed anew which is a real complex work. While in runtime verification, the monitor can be reused if the property does not changed, that means all things we should do is just running the system again and get the new execution trace.

5   Related Work

RV is a formal verification technique, which monitors a system at the runtime and judges whether the system satisfies a given property by checking the trace generated at runtime. The Model-Based Trace-Checking [17] is a similar technique that checks trace by using formal models, which can be state machines described as formal notations. Another technique is Parameterised Three-Valued Model Checking [18], which extends the traditional model to three-valued Kripke structure. In this approach, the uncertain part of model is represented by the constant value *unknown*, and the parameterization can be used to improve the precision of three-valued model. Comparing with two methods, the whole model of the system is not needed in RV for it only considers runtime behaviors of the system. RV's another feature is that it deals with finite traces instead of infinite traces, that means a prefix of an infinite trace should express the same meaning of the full infinite trace. For the goal, three-valued temporal logic is used in RV usually.

To the best of our knowledge, there is no report of runtime verification for PPTL in the literature. We give a brief review of the studies on RV that have somehow impacted our work. LTL_3 [13] extends LTL and evolves three truth values *true*, *false* and *inconclusive*. The given property can be described by LTL_3, and then translated into an automaton. Eventually, a runtime verification monitor is generated. It verifies whether the system satisfies the property by checking the trace generated at runtime. The monitor can ensure the impartiality and anticipation [19] because the underlying logic has three-valued semantics. ITLTracer [20] is another RV monitor that is based on Interval Temporal Logic (ITL) [21]. The basic partitions are based on the *chop* operator instead of states, which ensures the continuation of variables' values. After getting the monitored trace, ITL formulas can be used to describe the property and verify whether the property is satisfied.

6   Conclusions

Runtime verification is a lightweight verification technology, which has some advantages in verifying reactive systems compared with traditional verification techniques such as model checking and theorem proving. This paper introduces a method to construct a monitor for runtime verification based on $PPTL_3$, which translates $PPTL_3$ formulas into automata using the notions of normal form and normal form graph.

For future work, we are going to implement the monitor and verify whether the current execution satisfies a property by checking the runtime information.

References

1. Pnueli, A., Zaks, A.: PSL model checking and run-time verification via testers. In: Misra, J., Nipkow, T., Sekerinski, E. (eds.) FM 2006. LNCS, vol. 4085, pp. 573–586. Springer, Heidelberg (2006). doi:10.1007/11813040_38
2. Tian, C., Duan, Z., Zhang, N.: An efficient approach for abstraction-refinement in model checking. Theoret. Comput. Sci. **461**, 76–85 (2012)
3. Luo, Q., Zhang, Y., Lee, C., Jin, D., Meredith, P.O.N., Şerbănuţă, T.F., Roşu, G.: RV-Monitor: efficient parametric runtime verification with simultaneous properties. In: Bonakdarpour, B., Smolka, S.A. (eds.) RV 2014. LNCS, vol. 8734, pp. 285–300. Springer, Cham (2014). doi:10.1007/978-3-319-11164-3_24
4. Simmonds, J., Chechik, M., Nejati, S., Litani, E., O'Farrell, B.: Property patterns for runtime monitoring of web service conversations. In: Leucker, M. (ed.) RV 2008. LNCS, vol. 5289, pp. 137–157. Springer, Heidelberg (2008). doi:10.1007/978-3-540-89247-2_9
5. Milea, N.A., Khoo, S.C., Lo, D., Pop, C.: NORT: runtime anomaly-based monitoring of malicious behavior for windows. In: Khurshid, S., Sen, K. (eds.) RV 2011. LNCS, vol. 7186, pp. 115–130. Springer, Heidelberg (2012). doi:10.1007/978-3-642-29860-8_10
6. Zhao, L., Tang, T., Xu, T., Chai, M., Li, X.: Runtime verification and its applications in train control systems. J. China Railway Soc. **33**, 65–71 (2011)

7. Duan, Z.: Temporal Logic and Temporal Logic Programming. Science Press, Beijing (2005)
8. Duan, Z., Yang, X., Maciej, K.: Framed temporal logic programming. Sci. Comput. Program. **70**, 31–61 (2008)
9. Duan, Z., Tian, C., Zhang, L.: A decision procedure for propositional projection temporal logic with infinite models. Acta Inf. **45**, 43–78 (2008)
10. Tian, C., Duan, Z.: Model checking rate monotonic scheduling algorithm based on propositional projection temporal logic. J. Softw. **22**, 211–221 (2011)
11. Yu, Y., Duan, Z., Tian, C., Yang, M.: Model checking C programs with MSVL. In: Liu, S. (ed.) SOFL 2012. LNCS, vol. 7787, pp. 87–103. Springer, Heidelberg (2013). doi:10.1007/978-3-642-39277-1_7
12. Zhang, N., Duan, Z., Tian, C.: A cylinder computation model for many-core parallel computing. Theoret. Comput. Sci. **497**, 68–83 (2013)
13. Bauer, A., Leucker, M., Schallhart, C.: Runtime verification for LTL and TLTL. ACM Trans. Softw. Eng. Methodol. **20**, 14:1–14:64 (2011)
14. Bauer, A., Leucker, M., Schallhart, C.: Comparing LTL semantics for runtime verification. J. Logic Comput. **20**, 651–674 (2010)
15. Duan, Z., Tian, C.: A practical decision procedure for propositional projection temporal logic with infinite models. Theoret. Comput. Sci. **554**, 169–190 (2014)
16. Tian, C., Duan, Z.: Expressiveness of propositional projection temporal logic with star. Theoret. Comput. Sci. **412**, 1729–1744 (2011)
17. Howard, Y., Gruner, S., Gravell, A., Wrede, J.: Model-based trace-checking. https://www.researchgate.net/publication/51953541_Model-Based_Trace-Checking
18. Timm, N., Gruner, S.: Parameterised three-valued model checking. Sci. Comput. Program. **126**, 94–110 (2016)
19. Leucker, M.: Teaching runtime verification. In: Khurshid, S., Sen, K. (eds.) RV 2011. LNCS, vol. 7186, pp. 34–48. Springer, Heidelberg (2012). doi:10.1007/978-3-642-29860-8_4
20. Janicke, H.: ITLTracer: runtime verification of properties expressed in ITL. www.cse.dmu.ac.uk/~heljanic/sw/itltracer-presentation.pdf
21. Moszkowski, B.: Executing Temporal Logic Programs. Cambridge University Press, Cambridge (1986)

Applying SOFL to a Railway Interlocking System in Industry

Juan Luo[1], Shaoying Liu[2(✉)], Yanqin Wang[1], and Tingliang Zhou[1]

[1] Casco Signal Ltd., R&D Center, Shanghai, China
{luojuan,wangyanqin,zhoutingliang}@casco.com.cn
[2] Department of Computer Science, Hosei University, Tokyo, Japan
sliu@hosei.ac.jp

Abstract. This paper describes another application of the SOFL three-step specification approach in specifying a railway interlocking system in industrial setting. We also explore the way of deriving hazard conditions from formal specifications, and propose a way to analyze the conditions for the assurance of the safety of the interlocking system in the early stage of the development. Our experience shows that SOFL is much more accessible by ordinary practitioners than other existing well-known formal methods and effective in helping practitioners deepen their understanding of the system details.

Keywords: Formal specification · Hazard condition · Analysis · Interlocking system

1 Introduction

Railway signaling system is a kind of safety critical system whose failure is likely to cause catastrophic disaster. The reliability and safety of such a system can be achieved not only through the redundant architecture of hardware, but also the high quality of the software deployed for the control purpose in the system. High quality software must function as expected and must not trigger safety problems for the system.

To ensure the high quality for a software system, capturing correct and complete requirements is essential, simply because it is almost impossible to achieve a high quality implementation from incorrect or incomplete requirements. Traditional requirements analysis, design, and testing methods based on natural language descriptions can hardly guarantee that all functional and safety requirements are implemented correctly. In the industrial practice, system functional requirements are mainly documented in natural language and their implementation is verified by testing. Safety requirements are usually ensured by first using hazard log to record potential hazard and then carrying out hazard analysis in different development phases. However, this kind of practice suffers from the following two disadvantages:

(1) Requirements specifications in natural language are likely to cause ambiguity in design and implementation, which may lead to significant errors.

© Springer International Publishing AG 2017
S. Liu et al. (Eds.): SOFL+MSVL 2016, LNCS 10189, pp. 160–177, 2017.
DOI: 10.1007/978-3-319-57708-1_10

(2) Since test cases of traditional testing methods are mainly generated manually, the functional scenarios of an operation may not be considered completely, which is likely to result in the incompleteness of test case design.

It is well recognized that the later the faults are found, the higher the cost for removing the faults will become [1]. This is especially true of railway signaling systems that involve complex operations in both hardware and software.

To detect faults in requirements, especially those related to human decisions on both functional and safety requirements, formal methods are considered to be an effective technique [2]. Formal methods are built on strict mathematical definitions and have precise mathematical semantics. This advantage can help resolve requirements and property ambiguity in natural language descriptions. There are many well-known formal methods, such as VDM [3], Z [4], Event-B [5], SCADE [6], and SOFL [7], and each has its own characteristics. Although they share some common features, such as using the concepts of pre- and post-conditions in specifications, their differences in syntax, style, and requiring different level of mathematical skills provide different accessibility to practitioners, which help them make appropriate choices in practice.

We have been making all kinds of attempts to use several formal methods on our products in CASCO Shanghai. For example, we applied SCADE to the design of a zone controller subsystem, Event-B for modeling and verification of the zone control subsystem, and formal proof for verifying the interlocking system. After these attempts, we derive the following conclusions based on our experience:

(1) SCADE performs well for system design, but when it comes to requirements analysis phase, it becomes unsuitable due to the lack of effective mechanism for functional abstraction.

(2) Event-B can be used throughout the entire development process. The formal refinement adopted in Event-B is an ideal technique that integrates formal verification and design into refinement laws for developing correct programs, but since it requires too much mathematical knowledge and manipulation skills for the developers, our experience suggests that it is beyond our capability and not cost-effective as well.

(3) There are also some formal verification tools (e.g. Gatel and Prover iLock) that can be used to verify the safety and functional requirements, but they do not provide specific guidelines for carrying out formal modeling and formal verification of related properties. They do not seem to be able to guarantee the correctness of the system either, even if the verification is successfully done.

Due to the disadvantages above, we turn to SOFL. SOFL, standing for Structured Object-Oriented Formal Language, provides a formal engineering method for practical formal modeling and verification. In particular, the practicality of the formal modeling mainly comes from the SOFL three-step approach that emphasizes the importance of writing a formal specification based on the construction of an informal specification and a semi-formal specification. After about fourteen hours training, we realized that SOFL is easy to understand and to use; it also requires much less mathematical skills than Event-B. We therefore decided to apply it to the interlocking system specification and verification as a trial testing project.

Our major contributions in this paper are three fold. Firstly, we explain how practitioners with little experience of SOFL can use the SOFL three-step approach properly to writing formal specifications on the basis of first writing informal and then semi-formal specifications. We chose the interlocking system as the target for specification and discuss how the domain knowledge can be effectively utilized to formalize properly the requirements with different features. Secondly, we describe how hazard conditions can be systematically extracted from a formal requirements specification. A hazard condition is a logical formula whose implementation may cause hazards to the system. Finally, we present a testing-based verification method for analyzing the hazard conditions.

The rest of the paper is organized as follows. Section 2 briefly introduces the interlocking system model to pave the way for readers to understand the subsequent sections. Section 2 focuses on the construction of the informal, semi-formal, and formal specifications of the interlocking system. Section 3 describes how hazard conditions can be extracted from formal specifications. Section 4 discusses our experience of using SOFL and the interesting problems encountered during the application. Section 5 briefly introduces some related applications of formal methods to interlocking systems. Finally, in Sect. 6, we conclude the paper and point out future research directions.

2   Specification for Interlocking System

In this section, we first give a brief introduction to the interlocking system used in our project, and then describe how the formal specification for its functional requirements can be constructed based on an informal specification and a semi-formal specification.

2.1   Introduction of the Interlocking System

In railway signaling system, interlocking subsystem (calls CBI, Computer based interlocking) is a signal control system that completes interactive interlocking check between signal, switch and route to set routes for trains and to prevent conflicting movements of trains. Once the route is set and the other routes conflict with the set route, they are not allowed to set and the associated interlocking operations, such as point move, are not allowed to perform. CBI should be designed to make it impossible to display a dangerous status for signal in any case and to prevent from the mistakenly release of route to ensure the safety of train operations. Only when they satisfy required interlocking relations, are trains to be allowed to proceed to the planned route in order to prevent accidents or hazards, such as head-on collision, side collision, rear-end collision, inappropriate route entering, switch splitting, or trains derailing during operation. Since interlocking systems are safety-critical and must have safety integrity (meaning the likelihood of a system satisfactorily performing the required safety functions under all the stated conditions within a stated period of time), according to the European standard EN50129, the safety integrity level of interlocking system is defined as SIL4. Safety Integrity Level SIL of a function is determined by the Tolerable Hazard Rate THR per hour. If $10\text{-}9 \leq THR < 10\text{-}8$, then the SIL of the function is defined as SIL4, which is a number indicating the required degree of confidence that a system meets its specified safety functions with respect to systematic failures.

As Fig. 1 shows, the interlocking system used in our project is divided into three layers: *man-machine session layer, interlocking computation layer*, and *execution layer*. Each layer is divided into several functional modules according to the partition of the functions. The man-machine session layer is responsible for processing the man-machine interface information by means of three modules, *man-machine interface module, communication module*, and *information indication module*. The interlocking computation layer carries out the interlocking computing through a dispatching module or real time operating system and a group of other modules, such as *basic interlocking module, self-diagnosing module, special interlocking module*, and *adjacent interlocking system interface module*. The execution layer controls the output of commands to the field devices through the *field device state input module* and the *field device control command output module*.

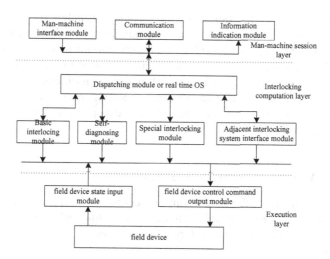

Fig. 1. The structure of an interlocking system

2.2   Basic Interlocking Function

We use SOFL mainly for the basic interlocking model that is used to realize the interlocking relations in the system. The devices controlled are mainly signals, switches, and track circuits, and these devices are controlled in a route or individually. Figure 2 is an example of part of some railway station layout that illustrates how field devices are arranged and related with each other in the interlocking system.

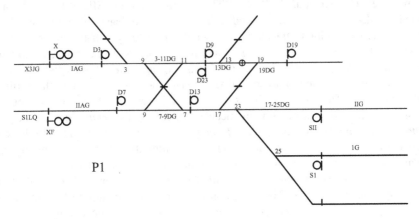

Fig. 2. Station layout example

The basic interlocking function is route controlling, including *route setting, route locking, signal opening, keeping signal opening, normal route release, abnormal route release, manual switch operation* and *general route call-on locking*. Since there are different kinds of routes, such as train route, shunting route, calling-on route, successive route, and special shunting route, and each function has different requirements for each kind of route, we need to first specify the functionality of operations for each kind of route and then investigate how the related specifications are connected to form the whole specification for the entire system.

2.3   Specific Ways to Write SOFL Specifications

As mentioned previously, the final formal specifications of various operations are achieved by means of writing an informal specification first and then refining it into a semi-formal specification, and finally formalizing the semi-formal specification into a formal specification.

2.3.1   Informal Specification

We build the informal interlocking requirements specification as advocated by the SOFL three-step approach. In this section, we focus our discussion on how the informal specification is written. According to the SOFL approach, an informal specification is composed of three sections: *functions, data resources,* and *constraints*.

The basic interlocking functional requirements are mainly learnt from the informal interlocking technical descriptions of the controlled devices, system states that need checking, and properties or constraints the system must satisfy. According to the form of SOFL informal specification, we treat the operations for checking the system states as bottom level functions, the devices (e.g., routes, signals, switches) to be controlled by the system as data resources, and the properties that the system must satisfy as constraints. For the sake of both confidentiality of the original specification and space limit, we only give the informal specification of a *switch normal operation* below as an example to show the general structure of an informal specification.

Informal specification for the switch normal operation:

1. *Functions:*
    1.1 *switch operation*
        1.1.1 *switch normal operation*
            1.1.1.1 *check that the switch is not locked*
            1.1.1.2 *check that the switch has position indication*
            1.1.1.3 *check that there is no reverse operation command output*
            1.1.1.4 *check that time is not out for the switch to operate*
        1.1.2 *switch reverse operation*
2. *Data resources*:
    2.1 *switch*
    2.2 *route*
3. *Constraints*:
    3.1 *If the switch is already in normal position when receiving a normal operation request, then the system will not output the normal operation command.*
    3.2 *If the max time for switch operation is expired, the operation for switch move must be stopped.*

In this informal specification, the description of each item is deliberately kept short and its style is not restrictive. However, to make the specification comprehensible, each functional description uses the *verb-object* structure; each data item is described using a noun; and each constraint is presented as a condition. The application of this principle can be flexible for other domains in practice.

2.3.2   Semi-formal Specification

After finishing the informal specification, we refine and transform it into a semi-formal specification. At this step, three things are done to fulfill the task. Firstly, we group the related functions, data resource items, and constraints in the informal specification into SOFL modules. Secondly, we declare all of the necessary constant identifiers, type identifiers, and state variables formally in SOFL. Finally, we define the functionality of each process in the module using pre- and post-conditions properly.

As far as constructing each module is concerned, we take the following guideline to define the corresponding items in the module. Each function in the informal specification is refined into a process in the SOFL module because each process fulfills a function by defining how its input can be used to produce its output. Each data resource item in the informal specification is transformed into a state variable declaration because it is likely to be shared by several processes. Each constraint in the informal specification is refined into either an invariant or part of some process functionality in the module, considering its role in the system.

For transforming the data resource items in the informal specification to the declarations in the semi-formal specification module, we apply the following principle. For each data resource item, we declare a state variable using a well-defined type in the module. If the type is not defined yet using the SOFL notation, we need to declare it properly in the section named "type" of the same module. For each declared type, its constraints, if any, can be defined as invariants in the section named "inv" of the same module. Each invariant is a condition described in natural language in the semi-formal specification. For each state variable, its properties that must be sustained throughout the entire system can also be defined as invariants in the "inv" section in the similar way to type invariants.

As far as refining each function in the informal specification into a process in the module is concerned, we use pre- and post-conditions to specify its functionality. To this end, we first need to determine all of the necessary input variables, output variables, and the state variables the process uses, and then formally declare them using well-defined types. The pre-condition presents a constraint on the input and state variables before the execution of the process, and the post-condition gives another constraint for the output and the updated state variables to satisfy. In the semi-formal specification, both the pre- and post-conditions are described in a structured natural language in order to strike a good balance between the usability and the rigor for a high cost-effectiveness. The structured natural language expression is actually a disjunctive normal form in which each term is described in natural language but the logical connectors are formally defined operators (e.g. *and, or, not*).

As an example, below we show part of the semi-formal specification of the process for the normal switch operation. The partial specification is expressed as a disjunction of several functional scenarios (FS). Each FS is a conjunction of terms described in English. Specifically, the semi-formal specification describes how the switch functions when the system receives a route setting request. First it needs to check the position of the switch. If the position is not the same as the route requests, the system should execute the switch normal or reverse operation. After the operation is done, the system should show the result. In this example, we only describe the semi-formal specification of normal switch operation.

Part of the semi-formal specification of the process for switch operation:

```
module switch_operation_Decom/switch_operation;
  type
CLOCK = nat0;/*time type*/

POSITION = composed of
            normal_indicate: bool
            reverse_indicate: bool
            end;

TIMER = composed of
        acc: CLOCK /*the current time value*/
        delay: nat0 /*maximum time delay*/
        start : bool /*timing flag*/
        end;

POINT = composed of
        sw_id: nat0
        track_id: nat0 /*track which the switch is in*/
        pos: POSITION /*switch position indication*/
        lock: bool /*switch lock state*/
        pt_timer: TIMER /*switch operation timer*/
        end;

ROUTE = composed of
        points: seq of POINT/*switches in the route*/
        pt_req_pos: seq of POSTION/*switch requested position by
                                    route*/
        tracks: set of TRACK/*tracks in the routes*/
        start_sig : SIGNAL/*start signal*/
        end_sig: SIGNAL/*end signal*/
        locked: bool/*route lock state*/
        permissive: bool/*route permissive state*/
        idle: bool /*route idle state*/
        end;

var
  rt: ROUTE
  pt: POINT
process switch_normal_operation(normal_request: sign | normal_cmd:
sign)normal_op_ok: sign | trail_alarm1: sign | normal_cmd: sign, nor-
mal_cmd_output: sign
ext wr pt
    wr rt
pre true
post
```

```
/*FS1: receives a normal operation request, outputs normal operation
command and starts the timer*/
normal operation request is received and
switch is not locked and
switch is in reverse position and
normal operation command is sent out and
the timer is started
or
/*FS2: switch is moving but not getting into normal position, time is
not out, output normal operation command and continue timing*/
the normal operation command in the last cycle is sent out and
switch is not locked and
switch is moving and
time is not out and
normal operation command is sent out and
timer is continuing
or
/*FS3: switch is already in normal position, output success flag*/
The switch is in normal position and
The success flag is sent out and
not normal operation command is sent out and
the timer is terminated and reset
or
/*FS4: switch is moving but time is out, not output normal operation
command and reset the timer, output fail flag*/
the normal operation command in the last cycle is sent out and
time is out and
not normal operation command is sent out and
the timer is terminated and reset
end_process;
process switch_position_check(route_set_req: sign)
normal_request: sign | no_operation: sign |reverse_request: sign
...
end_process;

process switch_reverse_operation(reverse_request: sign | reverse_cmd:
sign)reverse_op_ok: sign | trail_alarm2: sign | reverse_cmd: sign,
reverse_cmd_output: sign
...
end_process;
process switch_op_result(normal_op_ok: sign | trail_alarm1: sign |
no_operation: sign | reverse_op_ok: sign | trail_alarm2:
sign)switch_op_ok: sign | trail_alarm: sign
...
end_process;
end_module
```

2.3.3   Formal Specification

To ultimately resolve the ambiguity in the semi-formal specification, we need to completely formalize all of the informal expressions, such as "*switch is not locked*" in the above process for normal switch operation. However, since some processes in the specification may depend on other processes in terms of data flows, our experience suggests that it can reduce the chances of modifications of the formal specifications of the processes if their dependency relation can first be defined using a the graphical notation called Condition Data Flow Diagram (CDFD). Taking this into account, we need to fulfill two tasks in constructing the formal specification:

(1) *Draw a CDFD to describe the dependency relation between processes.*
(2) *Formalize the pre- and post-conditions of each process occurring in the CDFD.*

The CDFD not only reflects the dependency relation between processes, but also reflects the architecture of the system. In the architecture, the signature of each process in terms of its name, input, output, and the related data store variables is precisely defined, and all of the relevant processes are connected in terms of data flows and data stores.

When formalizing the pre- and post-conditions of each process in the corresponding module of the CDFD, we need to choose appropriate operators defined in the relevant data types to formally express the informal statements in the semi-formal specification. In some circumstances, we may find that some variables cannot be declared using existing types or some type definitions are not complete. In that case, we need to modify or add some type definitions.

As an example, we show the formal specification for the switch operation, which includes the CDFD in Fig. 3 and the corresponding module given below. For the sake of space, we only give the details of the formal specification of the process for switch normal operation.

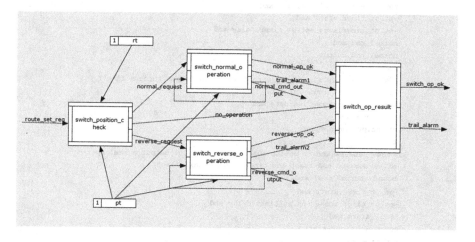

Fig. 3. CDFD of the switch operation module

```
module switch_operation_Decom/switch_operation;
type
… /*inherent from the semi-formal specification.*/
var
…
process switch_normal_operation(normal_request: sign | normal_cmd:
sign)normal_op_ok: sign | trail_alarm1: sign | normal_cmd: sign, nor-
mal_cmd_output: sign
ext wr pt
    wr rt

pre true

post
/*FS1: receives a normal operation request, outputs normal operation
command and starts the timer*/
bound(normal_request)and
not (~pt.locked) and
~pt.pos.reverse_indicate and
not ~pt.pos.reverse_indicate and
normal_cmd and
normal_cmd_output and
pt.pt_timer.start
pt.pt_timer.acc := 0
or
/*FS2: the switch is moving but not getting into normal position, time
is not out, output normal operation command and continue timing*/
bound(~normal_cmd) and
not (~pt.locked) and
not ~pt.pos.reverse_indicate and
not ~pt.pos.normal_indicate and
~pt.pt_timer.start and
~pt.pt_timer.acc< ~pt.pt_timer.delay and
normal_cmd and
normal_cmd_output
or
/*FS3: switch is already in normal position, output success flag*/
~pt.pos.normal_indicate and
not ~pt.pos.reverse_indicate and
success and
not pt.pt_timer.start
or
/*FS4: the switch is moving but time is out, not output normal oper-
ation command and reset the timer, output fail flag*/
bound(~normal_cmd) and
~pt.pt_timer.start and
~pt.pt_timer.acc>= ~pt.pt_timer.delay and
trail_alarm and
not pt.pt_timer.start
end_process;
… /*inherent from the semi-formal specification */
end_module
```

Since the formal specification preserves the structure of the corresponding semi-formal specification of the same process, we do not repeat the explanation of its meaning here for brevity.

3 Derivation and Analysis of Hazard Conditions

A complete formal specification of a safety critical system should be defined in the way that the functionality of the system must imply the required safety properties. To ensure this point, it is necessary to derive the hazard conditions from the relevant formal expressions that present a potential violation of the safety requirements and to check whether they are valid with respect to the safety requirements. A general distinction between a functional requirement and a safety requirement is that the functional requirement indicates that something must be done, while the safety requirement shows that the result of functional requirement do not lead to hazards [8]. In this section, we present a systematic way to derive hazard conditions from a formal process specification and then discuss how they can be analyzed to determine their validity.

3.1 Derivation of Hazard Conditions

Our previous research [9] shows that any formal process specification can be converted into an equivalent *functional scenario form* (FSF).

Definition 3.1. Let S_{pre} denote the pre-condition and S_{post} the post-condition of process S, respectively. Let $S_{post} = G_1$ *and* D_1 *or* G_2 *and* D_2 *or*...*or* G_n *and* D_n, where $G_i(i = ,...,n)$ is known as a *guard condition* containing only input variables and D_i is known as a *defining condition* containing at least one output variable. Then, the following form is called an FSF of S:

S_{pre} *and* G_1 *and* D_1 *or* S_{pre} *and* G_2 *and* D_2 *or*...*or* S_{pre} *and* G_n *and* D_n and each S_{pre} *and* G_i *and* D_i *is called a functional scenario* (FS), defining an independent function.

Our way to derive hazard conditions focuses on each functional scenario. Let T_i *and* D_i represents a general functional scenario, where $T_i = S_{pre}$ *and* G_i is called *test condition* of the scenario. Our discussions below always refer to this FS. The specific rules for hazard condition derivation are given as follows:

(1) If D_i defines a safety-related operation on some field device, then T_i *and not* D_i may describe a hazard condition. For example, suppose

*some switch on a route has no position indication **and** the start signal of the route is restrictive*

is a functional scenario in relation to the safety requirements, then we can derive the hazard condition:

*some switch on a route has no position indication **and not** (the start signal of the route is restrictive).*

This can further be simplified into the following more intuitive one:

*some switch on a route has no position indication **and** the start signal of the route is permissive.*

Obviously, this hazard condition is likely to produce a hazard if it is implemented in the system, because if some switch has no position indication and the start signal of the route is permissive, when the train runs into the route, it will likely derail or roll over.

(2) If T_i describes a critical guard condition (i.e., the violation of it may jeopardize the safety), then **not** T_i **and** D_i will become a hazard condition. For instance, suppose

*(all switches in the route are in right position **and** the route is out of obstacles **and** no conflicting route is set) **and** the start signal of the route is permissive*

is a functional scenario, then the following hazard condition can be derived:

***not** (all switches on the route are in right position **and** the route is out of obstacle **and** no conflicting route is set) **and** the start signal of the route is permissive.*

It can further be simplified into:

***not** all switches in the route are in right position **and** the start signal of the route is permissive **or** **not** the route is out of obstacles **and** the start signal of the route is permissive **or** **not** no conflicting route is set **and** the start signal of the route is permissive,*

which implies three different kinds of hazards.

To apply these rules effectively, the relevant functional scenarios have to be selected manually based on the safety-related knowledge in the domain in general. The reason is that formal expressions may not make sense if they are not interpreted in the context of the related domain. What our method can help is to systematically and automatically derive a hazard condition after the related specific functional scenario is selected.

3.2 Hazard Condition-Based Testing

After deriving all possible hazard conditions, we need to analyze whether each hazard condition is really implemented into code. To this end, a *hazard condition-based testing* can be carried out.

Specifically, for each derived hazard condition, we generate some test data for the input variables that satisfy the test condition of the hazard condition. Then, we use the test data to run the corresponding program that is supposed to implement the specified functionality of the related process. After obtaining the result of the test, which is the output of the program, we can evaluate the corresponding "defining" condition of the hazard condition. If the defining condition is true, that implies the hazard is already implemented in the code.

Given the hazard condition T_i **and not** D_i where T_i is the test condition and **not** D_i is the defining condition, applying the above technique, we can generate a test data, say t, to satisfy T_i, and then use t as the input to execute the corresponding program. Suppose we get the result r, then we need to check whether the following condition is true:

$$T_i(t) \Rightarrow \textbf{not}\, D_i(r)$$

If the implication evaluates to true, that indicates the fact that the hazard is implemented in the code. For example, considering the hazard condition:

*some switch on a route has no position indication **and not** the start signal of the route is restrictive.*

Suppose it is formalized as

$$switch\_trail \textbf{ and not } signal\_restrictive,$$

we generate a test data "true" for the boolean variable *switch_trail*, and use it to run the corresponding program, say P. Assume we get the value "false" as the result for the boolean variable *signal_restrictive*, we then substitute this value for the variable in the hazard condition to check whether the following implication is true:

$$switch\_trail \Rightarrow \textbf{not } signal\_restrictive.$$

Obviously, this is true because *switch_trail* is true and ***not** signal_restrictive* is true, which means the hazard may happen. This indicates the existence of bugs in the implementation of the related process specification. The same practice can be applied to the other hazard conditions.

As far as test data generation from a hazard condition is concerned, we can treat the hazard condition as a "normal" functional scenario derived from a process specification, and then apply the test data generation criteria proposed in our previous publications [10–12]. Since there is no new discovery about this point in our research, we omit the detailed discussions for brevity.

4   Experience and Difficulties

In this section, we first describe our experience of using SOFL in our project, and then point out some difficulties we have faced. Some of the difficulties have already been resolved through expert consultation, while a few still need to be addressed in the future practice.

4.1   Experience

Our project is planned as a one-year project and our experience of using SOFL so far can be summarized as the following points:

(1) When writing the semi-formal and formal specifications for a process, organizing the post-condition as a disjunctive normal form can significantly help the analyst (i.e., the person who writes the specification) write the specification, achieve its good readability, and check its completeness. The reason is that each conjunctive clause in the disjunctive normal form clearly defines a relatively independent functional scenario, showing under what condition what output is expected.

We found that the way also offers us a clear guideline by which we can rather systematically think about what to write in the specification.

(2) The mechanism for decomposing a high level process into a low level CDFD for defining its functionality in detail is effective to help us formalize some functionally complex processes. In particular, when the formal description of the process functionality inevitably involves the sequential operations, the decomposition of the process into a CDFD is rather straightforward and helpful, because the CDFD notation offers comprehensible graphical representation of sequential operations, parallel operations, and some simple data flow loop structures. One important thing in conducting the decomposition, however, is to keep the consistency between the interface of the high level process and that of the CDFD resulted from the decomposition.

(3) We found that the combination of semi-formal specifications and formal specifications for our system is cost-effective. For some complex processes whose functionality description requires necessary repetition of applying other processes, writing a complete formal specification can be difficult and time-consuming. In this case, we keep the description semi-formal in which only the process signature is precisely defined while the pre- and post-conditions are described in natural language.

4.2 Difficulties

We have also encountered some difficulties in applying SOFL, which include the following aspects:

(1) SOFL does not allow the invocation of another process in the formal specification of a process in order to avoid semantic ambiguity. But this may cause a difficulty for the practitioners who have got used to programming style. How to properly do abstraction in the formal specification to avoid the necessity of calling another process is a challenge to industrial practitioners. To handle this challenge, we turn to SOFL explicit specification. An explicit specification of a process is an abstract program in which the normal program constructs, such as sequence, selection, iterations, and process invocations, can be used to form the program structure and the data types and logical available in the SOFL notation can be used to form conditions and/or statements. However, since the explicit specification involves considerable considerations on the design of algorithm, it may not be suitable for abstract description of process functionality. Another perhaps more balanced way is to use semi-formal statements to express the idea of using another process's functionality in the pre- or post-conditions of the process under specification.

(2) Another problem we have faced is that the formal specification may not be clear enough for the programmer to understand the whole story of the entire system. This will require the programmer to make creative efforts in designing the program structure and the necessary algorithms. To help attack this difficulty, during the process of writing the semi-formal specification, we try to describe the state transitions of each device, which is declared as a data store variable in our

specification, and to get the feedback from the domain expert to clarify the ambiguities and to improve the specification. That is, we take an evolutionary approach to finally complete the formal specification.

5 Related Work

There are some studies about formal methods in railway systems. Haxthausen and Peleska present an abstract algebraic specification and verification for railway signaling system with simple railway network module [13]. The SACEM system [14] used in the RER line in Paris is a successful case of B method. Matra (now is part of Siemens) uses B method in the designing of many similar railway control systems. One of the famous applications is line 14 of RATP (Paris Metro), it used B method to refine the requirement specifications and correct some requirement errors [15]. Zou et al. studies how to formalize and verify the SRS (System Requirement Specification) of CTCS-3 (Chinese Train Control System 3) [16]. HCSP (Hybrid Communicating Sequential Processes) is used to model each basic functional scenario and HHL(Hybrid Hoare Logic) is used to describe the system attributes, and whether the specific HCSP model satisfies the given HLL attributes is formally verified. They also studied how to transform Simulink figures into HCSP and use the HHL to verify HCSP model. The related research results have been applied successfully in the verification of CTCS-3 [17]. Horste et al. formalizes the functional requirements about the ETCS (European Train Control System) [18]. The Ansaldo STS project uses model checking technique to verify the RBC subsystem of ECTS [19]. Many Interlocking systems in lines belonging to RATP (Paris Metro) and NYTC (New York City Transit Authority) were also verified using a model checking tool from Prover technology [20].There have been several years when CASCO started to study and try on formal methods, for the last several years the research is mainly about formal design and verification of ZC subsystem [21, 22]. And from this year, formal modeling and verification techniques have been applied on the interlocking system.

   After several years' research before our current project using SOFL, we realized that the formal methods used in the cases mentioned above are quite difficult for practitioners in our company to use, and may not be able to deliver expected results in a short period of time. We also found that the main difficulty for developing a highly reliable and safe system lies in the requirements analysis and specification phases. Our experience so far suggests that SOFL has a much better capability to help us effectively carry out requirements analysis and specification construction, and benefit the subsequent activities in design, coding, testing, and verification of the system.

6 Conclusion and Future Work

We discussed how the SOFL specification language and its three-step approach to writing formal specifications can be applied to an interlocking system in our company. The project is planned for one year and still ongoing. Currently, we have finished the semi-formal specification and part of the formal specification during which many ill-defined or incomplete requirements in natural language were identified. We are continuing the construction of the formal specification and the derivation of hazard conditions until the end of the project.

After the current project, we will try to carry out specification-based and hazard condition-based testing and verification for the implementation. We will further investigate how adequate test data can be generated from the specification and hazard conditions, and how bugs can be effectively uncovered. If our current project succeeds in terms of providing sufficient benefits or profits to our company, we will extend our experience and practice to more railway signaling systems in the future.

Acknowledgment. This work was supported by CASCO. Shaoying Liu was also partly supported by JSPS KAKENHI grant Number 26240008.

References

1. Boehm, B.W., Basili, V.R.: Software defect reduction top 10 list. IEEE Comput. **34**(1), 135–137 (2001)
2. Bowen, J., Stavridou, V.: Safety-critical methods and systems, formal standards. Softw. Eng. J. **8**(4), 189–209 (1993)
3. Bjørner, D., Jones, C.B. (eds.): The Vienna Development Method: The Meta-Language. LNCS, vol. 61. Springer, Heidelberg (1978). doi:10.1007/3-540-08766-4
4. Diller, A.: Z: an introduction to formal methods 23(9), 10–23 (1990). Wiley
5. Abrial, J.-R.: Modeling in Event-B System and Software Engineering. Cambridge University Press, Cambridge (2010), ISBN-13 978-0-521-89556-9
6. Efficient Development of Safe Railway Applications Software with EN 50128 Objectives Using SCADE Suite, 3rd edn.. Esterel Technologies, SA (2012)
7. Liu, S.: Formal engineering for industrial software development using the SOFL method. Springer, Heidelberg (2004), ISBN 3-540-20602-7
8. Halbwachs, N., Lagnier, F., Ratel, C.: Programming and verifying real-time systems by means of the synchronous data-flow language LUSTR. IEEE Trans. Softw. Eng. **18**(9), 785–793 (1992)
9. Liu, S., Chen, Y., Nagoya, F., McDermid, J.A.: Formal specification-based inspection for verification of programs. IEEE Trans. Softw. Eng. **38**(5), 1100–1122 (2012)
10. Liu, S., Chen, Y.: A relation-based method combining functional and structural testing for test case generation. J. Syst. Softw. **81**(2), 234–248 (2008)
11. Liu, S., Nakajima, S.: A decompositional approach to automatic test case generation based on formal specifications. In: 4th IEEE International Conference on Secure Software Integration and Reliability Improvement, Singapore, 9–11 June, pp. 147–155 (2010)
12. Liu, S., Nakajima, S: A "Vibration" method for automatically generating test cases based on formal specifications. In: 18th Asia Pacific Conference on Software Engineering (APSEC 2011), 5–8 December, pp. 73–80. IEEE CS Press, VNU-HCM, Vietnam (2011)
13. Haxthausen, A.E., Peleska, J.: Formal development and verification of a distributed railway control system. IEEE Trans. Softw. Eng. **26**(8), 369–387 (2000)

14. DaSilva, C., Dehbonei, B., Mejia, F.: Formal specification in the development of industrial applications: subway speed control system. In: IFIP Conference on Formal Description Techniques for Distributed Systems and Communication Protocols (FORTE), Perros-Guirec, France, 13–16 October, pp. 199–213 (1992)
15. Behm, P., Benoit, P., Faivre, A., Meynadier, J.-M.: Météor: a successful application of B in a large project. In: Wing, Jeannette M., Woodcock, J., Davies, J. (eds.) FM 1999. LNCS, vol. 1708, pp. 369–387. Springer, Heidelberg (1999). doi:10.1007/3-540-48119-2_22
16. Zou, L., Lv, J., Wang, S., Zhan, N., Tang, T., Yuan, L., Liu, Yu.: Verifying Chinese train control system under a combined scenario by theorem proving. In: Cohen, E., Rybalchenko, A. (eds.) VSTTE 2013. LNCS, vol. 8164, pp. 262–280. Springer, Heidelberg (2014). doi:10.1007/978-3-642-54108-7_14
17. Zou, L., Zhan, N., Franzle, M., Qin, S.: Verifying simulink diagrams via a hybrid hoare logic pover. In: International Conference on Embedded Software (EMSOFT), Montreal, QC, 29 September 2013–4 October 2013, pp. 1–10 (2013)
18. Horste, M., Hungar, A., Schnieder, E.: Modelling functionality of train control systems using petri nets. In: FM-RAIL-BOK Workshop, Madrid, Spain, September 23–24, 2013, pp. 46–50 (2013)
19. Cimatti, A., Corvino, R., Lazzaro, A., Narasamdya, I., Rizzo, T., Roveri, M., Sanseviero, A., Tchaltsev, A.: Formal verification and validation of ERTMS industrial railway train spacing system. In: Madhusudan, P., Seshia, Sanjit A. (eds.) CAV 2012. LNCS, vol. 7358, pp. 378–393. Springer, Heidelberg (2012). doi:10.1007/978-3-642-31424-7_29
20. Study cases of Prover technology, http://www.prover.com/company/casestudies/
21. Qian, J., Liu, J., Chen, X., Sun, J.: Formal design and verification of zone controller. In: 21st Asia-Pacific Conference on Software Engineering (APSEC 2014), 1–4 December 2014, pp. 375–382. IEEE CS Press, Jeju (2014)
22. Qian, J., Liu, J., Chen, X., Sun, J.: Modeling and verification of zone controller: the SCADE experience in china's railway systems. In: ICSE Workshop on Complex Faults and Failures in Large Software Systems (COUFLESS), 23 May 2015, pp. 48–54. IEEE, Florence (2015)

Model Checking

SMT-based Bounded Model Checking
for Cooperative Software
with a Deterministic Scheduler

Haitao Zhang[(⊠)] and Yonggang Lu

School of Information Science and Engineering, Lanzhou University,
Lanzhou 730000, China
{htzhang,ylu}@lzu.edu.cn

Abstract. The cooperative software, such as OSEK/VDX multi-tasks software and SystemC multi-threaded software, has been widely applied in the embedded system field. However, due to the flexible scheduling and complex cooperations between tasks or threads, the reliability of developed software is really difficult to be ensured by testing technique. To overcome this problem, model checking technique as a potential solution has attracted great attention in software industry. Recently, many model checking based methods have already been proposed and successfully applied in the verification of cooperative software, but most of them focus on the *non-deterministic* scheduler based cooperative software such as SystemC. The verification of *deterministic* scheduler based cooperative software is still at preliminary stage. In this paper, we propose an approach to verify this type of cooperative software. In our work, in order to make the proposed approach more general, the famous OSEK/VDX multi-tasks application is chosen as our target system. Furthermore, as to make the proposed approach more scalable, the advanced SMT-based bounded model checking is applied to carry out verification. We have investigated the effectiveness of our approach based on a series of experiments. The experiment results indicate that our approach can efficiently verify the cooperative software with a *deterministic* scheduler.

1 Introduction

The cooperative software, such as OSEK/VDX [29] and SystemC [1], has been widely applied in the embedded system field. In such software, the executions of tasks/threads are usually conducted by a scheduler, and tasks/threads can invoke application interfaces (APIs) or primitive functions to interact with each other via scheduler. Moreover, the invoked APIs and primitive functions will dynamically change the scheduling of tasks/threads. Compared with general concurrent software, it is more difficult to ensure the reliability of cooperative software using testing technique [8], because of flexible scheduling and complex cooperations between tasks/threads. In order to overcome this problem, model checking technique [2,17–19,22,33] as a potential solution has attracted great attention in software industry.

© Springer International Publishing AG 2017
S. Liu et al. (Eds.): SOFL+MSVL 2016, LNCS 10189, pp. 181–200, 2017.
DOI: 10.1007/978-3-319-57708-1_11

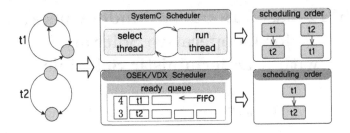

Fig. 1. Non-deterministic scheduler and deterministic scheduler.

Recently, for the *non-deterministic* scheduler based cooperative software, many model checking based methods have already been proposed [4,11,14,32] and successfully applied to verify practical programs such as SystemC multi-threaded programs. In these existing methods, since running thread cannot be explicitly fixed that is arbitrarily selected by scheduler, all of the possible cooperative states and interleavings of threads are checked the verification stage. For example, as shown in Fig. 1, if SystemC scheduler is used to dispatch threads t1 and t2, there exist two possible scheduling orders, one is (t1, t2), and the other is (t2, t1). In the verification stage, these two possible scheduling order will be verified by existing methods. Moreover, in order to make verification more explicit or accurate, in some works such as papers [4,11], scheduler are used to determine runnable threads and cooperative states for omitting the unnecessary verification states. Unfortunately, these existing methods are not suitable to verify the cooperative software with a deterministic scheduler such as OSEK/VDX multi-tasks application. This is because, in such cooperative software, the running task can be explicitly fixed by deterministic scheduler. For example, as depicted in Fig. 1, we assume that tasks t1 and t2 are currently in the ready queue and the priority of task t1 is higher than task t2. If OSEK/VDX scheduler is used to dispatch these two tasks, there just exist one scheduling orders that is (t1, t2). If we directly use existing methods to verify this type of cooperative software, a lot of unnecessary interleavings of takes/threads will be checked in the verification stage (the interleavings checked in the verification stage are larger than the realistic interleavings in deterministic scheduler based cooperative software). Furthermore, due to the unnecessary interleavings, the existing methods will often find a spurious bug which makes verification inaccurate. In order to accurately verify the deterministic scheduler based cooperative software using model checking technique, in this paper we describe and develop a new approach based on our previous work [25].

In our work, in order to make the proposed approach more general, the famous OSEK/VDX multi-tasks application is chosen as our target system. Furthermore, as to make the proposed approach more scalable, the advanced SMT-based bounded model checking is applied to carry out verification.

In OSEK/VDX application, tasks are concurrently executed under the scheduling of OSEK/VDX OS (a deterministic scheduler called static priority scheduler is adopted by OSEK/VDX OS to dispatch tasksm, in which a ready queue is used to manage the scheduling order of tasks). Moreover, tasks within application can invoke APIs to change the scheduling order and interact with each other, e.g., activate a task. In order to apply BMC to efficiently check an OSEK/VDX application, there are some challenges that should be addressed, e.g., how to deal with the APIs invoked from tasks, and how to construct an explicit transition system to reflect the executions of the application. In our approach, we develop an execution path generator (EPG) as intermediate translator to construct corresponding transition system for the target application. In EPG, an embedded OS model that conforms to OSEK/VDX standard is used to dispatch tasks and respond to the invoked APIs. In addition, several optimization strategies and an available tool named osek-bmc[1] are also implemented in our work.

There are two advantages in our approach. (*i*) EPG: we can construct an accurate transition system based on the generated execution paths since OS model is employed to explicitly determine the running task during generating execution paths, and moreover, the behaviors of OS model will not be taken into the verification because the OS model is embedded in the checking algorithm level (the idea on embedding scheduler model in checking algorithm benefits from papers [4,31]). (*ii*) SMT-based BMC: our approach can verify the complex programs, since SMT-based BMC can handle a large number of states. The contribution of the paper is that it can be considered as a guideline to verify other types of deterministic scheduler based cooperative software using SMT-based BMC technique.

To evaluate the efficiency of our approach, we have conducted a series of experiments based on the implemented tool. In the experiments, the related methods including Spin-based checking method [26] and Kratos [6] are considered as composition objects. Based on the experiment results, we find that our approach can efficiently verify the deterministic scheduler based OSEK/VDX applications.

Outline. The rest of the paper is structured as follows. The background of OSEK/VDX is presented in Sect. 2. Based on the execution characteristics of OSEK/VDX applications, the checking approach is shown in Sect. 3. As to evaluate our approach, some experiments are carried out in Sect. 5. The related work are discussed in Sect. 6. Conclusion and future work are placed in Sect. 7.

2 Background of OSEK/VDX

2.1 OSEK/VDX OS

OSEK/VDX, a standard of automobile OS, has been widely adopted by many automobile manufacturers to develop a vehicle-mounted OS, such as BMW, Opel, and Volkswagen. In general, as shown in Fig. 2, an OSEK/VDX OS consists of three primary process modules, scheduler module, synchronization event

---

[1] osek-bmc homepage: http://www.jaist.ac.jp/~s1220209/osek-bmc.htm.

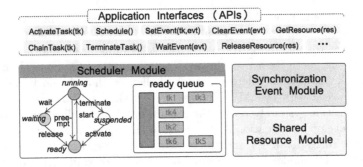

Fig. 2. The structure of OSEK/VDX OS.

module and shared resource module. In addition, these process modules also provide many useful APIs for applications to change the scheduling order of tasks, realize synchronous executions, and access shared resources. The process modules of OSEK/VDX OS and corresponding APIs are as follow.

Scheduler Module. OSEK/VDX OS can process two types of tasks, basic task and extended task. The states of a basic task consist of *running* state, *suspended* state, and *ready* state. Compared with basic task, the extended task can hold synchronization events and has an unique state called *waiting* state (the state transitions of basic task and extended task are shown in Fig. 2). In the scheduling process, the *static priority scheduling policy* with non-preemptive and full-preemptive strategies is adopted by scheduler to conduct the executions of tasks. Moreover, as shown in Fig. 2, scheduler manages a ready queue to indicate the scheduling order of tasks (the head task in the ready queue will be dispatched to executed by scheduler when *running* task is idle). Besides, scheduler can respond to four APIs (*TerminateTask*, *ActivateTask*, *ChainTask*, and *Schedule*) that can be invoked by tasks to switch task states. For instance, if the API *ActivateTask*(tk_1) is invoked by running task, then scheduler will move the activated task tk_1 from *suspended* state to *ready* state.

Event Process Module. In the event process module, OSEK/VDX OS provides a synchronization mechanism for implementing synchronous executions between tasks. Especially, only extended tasks can hold a definite number of events, and events are the criteria for the switching of task states from *running* state to *waiting* state or from *waiting* state to *ready* state. There are four APIs (*SetEvent*, *WaitEvent*, *ClearEvent*, and *GetEvent*) that can be responded by event process module, and tasks can invoke these APIs to implement the synchronous executions. E.g., when the running task tk_1 waits for the event evt_1 using API *WaitEvent*(evt_1), task tk_1 cannot continue until the event evt_1 is set by other tasks using API *SetEvent*(tk_1,evt_1).

Resources Process Module. The priority inversion and deadlock are two typical problems of common synchronization mechanism when several tasks access the same shared resource with different priorities. In order to avoid these two problems, OSEK/VDX OS adopts the *Priority Ceiling Protocol* [3] to coordinate the behaviors of accessing shared resources in the resource process module. The resource process module supports two APIs (*GetResource* and *ReleaseResource*) for tasks, and tasks can invoke these two APIs to construct a critical section for accessing a shared resource.

2.2 Motivating Application and Discussion

As shown in Fig. 3, an application developed based on OSEK/VDX OS consists of two files, one is source file, and the other is configuration file. The source file, which can be developed by C programming language, is used to present the concrete behaviors of the application. The configuration file is used to define tasks, events, and resources.

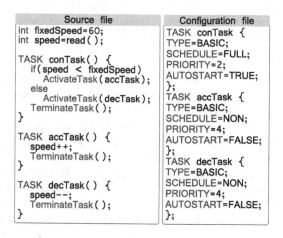

Fig. 3. The motivating application.

2.2.1 Motivating Application

As to clearly comprehend the execution characteristics of OSEK/VDX applications, an example is discussed in this part. In the simple example shown in Fig. 3, since only the attribute AUTOSTART[2] of *conTask* is set to be TRUE, *conTask* will be firstly moved to *running* state by scheduler and then *conTask* is executed. There are two branches in *conTask*, one is to activate *accTask*, and the other is to activate *decTask* (if a task is activated, scheduler will move the task from *suspended* state to *ready* state, and the task is placed in the corresponding queue). If the API *ActivateTask(accTask)* is invoked by *conTask*, scheduler will be loaded to responds to the API. For this moment, the context switch of tasks happens, since the priority of *accTask* is higher than *conTask* and the attribute

---

[2] AUTOSTART: if the attribute AUTOSTART of a task is set to be TRUE, the task starts from *ready* state in the initial state. Otherwise, the task starts from *suspended* state.

SCHEDULE[3] of *conTask* is set to be FULL. Therefore, scheduler will move *conTask* to *ready* state and dispatch *accTask* to *running* state. In this branch, the task execution sequence is *conTask*, *accTask*, *conTask* (the API *TerminateTask*() is used to terminate the executions of a task, and the terminated task will be moved from *running* state to *suspended* state by scheduler. If the *running* task is terminated, scheduler will dispatch the head task in the ready queue to run). Correspondingly, if the API *ActivateTask(decTask)* is invoked by *conTask*, the task execution sequence is *conTask*, *decTask*, *conTask* in the other branch.

Based on the executions of the simple application, we can find the following execution characteristics.

- Tasks within an application are concurrently executed based on the scheduling of OSEK/VDX OS, and the running task can be explicitly determined by OSEK/VDX scheduler.
- Tasks can invoke APIs to dynamically change the states of tasks, and the changed task states will affect the scheduling order of tasks.

2.2.2   Discussion

There are several methods that can be considered to check the OSEK/VDX applications using existing model checkers, e.g., we can use the model checker for concurrent software to check OSEK/VDX applications. As to accurately check an OSEK/VDX application using the model checker for concurrent software, all of the tasks within the application can be regarded as concurrent processes, and we can use some assistant statements to simulate the real executions of the application. However, there are some disadvantages in this method. E.g., (*i*) a lot of assistant statements such as branches will be verified. (*ii*) As to simulate the executions of the application, we should clearly know the states of tasks. Actually, for a complex application, it is difficult to clearly detect the states of tasks due to the intricate scheduling behaviours of OSEK/VDX scheduler and dynamic switches of task state caused by invoked APIs. Furthermore, for a general application, tasks also can invoke APIs to synchronously execute and access shared resources. It will significantly increase the checking complexity.

As to easily check an OSEK/VDX application using the model checker for concurrent software, the efficient way is to insert an OS model such as scheduler model in the constructed application model for responding to the invoked APIs and conducting the executions of application (where, the constructed checking model is a combination of application model and OS model). Nonetheless, in this method the states corresponding to the OS model will be checked, since the OS model is a part of constructed model. Moreover, it will increase the number of states in the checking process, especially the *state space explosion* will happen if the checked application invokes a lot of APIs (our experiments shown

---

[3] SCHEDULE: if the attribute SCHEDULE of a task is set to be FULL, the task can be preempted by higher priority tasks. Otherwise, the task will not leave *running* state until the API *TerminateTask*, *ChainTask* or *Schedule* is invoked, or waits for a synchronization event.

in Sect. 4.1 have proved it). In this paper, we present an alternative approach that can accurately and efficiently check OSEK/VDX applications using SMT-based BMC, which will be demonstrated in the next section.

3   The Checking Approach for OSEK/VDX Applications

3.1   The Overview of Checking Approach

The key processes of our approach are shown in Fig. 4. If our approach receives an OSEK/VDX application, it firstly calls C Intermediate Language (CIL) [24] to interpret the behaviours of tasks written in complex C programming language into the simple `goto` program. In the second step, to accurately construct a transition system, we develop an execution path generator (EPG) to generate all of the possible execution paths for the given application. In EPG, the path generator is used to produce execution paths in symbolic way according to the given loop bound and depth bound. The OS model corresponding to the OSEK/VDX OS standard is employed to determine running task and respond to the invoked APIs when meeting an API in the process of constructing an execution path (Note that, the states of OS model will not be poured into execution paths, since OS model is embedded in EPG to perform scheduling behaviours). Then, the transition system corresponding to the target application will be constructed based on the generated execution paths. Finally, the SMT solver Z3 [30] is used to check whether the constructed transition system satisfies a given property.

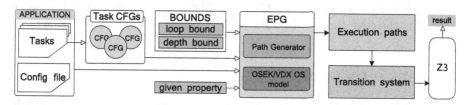

Fig. 4. The key processes of checking approach.

3.2   Task CFG

In the development of OSEK/VDX applications, developers can implement an application using C programming language. However, C code is often too complex to analyze in the static analysis. To automatically sequentialize an application developed in C programming language, like model checker CBMC [20], the application is firstly interpreted into the simple `goto` program based on the CIL, where complex structures such as `loops` and `structs` in C code are interpreted as branch statements with `goto` labels and general variables. Then, the behaviours of all tasks within the application are extracted and constructed as corresponding CFGs. The description of task CFG has been represented in Definition 1. For example, as shown in Fig. 5, we will construct three CFGs to represent each task included in motivating application.

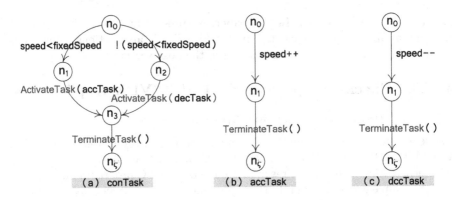

Fig. 5. CFGs of tasks shown in motivating application.

Definition 1: The CFG of a task is a tuple $\Omega^{tid} = (N^{tid}, n_0^{tid}, n_\varsigma^{tid}, \Sigma^{tid}, R^{tid}, V^{tid}, L^{tid})$. Where, tid is the identifier of tasks. N^{tid} is the set of nodes, n_0^{tid} is the start node, n_ς^{tid} is the end node. Σ^{tid} is the set of statements of task tid, the expression of a statement $\alpha \in \Sigma$ is as follows:

$$\alpha ::= condition \mid assignment \mid goto \mid assertion \mid API$$

$R \subseteq N^{tid} \times N^{tid}$ is the set of edges expressing a directed graph. $V^{tid} = V_{global} \cup V_{local}^{tid}$ is the set of variables. $L^{tid} : R^{tid} \rightarrow \Sigma^{tid}$ is the labelling function from edge $(n, n') \in R^{tid}$ to a statement $\alpha \in \Sigma^{tid}$, and $L^{tid}(n, n')$ denotes the statement α mapped in the edge (n, n'), where n, $n' \in N^{tid}$ and n' is the successor node of n.

3.3   OSEK/VDX OS Model

According to OSEK/VDX OS specification, we construct an OS model which is a combination of schedule model, event process model, and resource process model, as shown in Fig. 6. The definition of OSEK/VDX OS model is stated below.

Definition 2: The OS model is a tuple $\mathcal{O} = (N, n_0, n_\varsigma, R, F, L, D)$. Where N is the set of nodes, n_0 is the start node, n_ς is the end node. $R \subseteq N \times N$ is the set of edges expressing a directed acyclic graph (DAG). F is the set of functions defined in the OSEK/VDX OS specification. $L : R \rightarrow F$ is the labelling function from edge $(n, n') \in R$ to a function $\tau \in F$. $D = \{runTask, readyQueue, suspendList, waitList, evtBitArray, resAccessList\}$ is the set of data structures defined in the OSEK/VDX OS specification.

In D of OS model, $runTask$ which is a variable is used to store the tid of $running$ task (tid is task identifier). Since several tasks can share a same priority in the OSEK/VDX OS, the $readyQueue$ which is composed of queues with different priorities is used to store the $tids$ of tasks in the $ready$ state.

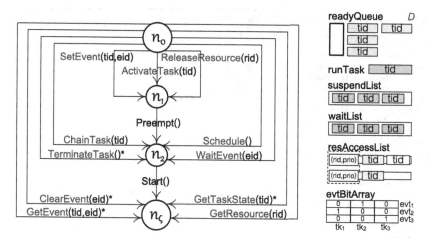

Fig. 6. OSEK/VDX OS model.

The data structures *suspendList* and *waitList* are used to store the *tids* of tasks in the *suspended* state and *waiting* state respectively. *evtBitArray* which is a matrix is used to store the event states of extended tasks (*eid* is event identifier). *resAccessList* which is composed of lists is used to indicate the state of resources accessed by tasks (*rid* is resource identifier). Note that, in the OS model the execution path ϖ for responding to an API is a function sequence which starts from node n_0 and ends at node n_ς, and the functions within ϖ will perform the concrete operations on the data structure D if OS model is employed to respond to an API.

3.4   EPG and Transition System

To verify a system using BMC, the challenge is how to use a transition system to reflect the executions of the target system. Based on the example shown in Fig. 3, we have found that the different APIs in different branches will lead to different task execution sequences, and the context switch of tasks will happen when an API is invoked. We have tried several ways to construct a transition system for OSEK/VDX application. Finally, we find that the best way is to explore the execution paths for constructing the transition system, because the execution trace of tasks in an execution path can be explicitly decided based on the scheduling of OS model. Based on this idea, we have developed an EPG as intermediate translator to generate the execution paths, the key processes of EPG are as follow,

p1. construct an execution path along the trace of *running* task CFG, and map the explored statement in the execution path.

p2. if meet a branches, select one branch to continue, and push the other branch and current OS data into `stack`.

Algorithm 1. Execution Paths Generator

Input: Tasks CFGs, configuration file of application
Output: Execution paths $\pi_1, \pi_2, \cdots$
1: initialize data structure set D within OS model according to application config. file
2: $pcs := [n_0^1, \ldots, n_0^m]$, where m is the number of tasks
3: $i := 0$, where i is the index of state of execution path
4: $j := 1$, where j is the index of execution paths
5: execute OS model function $Start()$ to compute $runTask$
6: **if** $runTask = null$ **then**
7:    goto 30
8: **end if**
9: $tid := tid$ of $running$ task
10: $\Delta := \{(n, n') \in CFG^{tid} | n = pcs[tid]\}$
11: $(n, n') :=$ one of the element of Δ
12: $\Delta := \Delta \setminus \{(n, n')\}$
13: **if** $|\Delta| > 0$ **then**
14:    $D \to osd$, the operator "$\to$" represents mapping the data within D into osd
15:    **for all** $(n, n') \in \Delta$ **do**
16:       $elem := (pcs, osd, i, (n, n'))$, $stack.push(elem)$
17:    **end for**
18: **end if**
19: **if** $L^{tid}(n, n')$ **is an API then**
20:    **if** $L^{tid}(n, n')$ **is** $TerminateTask()$ **then**
21:       $pcs[tid] :=$ the start node of task tid
22:    **end if**
23:    **compute the responding trace** ϖ **in OS model**
24:    **call corresponding functions within** ϖ **to compute** D **within OS model**
25: **end if**
26: $L^{tid}(n, n') \mapsto \langle s_i, s_{i+1}\rangle$, the operator "$\mapsto$" represents mapping a task statement in the edge $\langle s_i, s_{i+1}\rangle$ of execution path π_j
27: $i++$
28: update $pcs[tid]$ with target node n' of edge (n, n')
29: goto 6
30: **if** $stack.empty() = true$ **then**
31:    $output(\pi_j)$
32:    goto end
33: **end if**
34: $output(\pi_j)$
35: $(pcs, osd, i, (n, n')) := stack.pop()$
36: $\pi_{sub} := GetSubpath(\pi_j, i)$
37: $j++$
38: $\pi_j := \pi_{sub}$
39: $osd \to D$, the operator "$\to$" represents mapping the values within osd into D of OS model
40: $tid := runTask$ of D within OS model
41: goto 19
42: **return**

p3. if meet an API, call OS model to respond to the API and compute the *running* task. If *running* task is idle, pop an element from **stack** to construct the next execution path; otherwise, repeat p1, p2 and p3 until **stack** is empty.

The details of EPG are shown in Algorithm 1. In Algorithm 1, the element of stack is a tuple $elem = (pcs, osd, i, (n, n'))$, where pcs which is an array is used to record the current position of task CFGs, osd which is the set of values is used to record the data within D, i which is variable is used to record the position of branches, (n, n') is one of the branches. Since stack is used to construct the execution paths, the execution path π_j and the next execution path π_{j+1} will hold the same sub-path which starts from initial state and ends at the position of branch popped from stack. The function $GetSubpath(\pi_j, i)$ is used to extract the same sub-path from the execution path π_j for constructing the next execution path π_{j+1}. Δ which is a set is used to store the edges whose previous node n is equal to the current position of *running* task.

Based on the EPG, all of the execution paths with respect to the target application can be generated. Where, a generated execution path π is the task statement sequence $\pi = s_0 \xrightarrow{a} s_1 \xrightarrow{a} s_2 \xrightarrow{a} s_3 \xrightarrow{a} \cdots$, s is the state of execution path, which consists of the values of the global variables and local variables declared in the application. E.g., for the simple cruise control application, EPG will generate two execution paths. There are some advantages in EPG, (*i*) all of the execution paths can be generated, (*ii*) we can construct an accurate transition system based on the generated execution paths since the embedded OS is used to compute the running task in the process of generating an execution path, (*iii*) the behaviors of OS model will not be involved in the execution path since it is a component of EPG.

Based on the generated execution paths, we can construct an accurate transition system for the target application. Here, we use function $[\![\pi_j]\!]$ to convert an outputted execution path π_j into CNF expression in SMT-LIB format. The CNF expression for an execution path π_j is defined in the formula (1), where $\mathcal{L}\langle s_i, s_{i+1}\rangle$ represents a task statement α mapped in the edge $\langle s_i, s_{i+1}\rangle$ of execution path π_j. According to the formula (1), we can obtain the transition system $[\![M]\!]$ when translating all of the execution paths into CNF expression. The expression of transition system $[\![M]\!]$ is defined in the formula (2), where $I(s_0)$ which is the initial function is used to initialize each variable $v \in \bigcup V^{tid}$ in the initial state, w is the number of execution paths.

$$[\![\pi_j]\!] := \bigwedge_{i=0}^{|\pi_j|-1} [\![\mathcal{L}\langle s_i, s_{i+1}\rangle]\!] \tag{1}$$

$$[\![M]\!] := I(s_0) \wedge \bigvee_{j=1}^{w} (\bigwedge_{i=0}^{|\pi_j|-1} [\![\mathcal{L}\langle s_i, s_{i+1}\rangle]\!]) \tag{2}$$

3.5   Bounds

Based on the EPG, we can construct a transition system for a given application. However, there is a limitation in EPG, that is, EPG cannot terminate its executions if the given application contains infinite execution paths or loops. As to terminate the executions of EPG, two types of bounds are considered in our approach.

Depth Bound. In OSEK/VDX applications, tasks can invoke the API *ActivateTask(tid)* or *ChainTask(tid)* to activate a terminated task. It will possibly result in an infinite execution path in an application if two tasks within application mutually activate each other. For this type of applications, our approach provides a depth bound to limit the depth of infinite execution paths.

Loop Bound. In our approach, the computation of variables is performed by the back-end solver Z3 rather than EPG. Thus, in the process of constructing

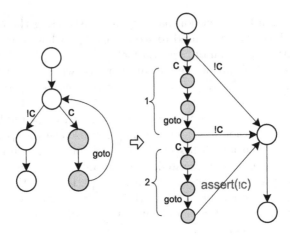

Fig. 7. The unfolding processes for loops, where loop bound is set to 2.

execution paths, the loop-condition cannot be decided by EPG. In order to terminate the execution of EPG and avoid the redundant translations of loops to be translated into the transition system, as shown in Fig. 7, like other bounded model checkers such as CBMC [16], a loop bound is provided. Especially, our approach also can judge whether a loop has been unfolded enough or not in the verification, if not, the loop will be reported.

3.6 Given Property

Based on the EPG and bounds, we can construct a transition system for the given application which contains infinite execution paths and loops. In this part, we will discuss what kinds of given properties can be checked by our approach.

Variable Property. In the practical checking process, we usually use assertion statements to check an interesting variable declared in the application. Based on the expression of transition system, we can find that all of the executions of target application have been translated into the transition system. Thus, our approach can be used to check variable property using assertion statement.

LTL Property. In addition to assertions, the given property which holds temporal operators is frequently used to check an application. For instance, we want to check whether the value of a variable will be changed to be zero in the future. To check such type of property, the property specified in Linear Temporal Logic (LTL) can be accepted by our tool. The conjunctive expression ψ of translation system and given property f specified in LTL is defined in the formula (3), where k is the state number of the longest execution path. The details about how to use BMC to check LTL property have been stated in the paper [7].

$$[\![\psi_k]\!] := I(s_0) \wedge \bigvee_{j=1}^{w} (\bigwedge_{i=0}^{|\pi_j|-1} [\![\mathcal{L}\langle s_i, s_{i+1}\rangle]\!]) \wedge \neg f_k \tag{3}$$

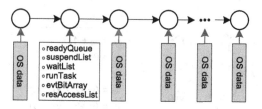

Fig. 8. Mapping OS data into path states.

OS Data Property. When an application runs on the OSEK/VDX OS, it is difficult to judge the execution situations of the application, since the executions of OSEK/VDX applications are conducted by the scheduler, and tasks within application can invoke APIs to synchronously execute and access shared resources. As to clearly detect the execution situations of an application, the states of tasks, events, and resources are often considered as a checking point. To check this type of property (which is named as OS data property in our paper), the transition system should hold the data within D of OS model. In our approach, as shown in Fig. 8, the OS data is mapped into each state of execution paths by EPG when constructing execution paths. Based on the mapping process, the OS data property can be checked by our tool, e.g., we can check whether the running task will be moved into ready queue after $ActivateTask(tid)$ is invoked.

4 Optimization of Checking Approach

4.1 Reduction of Execution Paths

Based on the given example shown in Fig. 3, we have found that the different APIs in different branches will lead to different task execution sequences. Therefore, as to accurately construct the transition system, we have to explore all of the execution paths. However, if the target application holds a lot of branches, it will slow down the performance of our approach. Actually, for the general branches which do not hold the APIs, we do not need to explore these branches in the process of constructing execution paths. In our approach, as shown in Fig. 9, in order to reduce the number of execution paths, we use *static single assignment* (SSA) form [12] to combine the branches which do not hold APIs.

4.2 Acceleration of Bug Detection

To quickly detect bugs from target applications according to the given properties, two acceleration strategies are proposed in our approach.

The first strategy named *assert-guided* is applied in the process of constructing execution paths. As shown in the left side of Fig. 10, the right-hand branch within a task CFG holds an assertion statement. In our approach, the right-hand branch will be firstly selected by EPG to generate execution paths. Based on this process, in the verification stage, the assertion will be checked in advance.

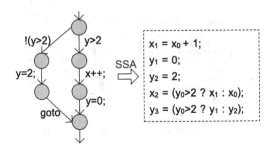

Fig. 9. The SSA form of branches

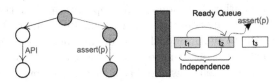

Fig. 10. Assert-guided and scheduling-accelerated strategies for bug detection.

The second strategy named *scheduling-accelerated* is applied in the scheduling queue. If two tasks in the ready queue are independent, we will swap the execution order of these two tasks in order to make the task which holds the assertion statement to be firstly executed, as shown in the right side of Fig. 10. This strategy benefits from the partial order reduction (POR) [10]. However, compared with the general POR technique, the APIs and priorities of tasks should be considered in the swap process, because APIs and priority will affect the scheduling order of tasks. We have summarized the swap condition based on some examples, the swap condition is: if two adjacent tasks locating at the same priority-queue are independent and just hold the APIs which will not lead to the rescheduling point (the APIs have been labelled with '*' in OS model), the execution order of these two tasks can be swapped in the scheduling queue.

4.3   Non-deterministic Input

In the OSEK/VDX application, tasks often get a value from a sensor. However, it is difficult to determine the values inputted from sensors in the verification, since the values are usually in some ranges. In our approach, we can easily implement the non-deterministic inputs, because the advanced SMT solver is used to

```
x = sensor value (0,10);        (x > 0)∧(x < 10)∧
y = x² - 2x + 1;          ⟹     (y = x² - 2x + 1)∧
assert(!(y > 0));               (y > 0)
```

Fig. 11. The non-deterministic inputs and verification.

perform the verification. For example, as shown in Fig. 11, we can translate the program into CNF formulae, and then employ Z3 to solve the program.

5   Experiment and Evaluation

To evaluate our approach, we have conducted many experiments using the implemented tool osek-bmc. In the experiments, related methods including Spin-based checking method and Kratos [6] are considered as comparison objects. All of the experiments are conducted on the Intel Core(TM)i7-3770 CPU with 32 G RAM, and we set the time limit and memory limit to 600 s and 1 GB respectively. In the result Tables 1 and 2, #t is the number of tasks, #l is the number of loops with APIs, #s is the number of explored transitions. " Mb" and "time" are the memory and time consumptions measured in Mbyte seconds, respectively.

5.1   Comparison to Spin-Based Checking Method

As to accurately check OSEK/VDX applications using Spin [23], we developed an OSEK/VDX OS model with promela, and the developed OS model as a special process is inserted into checking model to respond to the invoked APIs and conduct the executions of tasks (where, all of the tasks within the application and OS model are regarded as the process type). Moreover, channel is employed to simulate the interactive behaviors between OS model and application model. In this part, we will evaluate the checking performance between Spin-based checking method and our approach. All of the experiment results have been listed in Table 1. In the shown experiments, we investigated three aspects including task number, API number, and loop number. Note that, in the experiments the jSpin is selected as comparison object, and the "C complier" is configured to "-DVECTORSZ = 16384 -DBITSTATE", the max depth is set to "20,000,000".

There are some noticeable results in the Table 1. In all of the conducted experiments, Spin-based checking method will check more states than osek-bmc. Moreover, if we increase the task number (lines 1–4) and APIs number (lines 5–8), Spin will run out of memory and time (line 4 and 8). Compared with Spin-based checking method, our approach can successfully check these examples with lesser states, and spends lower cost (time and memory) than Spin. It is easy to explain why our approach is excellent in the verification. In Spin-based checking method, since the OS model is a part of constructed checking model, all of the states with respect to both tasks and OS model will be stored in the memory in the checking process. In addition, Spin will not only check the behaviors of tasks but also verify the OS model behaviors. In contrast with Spin-based checking method, (i) in our approach the OS model is embedded in the EPG to conduct the executions of application, that is, the executions of OS model will not be taken into the verification, (ii) our approach just puts one execution path in the memory when checking an application, and (iii) the advanced SMT solver is employed to check obtained transition system. These efforts make our approach much faster than Spin on handling the same application.

Table 1. Spin-based checking method VS our approach (`osek-bmc`)

Benchmark	Size				Spin				osek-bmc			
	#t	#l	Loop bound	#API	#s	Mb	Time(s)	Result	#s	Mb	Time(s)	Result
1 passCnt1	4	0	-	4	480	755	0.19	sat	18	2.13	0.093	sat
2 passCnt2	10	0	-	10	137225	768	3.76	sat	46	2.13	0.097	sat
3 passCnt3_bug	15	0	-	15	670176	798	17.6	unsat	29	2.14	0.231	unsat
4 passCnt4_bug	20	0	-	20	-	M.O.	T.O.	-	41	2.15	**0.301**	unsat
5 increAPI1_bug	10	1	10	200	2955686	832	59.9	unsat	333	2.23	2.923	unsat
6 increAPI2_bug	10	1	20	400	5905975	891	116	unsat	663	2.24	6.130	unsat
7 increAPI3_bug	10	1	30	600	8897424	937	174	unsat	993	2.27	10.24	unsat
8 increAPI4_bug	10	1	40	800	-	M.O.	-	-	1323	2.31	**15.23**	unsat
9 cyclic1	6	16	5	86	4025	757	**0.26**	sat	605	2.41	10.76	sat
10 cyclic2	9	28	10	289	21803	761	**1.31**	sat	1135	2.61	53.51	sat
11 cyclic3	12	40	10	412	116432	768	**3.97**	sat	939	2.80	94.94	sat
12 cyclic4	15	56	10	575	1110057	799	**29.4**	sat	1239	3.06	198.4	sat

However, if the target application contains a few tasks but many loops with APIs (lines 9–12), Spin will defeat our approach in time consumption. This is because, in our approach all of the loops with APIs will translated into branches with APIs under the loop bound. Therefore, when the target application holds a lot of loops with APIs, our approach will check a large number of execution paths and a large number of the same sub-paths will be repeatedly verified in the verification, which will slow down the performance of our approach. In contrast with our approach, in Spin-based checking method, loops will not be unfolded in the checking process.

Based on the shown experiments, there are two important evaluation results. (*i*) For the simple application which contains a few tasks (less than 15) but many loops, Spin-based checking method will spend more memory than our approach but faster than our approach. (*ii*) For the complex application which contains many tasks and APIs, our approach is more efficient than Spin-based checking method. According to the above evaluation results, we would say that, for the applications which hold a few tasks but many loops, the Spin-based checking method is enough to handle them. However, for the complex applications, we should use our approach to verify these applications.

5.2   Comparison to Kratos

Kratos is a model checker for checking the safety property of System C program with assertions, which is an implementation of the ESST technique [4] with POR. In Kratos, the SystemC scheduler [15] is embedded in the checking algorithm to conduct the executions of threads, and the predicate abstraction technique is used to find bugs. Although the scheduling policy between OSEK/VDX and SystemC is different, there is one kind of OSEK/VDX or SystemC programs that can be checked by both our approach and Kratos without any modifications, e.g., the program in which the threads are synchronously executed and only one thread is in the runnable or ready state during running. As to evaluate the effectiveness of our approach, we have conducted several experiments. The benchmarks used in the experiments are selected and adapted from Kratos homepage (note that, the selected benchmarks are fair to Kratos and our approach, because all of them represents the same scheduling execution behaviors). The experiment results have been shown in Table 2.

Table 2. Kratos VS our approach (osek-bmc)

Benchmark	Size				Kratos			osek-bmc		
	#t	#l	Loop bound	#API	#s	Time(s)	Result	#s	Time(s)	Result
1 token_ring3	3	3	2	9	23	0.27	sat	151	1.43	sat
2 token_ring7	8	8	3	21	43	525	sat	389	**2.93**	sat
3 token_ring9	10	10	4	24	-	T.O.	-	573	**4.78**	sat
4 token_ring9x	10	10	unbound	24	53	13.38	sat	-	-	-
5 token_ring11	12	12	5	36	-	T.O.	-	889	**7.96**	sat
6 token_ring11x	12	12	unbound	36	63	561	sat	-	-	-
7 transmitter4_bug	5	5	5	9	24	25.1	unknown	108	**2.51**	unsat
8 transmitter4x_bug	5	5	unbound	9	20	0.48	unsat	-	-	-
9 token_Ring	12	12	**100**	36	-	T.O.	-	15881	**596**	sat
10 transmitter8_bug	9	0	-	16	28	1.42	unsat	15	**0.19**	unsat
11 transmitter9	10	0	-	18	31	11.62	sat	38	**0.08**	sat
12 transmitter10_bug	11	0	-	20	34	16.61	unsat	19	**0.20**	unsat

There are some interesting results in the result table. To the small benchmark (line 1), Kratos can report the checking result with a shorter time and smaller states compared with our approach. However, when we increase the size of the programs (line 2), Kratos takes longer to verify the target programs and even runs out of time (line 3). This is an amazing result, since in our approach all of the execution paths corresponding to the loops with APIs are constructed according to the set bound, and these constructed execution paths are verified in the checking process, our approach should spend more time to check more states compared with Kratos, because the large block encoding technique [13] is used by Kratos to reduce the number of paths. As to confirm the results, we then conducted seven experiments (lines 3–9). In these experiments, the benchmarks which contain unbounded and bounded loops are checked by Kratos and our approach (where, the unbounded loop is like while(true) {···}). The results show that, to the same programs (e.g., lines 3 and 4), if we set the loop-condition to be true (unbound), Kratos is efficient, however, if we set a bound to the loops, Kratos is not efficient compared with our approach. Based on the experiment results, we would like to report that, (i) Kratos is an exhaustive technique in checking the unbounded loop programs, since we do not need to consider the loop bound when using predicate abstraction technique to verify a program (in bounded model checking, we usually need to set a bound for loops). However, (*ii*) for the bounded loop programs, our approach is better than Kratos, because we do not need to speed extra time to refine the abstract when using BMC to verify a program. Besides, we also conducted some other experiments (line 10–12). The experiment results show, our approach is more efficient than Kratos in checking the programs which do not hold branches.

In addition, compared with Kratos, our approach holds the following advantages in checking the safety property of OSEK/VDX applications. (*i*) our approach supports both non-preemptive and full-preemptive scheduling strategies. (*ii*) The property specified in LTL formula and OS data property can be checked by our approach. To the best of our knowledge, Kratos for now does not support the full-preemptive scheduling strategy and LTL property. In summary, our approach is a more complete technique to check OSEK/VDX applications compared with Kratos, and our approach is more efficient than Kratos in checking the OSEK/VDX applications which do not hold the unbound loops.

6   Related Work

As to verify complex SystemC programs, Cimatti et al. describe a new method named ESST [4] based on the predicate abstraction [21]. Our approach is similar to this method in embedding scheduler model in the checking algorithm, but we handle the OSEK/VDX applications instead of SystemC, use BMC instead of predicate abstraction. The challenge in our research is how to construct an accurate transition system for the cooperative software with a deterministic scheduler, which is different from the ESST technique. In this paper, we have compared our approach with ESST based on the several experiments. The comparison results shown in Sect. 4.2 indicate that, to the same benchmarks which represent the same scheduling execution behaviors, the ESST method is an exhaustive technique in checking the unbounded loop programs, but is not efficient to verify the programs which hold many bounded loops. Compared with ESST method, our approach is more efficient to detect bugs from the programs which holds many bounded loops, but the completeness of our approach for the unbounded loop programs is under the set bound.

In the field of BMC [7], a lot of researches are proposed and have been successfully applied to detect subtle errors from the complex system. However, most works focus on the sequential programs [5] and general multi-threaded programs [27]. In these existing works, the interactive behaviors between threads and scheduler are not taken into account. If we use these existing works to check the cooperative software with a deterministic scheduler, it will significantly increase the checking complexity.

To verify the design model of OSEK/VDX applications, the paper [28] proposed a method to check the timing property based on the UPPAAL [9]. However, to the best of our knowledge, there is no work that considers a SMT-based BMC method to check the safety property of the OSEK/VDX applications except our previous work [25]. The main contribution of our paper is that, we firstly apply SMT-based BMC in the verification of the cooperative software with a deterministic scheduler.

7 Conclusion and Future Work

In this paper, based on the OSEK/VDX applications, we presented an approach that can formally verify the cooperative software with a deterministic scheduler using SMT-based BMC. We have investigated the effectiveness of the approach using implemented tool based on a series of experiments. The experiment results shown that our approach is capable of checking the safety property of deterministic scheduler based OSEK/VDX applications. We also compared our approach with other methods. The comparison results indicate, in contrast with Spin-based checking method, our approach can handle more complex program which hold a lot of tasks and APIs. In addition, compared with ESST technique, our approach is a more complete technique to check the cooperative software with a deterministic scheduler. In the future, we will extend our work to verify other types of deterministic scheduler based cooperative software, such as round robin scheduler based multi-tasks/threaded software.

Acknowledgements. This work is supported by the National Science Foundation of China (Grants No. 61602224 and No. 61272213) and the Fundamental Research Funds for the Central Universities (Grants No. lzujbky-2016-142 and No. lzujbky-2016-k07).

References

1. IEEE 1666: SystemC language Reference Manual (2005)
2. Clarke, E.M., Emerson, E.A., et al.: Model checking: algorithmic verification and debugging. Commun. ACM **152**(11), 74–84 (2009)
3. Burns, A., Wellings, A.: Real-Time Systems and Programming Languages, 4th edn. Addison Wesley Longman, New York (2009)
4. Cimatti, A., Micheli, A., Narasamdya, I., Roveri, M.: Verifying SystemC: a software model checking approach. In: FMCAD, pp. 51–59 (2010)
5. Alessandro, A., Jacopo, M., Lorenzo, P.: Bounded model checking of software using SMT solvers instead of SAT solvers. Int. J. Softw. Tools Technol. Transf. (STTT) **11**(1), 69–83 (2009)
6. Cimatti, A., Micheli, A., Narasamdya, I., Roveri, M.: Kratos Homepage (2010). https://es-static.fbk.eu/tools/kratos/
7. Armin, B., Clarke, E.M., Zhu, Y.: Bounded model checking. Adv. Comput. **58**(11), 117–148 (2003)
8. Basili, V.R., Selby, R.W.: Comparing the effectiveness of software testing strategies. TSE **13**, 1278–1296 (1987)
9. Behrmann, G., David, A., Larsen, K.G.: A tutorial on UPPAAL. In: Formal Methods for the Design of Real-Time Systems: 4th International School on Formal Methods for the Design of Computer Communication, and Software Systems, pp. 200–236 (2004)
10. Flanagan, C., Godefroid, P.: Dynamic partial-order reduction for model checking software. In: POPL, pp. 110–121 (2005)

11. Traulsen, C., Cornet, J., Moy, M., Maraninchi, F.: A SystemC/TLM semantics in PROMELA and its possible applications. In: Bošnački, D., Edelkamp, S. (eds.) SPIN 2007. LNCS, vol. 4595, pp. 204–222. Springer, Heidelberg (2007). doi:10. 1007/978-3-540-73370-6_14

12. Cytron, R., Ferrante, J., Rosen, B.K., Wegman, M.N., Zadeck, F.K.: An efficient method of computing static single assignment form. In: POPL, pp. 25–35 (1989)

13. Beyer, D., Cimatti, A., Griggio, A., Keremoglu, M.E., Sebastiani, R.: Software model checking via large-block encoding. In: FMCAD, pp. 25–32 (2009)

14. Kroening, D., Sharygina, N.: Formal verification of SystemC by automatic hardware/software partitioning. In: MEMOCODE, pp. 101–110 (2005)

15. Tabakov, D., Kamhi, G., Vardi, M.Y., Singerman, E.: A temporal language for SystemC. In: FMCAD, pp. 1–9 (2008)

16. Kroening, D., Clarke, E., et al.: The CBMC Homepage (2004). http://www.cprover.org/cbmc/

17. Duan, Z.: Temporal Logic and Temporal Logic Programming. Science Press, Beijing (2005)

18. Duan, Z., Tian, C., Zhang, L.: A decision procedure for propositional projection temporal logic with infinite models. Acta Informatica 45(1), 43–78 (2008)

19. Duan, Z., Yang, X., Koutny, M.: Framed temporal logic programming. Sci. Comput. Program. 70(1), 31–61 (2008)

20. Clarke, E., Kroening, D., Lerda, F.: A tool for checking ANSI-C programs. In: Jensen, K., Podelski, A. (eds.) TACAS 2004. LNCS, vol. 2988, pp. 168–176. Springer, Heidelberg (2004). doi:10.1007/978-3-540-24730-2_15

21. Clarke, E.M., Kroening, D., Sharygina, N., Yorav, K.: SATABS: SATBased predicate abstraction for ANSI-C. In: TACAS, pp. 570–574 (2005)

22. Clarke, E.M., Grumberg, O., Long, D.E.: Model checking and abstraction. ACM Trans. Program. Lang. Syst. (TOPLAS) 16(5), 1512–1542 (1994)

23. Holzmann, G.J.: The Spin Model Checker: Primer and Reference Manual. Lucent Technologies Inc., Bell Laboratories, Boston (2003)

24. George, C.N., Scott, M., Shree, P.R., Westley, W.: CIL: intermediate language and tools for analysis and transformation of C programs. In: Proceedings of the 11th International Conference on Compiler Construction, pp. 213–228 (2002)

25. Zhang, H., Aoki, T., et al.: SMT-based bounded model checking for OSEK/VDX applications. In: 20th APSEC, pp. 307–314 (2013)

26. Zhang, H., Aoki, T., Chiba, Y.: A spin-based approach for checking OSEK/VDX applications. In: 3rd International Workshop FTSCS in ICFEM, pp. 239–255 (2014)

27. Cordeiro, L., Fischer, B.: Verifying multi-threaded software using SMT-based context-bounded model checking. In: ICSE 2011, vol. 3(9), pp. 331–340, May 2011

28. Waszniowski, L., Hanzlek, Z.: Formal verification of multitasking applications based on timed automata model. Real-Time Syst. 38(1), 39–65 (2008)

29. Lemieux, J.: Programming in the OSEK/VDX environment. CMP, Suite 200 Lawrence, KS 66046, USA (2001)

30. de Moura, L., Passmore, G.: Z3 Homepage. http://z3.codeplex.com/

31. Blanc, N., Kroening, D.: Race analysis for SystemC using model checking. In: ICCAD, pp. 356–363 (2008)

32. Blanc, N., Kroening, D., Sharygina, N.: SCOOT: a tool for the analysis of SystemC models. In: Ramakrishnan, C.R., Rehof, J. (eds.) TACAS 2008. LNCS, vol. 4963, pp. 467–470. Springer, Heidelberg (2008). doi:10.1007/978-3-540-78800-3_36

33. Tian, C., Duan, Z., Zhang, N.: An efficient approach for abstraction-refinement in model checking. Theor. Comput. Sci. 461, 76–85 (2012)

Model Checking of a Mobile Robots Perpetual Exploration Algorithm

Ha Thi Thu Doan[✉], François Bonnet, and Kazuhiro Ogata

School of Information Science, JAIST, Nomi, Japan
{doanha,f-bonnet,ogata}@jaist.ac.jp

Abstract. Distributed mobile computing has been recently an active field of research, resulting in a large number of algorithms. However, to the best of our knowledge, few of the designed algorithms have been formally model checked. This paper presents a case study of how to specify and model check a given robot algorithm. We specify the system in Maude, a rewriting logic-based programming and specification language. To check the correctness of the algorithm, we express in LTL the properties it should enjoy. Our analysis leads to a counterexample which implies that the proposed algorithm is not correct.

Keywords: Automatic verification · Maude · Mobile robots · Model checking · Perpetual exploration

1 Introduction

For the last two decades, the Distributed Computing community has been investigating what can be solved by a team of autonomous mobile robots. Following a different approach compared to the AI and Robotic communities, researchers started to propose formal models for these systems and design algorithms solving some predefined tasks. Most papers focus on the computability of mobile robots and consider teams of identical robots with limited capabilities; one of the main goals is usually to find the weakest assumptions (on the robots and/or on the model) that make a problem solvable or unsolvable.

There exist many different models, but they can be classified in two main classes: (i) continuous models in which entities move on a continuous space (1D [9], 2D [7,10], or even 3-dimensional space [11]), and (ii) discrete models in which movement are restricted on a graph [3,4,6]. For both cases, a large variety of tasks have been considered such as gathering, pattern formation, scattering, flocking for continuous environments, and gathering, exploration, patrolling for discrete environments. For more details, we invite the interested reader to check the book [7] of Flocchini *et al.* that surveys many results (mostly on continuous models).

Any publication of mobile robot algorithms usually includes proofs of correctness. Most of these proofs are handmade and may consist of a large number of cases, especially when the algorithm is given explicitly as a set of transition rules (*e.g.* [3]) in opposition to a more abstract algorithm where movements are

© Springer International Publishing AG 2017
S. Liu et al. (Eds.): SOFL+MSVL 2016, LNCS 10189, pp. 201–219, 2017.
DOI: 10.1007/978-3-319-57708-1_12

implicitly given by some mathematical rules (*e.g.* [6]). This is not easy and not trustful to check the correctness of these algorithms only by hand. We believe that the research field of distributed mobile robots is now mature; some main models have emerged and have been adopted by the community. It is time to study how to automatically verify such algorithms and this paper presents an example of automatic verification.

The main contribution of our research consists in using the model checking approach to automatic verification of a perpetual ring exploration algorithm. We formally specify the algorithm in Maude, a language and a system supporting executable specification and declarative programming in rewriting logic. The two significant properties which the algorithm should satisfy have been specified as Linear Temporal Logic (LTL) formulas [8]. We then model check the two properties for the algorithm with LTL model checker in Maude. As the result of our model checking for the algorithm, a counterexample has been found. This states that the algorithm is not correct since it does not satisfy the two properties.

It is worth mentioning that this algorithm has already been model checked in a recent paper using DiVinE and ITS tools [2]. While the results are fortunately similar[1], we propose here a different modeling approach. Bérard *et al.* [2] consider robots independently; each of them being modeled by its own automaton. Differently, we consider only global configurations of the system. Our method leads to slightly faster model checking. Both contributions use LTL to state the properties that must be satisfied by the algorithm, but the model checking tool is different.

Outline. Section 2 proposes a brief introduction to Maude. Section 3 describes the model, the problem, and the algorithm that is analyzed. Section 4 provides the formal specification of the protocol in Maude. Section 5 explains how to check its correctness and shows the counter-example. Section 6 finally concludes the paper and brief gives some future research directions.

2   Maude

Maude is a rewriting logic-based programming and specification language and equipped with a powerful system (or environment) [5]. Rewriting logic makes it possible to naturally specify dynamic systems, and the Maude system has a linear temporal logic model checker. Therefore, Maude allows to model check if dynamic systems specified in Maude enjoy properties expressed in LTL. A simple example is used to briefly describe Maude and its LTL model checker.

The simple system is a ring-shaped network consisting of four nodes whose identifications are 0, 1, 2, and 3 clockwise (see Fig. 1). There is one mobile robot in the system, located at one node. Initially, the robot is located at node 0. We take two versions of the system into account: System 1 and System 2. System 1

---

[1] We confirm the incorrectness of the algorithm by obtaining the same counter-example. Any other result would be worrisome.

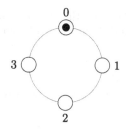

Fig. 1. Initial configuration of the system.

has four transitions: if the robot is located at node N, then one of the four transition moves the robot at node $(N + 1)$ mod 4. System 2 has four more transitions as well: if the robot is located at node N, then one of the four transition moves the robot at node $(N - 1)$ mod 4. We take two properties into account. One property is that the robot never visits node 4, and the other property is that the robot visits node 3 infinitely many times. The two properties are denoted nv4 and v3im, respectively. nv4 is a safety property, while v3im is a liveness property.

The state in which the robot is located at N is expressed as term {N}. First we declared the following functional module:

```
fmod NAT+MOD4 is
  sort NatMod4 .
  ops 0 1 2 3 4 : -> NatMod4 [ctor] .
  op inc : NatMod4 -> NatMod4 .
  op dec : NatMod4 -> NatMod4 .
  eq inc(0) = 1 . eq inc(1) = 2 . eq inc(2) = 3 . eq inc(3) = 0 .
  eq dec(0) = 3 . eq dec(1) = 0 . eq dec(2) = 1 . eq dec(3) = 2 .
endfm
```

where NatMod4 is a sort, 0, 1, 2, 3 and 4 are constants of NatMod4, and inc and dec are operators that are defined in the following equations. The constants 0, 1, 2 and 3 of NatMod4 are used to denote the node identifications. The constant 4 of NatMod4 is used for expressing the property nv4. ctor stands for constructor, meaning that the operators concerned are used to construct data. The operators inc and dec are the ordinary ones for natural numbers modulo 4.

The following module CONFIG is declared:

```
fmod CONFIG is
  pr NAT+MOD4 .
  sort Config .
  op {_} : NatMod4 -> Config [ctor] .
endfm
```

The module is imported in the protecting mode. As written, {N} denotes the state in which the robot is located at node N.

The four transitions in System 1 can be described as the following rewriting rule:

```
rl [rr] : {X} => {inc(X)} .
```

where `rr` is the label of the rule. Note that the rule has four instances for $N = 0$, 1, 2 and 3. The other four transitions in System 2 can be described as the following rewriting rule:

```
rl [lr] : {X} => {dec(X)} .
```

The two rewriting rules are declared in the following module SYSTEM:

```
mod SYSTEM is
  inc CONFIG .
  var X : NatMod4 .
  rl [rr] : {X} => {inc(X)} .
  rl [lr] : {X} => {dec(X)} .
endm
```

For System 1, the second rule is commented out or deleted.

To express the two properties in LTL, we need to prepare one proposition (at N) checking if the robot is located at node N in a given state. The proposition is declared in the following module SYS-PROP:

```
mod SYS-PROP is
  pr SYSTEM .
  inc SATISFACTION .
  subsort Config < State .
  op at_ : NatMod4 -> Prop .
  var X : NatMod4 .
  var C : Config .
  var P : Prop .
  eq {X} |= (at X) = true .
  eq C |= P = false [owise] .
endm
```

SATISFACTION is one module provided in the file model-checker.maude available in the Maude distribution. In the module, model satisfaction relation _|=_ and some more are declared. SATISFACTION is imported in the including mode. The first equation in the module says that (at X) holds in the state {X}. owise stands for otherwise. The second equation in the module says that (at X) does not hold in any other states.

The two properties are defined in the following module SYS-FORMULA:

```
mod SYS-FORMULA is
  inc SYS-PROP .
  inc MODEL-CHECKER .
  inc LTL-SIMPLIFIER .
  ops nv4 v3im : -> Formula .
  eq nv4 = [] ~(at 4) .
  eq v3im = [] <> (at 3) .
endm
```

The operator []_ is the always temporal operator, and <>_ is the eventually temporal operator. [] ~(at 4) says that the robot never visits node 4, and [] <> (at 3) says that the robot visits node 3 infinitely many times. The two properties are model checked as follows:

```
red in SYS-FORMULA : modelCheck({0},nv4) .
red in SYS-FORMULA : modelCheck({0},v3im) .
```

The Maude LTL model checker concludes that System 1 enjoys both properties, while System 2 enjoys **nv4** but does not **v3im**. The counterexample shown is as follows:

```
result ModelCheckResult: counterexample({{0},'rr}, {{1},'rr} {{2},'lr})
```

saying that once the robot moves to node 1 from node 0, the robot always moves clockwise when it is located at node 1 and always moves counterclockwise when it is located at node 2, never visiting node 3. If we assume Strong Fairness of transitions to model check **v3im**, then even System 2 enjoys **v3im**, an extended version of the Maude LTL model checker that facilitates model checking liveness properties under fairness has been developed [1].

3 Exclusive Perpetual Exploration of the Ring

In this paper, we consider the *exclusive perpetual exploration* of the *ring* and we analyze one of the first algorithm proposed to solve this problem. More specifically we focus on the algorithm designed for *three robots*[2] by Blin *et al.* [3].

In the remaining of this section, we present successively the model, the problem, and the algorithm under study. For each part, a more complete description can be found in the original paper [3].

3.1 Model

This model description is adapted from [4] for our specific context. The ring is *anonymous*, that is, there is neither node nor edge labeling. The robots are *identical*, i.e., they are indistinguishable and all execute the same algorithm. Moreover, the robots are *oblivious* and *disoriented*, meaning that they have no memory of past actions, and they share no common orientation (no chirality).

The robots cannot explicitly communicate, but have the ability to sense their environment and see the relative positions of the other robots, in their local coordinate system. Robots follow a three-phase behavior: *Look*, *Compute*, and *Move*. During its Look phase a robot takes a snapshot of all robots' positions. The collected information (position of the other robots in the egocentric view) is used in the Compute phase during which the robot may decide to move or stay idle. In the Move phase, the robot may move to one of the two adjacent nodes, as computed in the previous phase. The moves are assumed to be instantaneous which means that, during a Look phase, robots can be located on nodes only.

The computational model we consider is the classical asynchronous ASYNC model [7]. It means that, the start and duration of each Look-Compute phases and the start of each Move phase of each robot are arbitrary and determined by an adversary. Note that it is possible for a robot to make a move based on a previously observed configuration which is not the current one anymore (*e.g.* if its Look phase occurred before the Move phase of another robot).

We call a *pending move* a move that has been computed (during a Compute phase) but not yet executed (in the subsequent Move phase).

---

[2] It is natural to consider 3-robot algorithms, since, for non-trivial rings, any exploration algorithm requires at least three robots.

3.2 Problem

The *perpetual* exploration problem requires each agent to visit each location (here, nodes of the ring) infinitely often. Moreover the *exclusive* nature of the exploration implies that two agents are not allowed to be on the same location at the same time; two robots cannot be on the same node and two robots cannot cross each-other on the same edge.

In order to verify the correctness of an algorithm, two properties have to be model-checked (see Sect. 5):

- The perpetual exploration property,
- The mutual exclusion property,

where the former is a liveness property, while the latter is a safety property.

3.3 Algorithm

We recall here first some notations used to describe configurations and algorithms, and then present succinctly the 3-robot exploration algorithm.

Configuration encoding. In order to represent in a concise way any configuration of the system, we use the classical encoding as the sequence of occupied/free nodes of the ring. For example the configuration of Fig. 2 depicting 3 robots on a 10-node ring is encoded as (R_2, F_2, R_1, F_5) since there are 2 adjacent *Robots* followed by 2 *Free* nodes, followed by 1 *Robot*, followed finally by 5 *Free* nodes. Note that, due to the lack of orientation and origin, the very same configuration could also be encoded differently, for example with the sequence (R_1, F_2, R_2, F_5).

Fig. 2. Configuration (R_2, F_2, R_1, F_5) with 3 robots on a 10-node ring.

The configurations can be parametrized with integer variables when the size of the ring is unknown. For example, one can consider the configurations (R_2, F_2, R_1, F_z) in which there are two adjacent robots separated from the third robots by a gap of two empty nodes on one side, and z empty nodes on the side. Such notations allow to define generic algorithms for arbitrary size of ring.

Similar encoding will be used in the formal specification of the algorithm (see Sect. 4) in Maude. The only difference is that we use the number of edges between two robots, instead of counting the number of free nodes.

Move encoding. According to Sect. 3.1, each robot computes its next move based on the position of other robots. Therefore, designing an algorithm means giving the function that associates a move to any possible snapshot. A concise way of representing such algorithm is to write transition rules such as:

$$(R_2, F_2, R1, F_z) \rightarrow (R_1, F_1, R1, F_2, R_1, F_z)$$

Such a rule encodes the computed movement of each of the three robots when they take a snapshot corresponding to the configuration on the left. For example, in this case (see Fig. 3), the isolated robot (corresponding to R_1) should not move, and among the two other robots (corresponding to R_2), only the furthest one (wrt. the isolated robot) should compute a move to go away.[3]

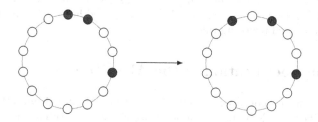

Fig. 3. Rule RL1: $(R_2, F_2, R_1, F_z) \rightarrow (R_1, F_1, R_1, F_2, R_1, F_z)$.

Again, a similar encoding will be used in the formal specification of the algorithm (see Sect. 4). Each rule of the algorithm has a corresponding conditional rewriting rule in Maude.

Algorithm rules. The algorithm for three robots designed by Blin *et al.* [3] works in two phase. First there is a *Convergence Phase* which guarantees that starting from any initial configuration, the system reaches one of the three *legitimate*[4] configurations. Then during the *Legitimate Phase*, the system cycles between three configurations to explore perpetually the ring. The Legitimate Phase consist of the three rules RL1,

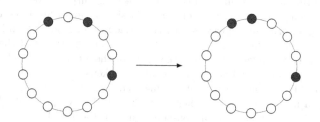

Fig. 4. Rule RL2: $(R_1, F_1, R_1, F_2, R1, F_z) \rightarrow (R_2, F_3, R_1, F_z)$.

---

[3] On Fig. 3, the computed move is anti-clockwise.
[4] The terminology comes from the Self-Stabilization concept. One can understand such configurations as "good" configurations.

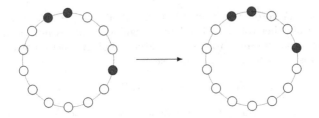

Fig. 5. Rule RL3: $(R_2, F_3, R_1, F_z) \rightarrow (R_2, F_2, R_1, F_{z+1})$.

RL2, and RL3 represented[5] on Figs. 3, 4, and 5. One can "easily check" that applying successively these rules to the three robots indeed solves the perpetual exploration.

The set of rules for the Convergence Phase is omitted here, but appears in Sect. 4 as a list of conditional rewriting rules.

4   System Specification of the Algorithm

The system in which robots operate under the control of the algorithm will be modeled and then specified in order to model check the algorithm. This section describes our way to formalize the system and specify it in Maude. The system is specified in our system module EXPLORATION, which defines the behavior of the system. We consider first how to express the states of the system and then the state transitions for the system.

4.1   State Expressions for the System

Robots are denoted as r1, r2, ..., and the sort is Robot. In the Compute phase, a robot, based on the perceived configuration, makes a decision to stay idle or move to one of its adjacent nodes: either the node on the right or the node on the left. *Pending moves* are denoted as L, R, and nil corresponding respectively to moving to the right, moving to the left, and staying idle, and the sort is Pending.

Since the algorithm works on a ring shape network, our modeling of the system respects the ring. Although the ring is an anonymous ring without orientation and the robots on the ring are anonymous, for model checking purpose, we name the robots and number the nodes of the ring. For a ring of size n, nodes are labeled from 0 to $n - 1$ following an arbitrary clockwise ordering. Each robot is given a different name. We want to note that this does not affect the fact that the ring and the robots are anonymous since our implementation of the rules for the algorithm, which is presented in Sect. 4.2, recognizes the robots are identical, and likewise with the nodes.

Each robot is located at one node of the ring. When a node is occupied by robots, the node is called a non-empty node. Otherwise, it is called an empty node. We actually represent the ring by the set of all non-empty nodes. Each such node is denoted as <r,d,p>, where r is the name of the robot, d is the label of the node, and p is the pending move of the robot. The corresponding sort is Node.

---

[5] Pictures represent a ring of size 14, but the rules are defined for arbitrary size, as written in the corresponding captions.

The ring is denoted as a commutative and associative set of these non-empty nodes and the sort is `Ring`. Rings without any robots are called empty rings and we use `empR`, a constant of the sort `Ring`, for them.

```
subsort Node < Ring .
op <_,_,_> : Robot Nat Pending -> Node [ctor] .
op empR : -> Ring [ctor] .
op __ : Ring Ring -> Ring [ctor assoc comm id: empR] .
```

where `Nat` is the sort for natural numbers.

We define the sort `Size` for the size of a ring. This sort is a super-sort of the sort `Nat`. The constant `size`, an element of the sort `Size`, is used for the size of a ring. The configuration of a system is denoted as `{R}`, where `R` is an element of the sort `Ring`, and the sort is `Config`. The system is described by the configuration and the size of the ring.

```
op {_} : Ring -> Config .
op size : -> Size .
```

Some examples of how to describe a system are showed in Fig. 6. In any initial configuration of the system, there is no two robots located on the same node and the pending move of any robot is nil.

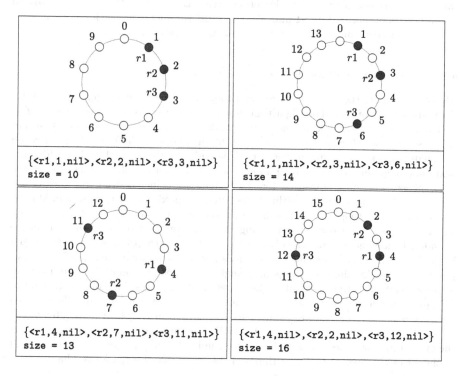

Fig. 6. Describing a system by the configuration and the size of the ring

We define two important concepts: *interval* and *order*. Given two robots r1 and r2 located respectively on the nodes n1 and n2, we define the intervals between the two robots as the number of edges between n1 and n2. Since the environment is a ring, for each pair of robots there are two different intervals, (1) the clockwise interval which counts edges from n1 to n2 following the clockwise orientation, and (2) the counter-clockwise interval, which counts edges in the other direction.

The latter concept takes into account the order of robots on the ring. Since the algorithm under study works for three robots, we define the notion only for this case. It is possible to extend the notion for arbitrary number of robots. Given three robots r1, r2, and r3 located respectively in the node n1, n2, and n3, the three robots are said to be in the right (or clockwise) order if and only if n2 is between n1 and n3 on the ring according to the clockwise orientation (*e.g.* the three first configurations of Fig. 6). Conversely, the three robots are said to be in the left (or counter-clockwise) order if and only if n2 is after n1 and before n3 on the ring according to counter-clockwise orientation (*e.g.* the last configuration of Fig. 6). We calculate the interval of two robots and the order of three robots by using the following functions:

```
op order : Nat Nat Nat -> Pending .
op interval : Nat Nat Pending -> Nat .
```

The function `order(N1, N2, N3)` returns the order of three robots located in the nodes N1, N2, and N3. The order can be L (left order), R (right order), or `nil` in case the three robots are not in any order.[6] Function `interval(N2, N1, M)` returns the interval of the two robots located on N1 and N2. The third parameter M, which can be L, R, or `nil`, is used to determine which way we calculate the interval.

4.2   State Transitions for the System

All robots execute the same algorithm and they do not have the ability to distinguish themselves from others. The algorithm is given as the set of rules as presenting in Sect. 3.3. A robot first looks at the system in the Look phase to capture the snapshot of the system, which contains the positions of all robots on the ring. Then based on the snapshot and according to the set of the rules of the algorithm, it decides the next movement in the Compute phase. The pending move will be executed in the Move phase. The state transition for the system is conducted from the rules of the algorithm. The rules of the algorithm will be implemented as rewriting rules in Maude. The following rewriting rules do not identify robots and also nodes. They totally depend on the positions of all robots on the ring. This ensures that the ring and robots are considered anonymous. Since the Compute phase uses the snapshot of the system taken in the Look phase as input and a robot does not perform any movements during two phases, we combine the two phases in a single one called the Look-Compute phase in which a robot takes the snapshot of the system and computes the movement. A robot decides to take a snapshot of the system and calculate a movement only when it does not hold a pending move. The pending move is stored in the third parameter of the notation of a non-empty node as `<r,d,p>`. We separate the set of rewriting rules for the system into two sets: the set of rules for the Look-Compute phases corresponding to the set of the rules of the algorithm and the set of rules for the Move phase.

---

[6] When two robots are located on the same nodes, there is no order.

The Rules for the Look-Compute Phase. Each of the following rewriting rule corresponds to one rule in the set of rules of the algorithm. For each rule, we keep the same name as in the original paper [3] to easily match them. In the following part, R1, R2, and R3 are variables of the sort Robot; N1, N2, and N3 are variables of the sort Nat; and M, M1, M2, and M3 are variables of the sort Pending.

1. The rewriting rule corresponding to the rule RL1 given on Fig. 3:

```
crl [RL1] : { <R1,N1,nil> <R2,N2,M2> <R3,N3,M3> }
          => { <R1,N1,change(M)> <R2,N2,M2> <R3,N3,M3> }
          if M := order(N1,N2,N3) /\ interval(N2,N1,M) == 1
                                  /\ interval(N3,N2,M) == 3 .
```

where the function change(M) returns the opposite value of M. If M is L then it returns R, if M is R then it returns L, and nil otherwise.

The lefthand side and the conditional part of the rule encodes the initial configuration of the rule RL1 (*i.e.* the left picture of Fig. 3). The initial configuration contains three robots such that, given an orientation (clockwise or counterclockwise), the two first robots are at distance 1 (*i.e.* neighbors) and the third robot is at distance 3 from the second one; both distances/intervals being computed in the same orientation.

The topmost robot of Fig. 3 corresponds to robot R1 of the Maude rule. According to the rule RL1, this robot has to move if it takes a snapshot of this configuration. In Maude, it is specified by having no pending move initially (the parameter nil on the lefthand side), while having a pending move (change(M) on the righthand side). The direction of the pending move is chosen to match the direction of the move in rule RL1.

Since the two other robots are not supposed to move in RL1; the parameters M2 and M3 respectively are not updated in the conditional rule.

Note that the rule RL1 could have equivalently be written by exchanging the roles of the first and third robot, as proposed below. We choose the previous specification to match as closely as possible the rules given in the original paper.

```
crl [RL1] : { <R1,N1,M1> <R2,N2,M2> <R3,N3,nil> }
          => { <R1,N1,M1> <R2,N2,M2> <R3,N3,M> }
          if M := order(N1,N2,N3) /\ interval(N2,N1,M) == 3
                                  /\ interval(N3,N2,M) == 1 .
```

2. The rewriting rule corresponding to the rule RL2 given on Fig. 4.

```
crl [RL2] : { <R1,N1,M1> <R2,N2,nil> <R3,N3,M3> }
          => { <R1,N1,M1> <R2,N2,change(M)> <R3,N3,M3> }
          if M := order(N1,N2,N3) /\ interval(N2,N1,M) == 2
                                  /\ interval(N3,N2,M) == 3 .
```

3. The rewriting rule corresponding to the rule RL3 given on Fig. 5.

```
crl [RL3] : { <R1,N1,M1> <R2,N2,M2> <R3,N3,nil> }
          => { <R1,N1,M1> <R2,N2,M2> <R3,N3,change(M)> }
          if M := order(N1,N2,N3) /\ interval(N2,N1,M) == 1
                                  /\ interval(N3,N2,M) == 4 .
```

4. The rewriting rule corresponding to the rule RC1.

```
crl [RC1] : { <R1,N1,M1> <R2,N2,M2> <R3,N3,nil> }
          => { <R1,N1,M1> <R2,N2,M2> <R3,N3,change(M)> }
          if M := order(N1,N2,N3) /\ interval(N2,N1,M) == 1
                                  /\ interval(N3,N2,M)> 4
             /\ (interval(N3,N2,M) < interval(N1,N3,M)) .
```

5. The rewriting rule corresponding to the rule RC2.

```
crl [RC2] : { <R1,N1,M1> <R2,N2,M2> <R3,N3,nil> C }
          => { <R1,N1,M1> <R2,N2,M2> <R3,N3,M> C }
          if M := order(N1,N2,N3) /\ (interval(N2,N1,M)> 0)
                                  /\ (interval(N3,N2,M)> 1)
             /\ (interval(N3,N2,M) == interval(N1,N3,M)) .
```

6. The rewriting rule corresponding to the rule RC3.

```
crl [RC3] : { <R1,N1,M1> <R2,N2,nil> <R3,N3,M3> C }
          => { <R1,N1,M1> <R2,N2,change(M)> <R3,N3,M3> C }
          if M := order(N1,N2,N3)
             /\ (interval(N3,N2,M) > interval(N2,N1,M))
             /\ (interval(N1,N3,M) > interval(N3,N2,M))
             /\ (interval(N2,N1,M) > 1) .
```

7. The rewriting rule corresponding to the rule RC4.

```
crl [RC4] : { <R1,N1,nil> <R2,N2,M2> <R3,N3,M3> C }
          => { <R1,N1,change(M)> <R2,N2,M2> <R3,N3,M3> C }
          if M := order(N1,N2,N3)
             /\ (interval(N2,N1,M) == 1)
             /\ (interval(N3,N2,M) == 1) .
```

This rule is more subtle than other rules and the formalization from the original rule is less straightforward. The initial configuration (lefthand side of the rewriting rule) is symmetrical; three robots are adjacent to each other. The commutativity of the sort Ring and our notions of order and interval guarantee that this specification is conform to the original rule; it is possible than either one or two robots compute a move.

8. The rewriting rule corresponding to the rule RC5.

```
crl [RC5] : { <R1,N1,M1> <R2,N2,M2> <R3,N3,nil> C }
          => { <R1,N1,M1> <R2,N2,M2> <R3,N3,M> C }
          if M := order(N1,N2,N3)
             /\ (interval(N2,N1,M) == 1)
             /\ (interval(N3,N2,M) == 2) .
```

The Rules for the Move Phase. Each robot may move to its adjacent node on the left, its adjacent node on the right, or stay idle. This movement is based on its pending move. In the following, the function moveL(N) is to move the robot located on the node N to the adjacent node on the left and the function moveR(N) is to move the robot located on the node N to the adjacent node on the right.

1. If the stored pending move is L, the robot will move to the adjacent node on the left.

```
rl [RL-Lpending] : { <R1,N1,L> C } => { <R1,moveL(N1),nil> C } .
```

2. If the stored pending move is R, the robot will move to the adjacent node on the right.

```
rl [RL-Rpending] : { <R1,N1,R> C } => { <R1,moveR(N1),nil> C } .
```

5   Model Checking

The perpetual exploration property guarantees that each robot visits infinitely often each node. It is a liveness property which ensures that something good eventually happens. The mutual exclusion property ensures that no two robots are located on any node at any given time. This property is a safety property, which guarantees that something bad never happens. Maude is equipped with an LTL model checker [5,8]. These two properties can be expressed in the LTL used by Maude.

5.1   State Predicates

We define the state predicates **perexp** and **mutual** which are used to specify the two properties as LTL formulas. The two predicates are specified in the module EXPLORATION-PREDS, which protects the module EXPLORATION and includes the module SATISFACTION. The sort Config is chosen as our kind for states and declared as sub-sort of the sort State.

```
mod EXPLORATION-PREDS is
  pr EXPLORATION .
  inc SATISFACTION .
  subsort Config < State .
  ...
endm
```

where '...' indicates the part in which the syntax and semantics of the state predicates are specified. The specification of predicate perexp(R, N) is as follows:

```
op perexp : Robot Nat -> Prop .
eq { < R, N, M > C } |= perexp(R, N) = true .
eq { C }             |= perexp(R, N) = false [owise] .
```

where R is a variable of the sort Robot, N a variable of the sort Nat, and M a variable of the sort Pending. The predicate perexp(R, N) is true in the configuration S if and only if the robot R is located at the node N in S, as <R,N,M>, and false otherwise. The mutual predicate is specified as follows:

```
op mutual : -> Prop .
op checkMutual : Config -> Bool .
op checkMutual1 : Robot Nat Config -> Bool .

eq { C } |= mutual = checkMutual({ C }) .
```

```
eq checkMutual({ empR }) = false .
eq checkMutual({ < R1, N1, M1 > C }) =
   checkMutual1(R1, N1, { C }) or checkMutual({ C }) .

eq checkMutual1(R1, N1, { empR }) = false .
eq checkMutual1(R1, N1, { < R2 , N2, M2 > C }) =
   (N1 == N2) or checkMutual1(R1, N1, { C }) .
```

where R1 and R2 are variables of the sort Robot, N1 and N2 are variables of the sort Nat, M1 and M2 are variables of the sort Pending, and C is a variable of the sort Ring.

The value of the predicate mutual depends on the result of the function checkMutual which is false if and only if there are no two robots located at the same node and true otherwise.

5.2 Property Specifications as LTL Formulas

The perpetual exploration property and the mutual exclusion property will be specified as LTL formulas. The LTL formula saying that the robot r eventually visits the node 0, eventually visits the node 1, ..., and eventually visits the node n-1 is as follows:

```
([]<> (perexp(r, 0))) /\ ([]<> (perexp(r, 1)))
   /\ ([]<> (perexp(r, 2)))    /\  ...
   /\ ([]<> (perexp(r, n-2))) /\ ([]<> (perexp(r, n-1))) .
```

where n is the size of the ring.

We define a function named perexpGen as the following function to automatically generate this formula:

```
op perexpGen : Robot Nat -> Formula .
eq perexpGen(R, 0) = ([]<> (perexp(R, 0))) .
ceq perexpGen(R, N) = ([]<> (perexp(R, N)))
                         /\ perexpGen(R, sd(N, 1)) if N > 0 .
```

where R and N are variables of the sort Robot and Nat respectively.

The perpetual exploration property is satisfied if and only if the LTL formula perexpGen(r,n) is satisfied for all robots r in the system of a n-node ring:

```
perexpGen(r1,n) and perexpGen(r2,n) and ...  and perexpGen(rk,n) .
```

where k is the number of robots in the system.

The mutual exclusion property is expressed as the following LTL formula:

```
[]~ (mutual)
```

This formula says that mutual predicate is always false, meaning that the mutual exclusion will never happen.

5.3 Experiments and Counterexample

The system module EXPLORATION specifying the system in which robots execute the algorithm has been given. In the module EXPLORATION-PREDS, which protects the module EXPLORATION, the two predicates and their semantics have been defined. The two properties have been specified as LTL formulas. All requirements to perform the model checking are satisfied. We define a new module, called EXPLORATION-CHECK. The module EXPLORATION-CHECK imports the module MODEL-CHECKER, which supports for LTL model checking. We then model check the two given LTL formulas specifying the two properties for a given initial configuration. An initial configuration is defined as the constant initial of the sort Config in the module EXPLORATION-CHECK. First, we perform the model checking for the ring of size 10.

```
op initial : -> Config .
ops r1 r2 r3 : -> Robot .
eq initial = { < r1, 1, nil > < r2, 2, nil > < r3, 3, nil > } .
eq size = 10 .
```

We are now ready to model check the two properties. We use the key operator modelCheck, which takes a state and the LTL formula and returns either the Boolean true if the formula is satisfied, or a counterexample when it is not satisfied. The first property to check is perpetual exploration:

```
red modelCheck(initial, perexpGen(r1, 9))   .
red modelCheck(initial, perexpGen(r2, 9)) .
red modelCheck(initial, perexpGen(r3, 9)) .
```

The second property to check is mutual exclusion:

```
red modelCheck(initial, []~ (mutual)) .
```

For the ring of size 10, we can define all possible initial configurations of the system. It takes less than 30 s to model check both properties for all initial configurations. For the ring of size 10, there is one initial configuration for which the model checker finds a counterexample for each formula; this is the initial configuration with three adjacent robots. The counterexample is showed as follows:

```
reduce in M-CHECK : modelCheck(initial6, []~ mutual) .
rewrites: 284597 in 89ms cpu (91ms real) (3163946 rewrites/second)
result ModelCheckResult: counterexample(...)

reduce in M-CHECK : modelCheck(initial6, perexpGen(r1, 9)) .
rewrites: 284597 in 89ms cpu (91ms real) (3163946 rewrites/second)
result ModelCheckResult: counterexample(...)

reduce in M-CHECK : modelCheck(initial6, perexpGen(r2, 9)) .
rewrites: 284597 in 89ms cpu (91ms real) (3163946 rewrites/second)
result ModelCheckResult: counterexample(...)

reduce in M-CHECK : modelCheck(initial6, perexpGen(r3, 9)) .
rewrites: 284597 in 89ms cpu (91ms real) (3163946 rewrites/second)
result ModelCheckResult: counterexample(...)
```

where '...' is the following counterexample:

```
{{< r1,1,nil > < r2,2,nil > < r3,3,nil>},'RC4}
{{< r1,1,L > < r2,2,nil > < r3,3,nil >},'RC4}
```

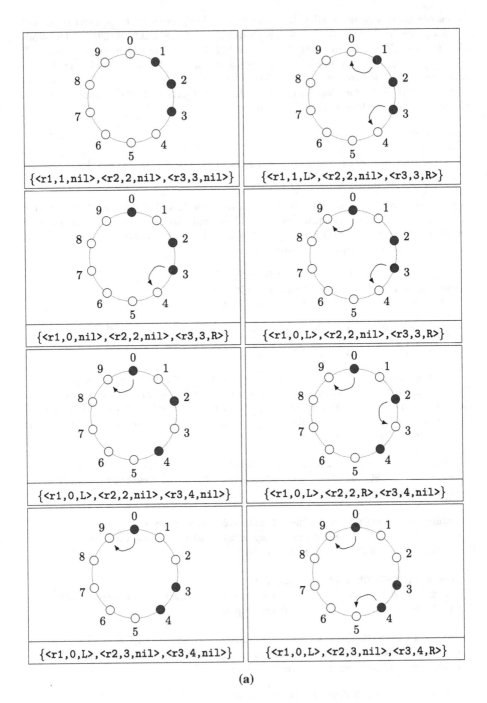

Fig. 7. (a) and (b) Scenario of the counterexample

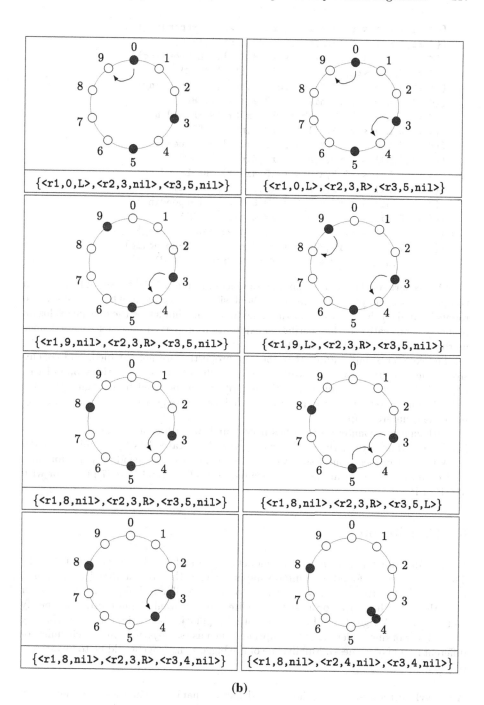

(b)

Fig. 7. (*continued*)

```
{{< r1,1,L > < r2,2,nil > < r3,3,R >},'RL-Lpending}
{{< r1,0,nil > < r2,2,nil > < r3,3,R >},'RC5}
{{< r1,0,L > < r2,2,nil > < r3,3,R >},'RL-Rpending}
{{< r1,0,L > <r2,2,nil > < r3,4,nil >},'RC2}
{{< r1,0,L > < r2,2,R > < r3,4,nil >},'RL-Rpending}
{{< r1,0,L > < r2,3,nil > < r3,4,nil >},'RL1}
{{< r1,0,L > <r2,3,nil > < r3,4,R >},'RL-Rpending}
{{< r1,0,L > < r2,3,nil > < r3,5,nil>},'RL2}
{{< r1,0,L > < r2,3,R > < r3,5,nil >},'RL-Lpending}
{{< r1,9,nil > < r2,3,R > < r3,5,nil >},'RC2}
{{< r1,9,L > < r2,3,R > < r3,5,nil >},'RL-Lpending}
{{< r1,8,nil > < r2,3,R > < r3,5,nil >},'RL2}
{{< r1,8,nil > < r2,3,R > < r3,5,L >},'RL-Lpending}
{{< r1,8,nil > < r2,3,R > < r3,4,nil >},'RL3}
{{< r1,8,L > < r2,3,R > < r3,4,nil >},'RL-Lpending}
{{< r1,7,nil > < r2,3,R > < r3,4,nil >},'RL-Rpending}
{{< r1,7,nil > < r2,4,nil > < r3,4, nil >},deadlock}
```

The scenario of the counterexample is depicted in Fig. 7 (slightly simplified to fit in two pages). We can recognize that a deadlook situation occurs, in which there are two robots located on the same node at the same time. This shows that the mutual exclusion property is not satisfied. The perpetual exploration property is also not satisfied since no robot can move anymore (deadlook).

The counterexample states that the two properties are not satisfied, and conclusively, the algorithm does not work correctly. While being outside the scope of this paper, it is worth mentioning that the algorithm can be fixed by changing the rule RC5. Unfortunately, it is not possible to deduce the required modification directly from the counterexample.

Although the counterexample has been found, we still conduct some more experiments for other sizes of rings. In our experiments, it takes less than 5 min to model check the first property and less than 30 s to model check the second property for rings of size up to 20. Computations were executed on a 4 GHz Intel Core i7 processor with 32 GB of RAM.

6   Conclusion

We have described how to specify and model check a mobile robot algorithm in Maude. The model checker found a counterexample showing that the analyzed algorithm is not correct. As future work, we consider to apply similar techniques to verify other algorithms that have been proposed in the literature. It would be interesting to specify and model check algorithms designed for other topologies (*e.g.* grid, torus, or arbitrary graphs) or working under other assumptions (such as (semi-)synchronous scheduler, or different notion of fairness). Finally, one of the biggest challenge would be to investigate continuous topologies.

Acknowledgments. The authors would like to thank Adrián Riesco for his useful comments on the specification in Maude. This work has been partially supported by Kakenhi 26540024 and 26240008.

References

1. Bae, K., Meseguer, J.: Model checking linear temporal logic of rewriting formulas under localized fairness. Sci. Comput. Program. **99**, 193–234 (2015)
2. Bérard, B., Lafourcade, P., Millet, L., Potop-Butucaru, M., Thierry-Mieg, Y., Tixeuil, S.: Formal verification of mobile robot protocols. Distrib. Comput. **29**, 1–29 (2016). (to appear, published online)
3. Blin, L., Milani, A., Potop-Butucaru, M., Tixeuil, S.: Exclusive perpetual ring exploration without chirality. In: Lynch, N.A., Shvartsman, A.A. (eds.) DISC 2010. LNCS, vol. 6343, pp. 312–327. Springer, Heidelberg (2010). doi:10.1007/978-3-642-15763-9_29
4. Bonnet, F., Potop-Butucaru, M., Tixeuil, S.: Asynchronous gathering in rings with 4 robots. In: Mitton, N., Loscri, V., Mouradian, A. (eds.) ADHOC-NOW 2016. LNCS, vol. 9724, pp. 311–324. Springer, Cham (2016). doi:10.1007/978-3-319-40509-4_22
5. Clavel, M., Durán, F., Eker, S., Lincoln, P., Martí-Oliet, N., Meseguer, J., Talcott, C.: All About Maude - A High-Performance Logical Framework. LNCS, vol. 4350. Springer, Heidelberg (2007)
6. D'Angelo, G., Di Stefano, G., Navarra, A., Nisse, N., Suchan, K.: Computing on rings by oblivious robots: a unified approach for different tasks. Algorithmica **72**(4), 1055–1096 (2015)
7. Flocchini, P., Prencipe, G., Santoro, N.: Distributed Computing by Oblivious Mobile Robots. Morgan & Claypool Publishers, San Rafael (2012)
8. Huth, M., Ryan, M.: Logic in Computer Science: Modelling and Reasoning about Systems. Cambridge University Press, Cambridge (2004)
9. Kawamura, A., Kobayashi, Y.: Fence patrolling by mobile agents with distinct speeds. Distrib. Comput. **28**(2), 147–154 (2015)
10. Suzuki, I., Yamashita, M.: Distributed anonymous mobile robots: formation of geometric patterns. SIAM J. Comput. **28**(4), 1347–1363 (1999)
11. Yamauchi, Y., Uehara, T., Kijima, S., Yamashita, M.: Plane formation by synchronous mobile robots in the three dimensional Euclidean space. In: Moses, Y. (ed.) DISC 2015. LNCS, vol. 9363, pp. 93–106. Springer, Heidelberg (2015). doi:10.1007/978-3-662-48653-5_7

A Visual Modeling Language for MSVL

Xinfeng Shu$^{(\boxtimes)}$, Chao Li, and Chang Liu

School of Computer Science and Technology,
Xi'an University of Posts and Communications, Xi'an 710061, China
`shuxf@xupt.edu.cn`

Abstract. Modeling, Simulation and Verification Language (MSVL) is a useful formalism for specification and verification of concurrent systems. To make it easy to use, we define a visual formalism, called vMSVL, which is the extension of the classic flowchart used in software design and helps the engineer to model the structure and behaviour of a system in a visual, hierarchical way. Besides, the technique for automatical translation of vMSVL model into MSVL model is also presented. The formalism combines the benefits of the classical visualized specification method with the power of model checking, which helps to popularize the application of model checking in industry.

Keywords: Temporal logic programming · Formal verification · Visual languages · System modeling

1 Introduction

Modeling, Simulation and Verification Language (MSVL) [1,2], an executable subset of Projection Temporal Logic (PTL) [3–7] with framing technique, is a useful formalism for specification and verification of concurrent and distributed systems [8–15]. It provides a rich set of data types (e.g., char, integer, pointer, string), data structures (e.g., array, list), as well as boolean and arithmetic expressions [16]. Besides, MSVL supports not only the commonly used statements in most of imperative programming languages (e.g. C and Java) such as assignment, sequential $(S_1; S_2)$, branch (if b then S_1 else S_2), loop (while b do S) statements, but also parallel and concurrent statements such as conjunct $(S_1$ and $S_2)$, parallel $(S_1 \| S_2)$ and projection $((S_1, \ldots, S_m)$ prj $S)$. Further, Propositional Projection Temporal Logic (PPTL), the propositional subset of PTL, has the expressiveness power of the full regular expressions [17], which enable us to model, simulate and verify the concurrent and reactive systems within a same logical system [18].

System modeling is the kernel process of model checking, and the correctness and rationality of the model greatly affects the validity of the model checking

This research is supported by the Natural Science Foundation of Education Bureau of Shaanxi Province, China (No. 11JK1037), the Industrial Research Project of Shaanxi Province (No. 2016GY-089).

S. Liu et al. (Eds.): SOFL+MSVL 2016, LNCS 10189, pp. 220–237, 2017.
DOI: 10.1007/978-3-319-57708-1_13

result. As a logic programming language, MSVL differs greatly from other traditional programming language (such as C language) in modelling, and it's not easy to be mastered by ordinary engineers. Besides, MSVL being a scripting language, the system model described by MSVL cannot be analyzed in an intuitively visible way, it is very difficult to model a complex system and guarantee the correctness of the model.

Therefore, we are motivated to define a visual modelling language, named vMSVL, for MSVL by extending the software-programming flowchart [19]. Thus, the system design model and the model checking model can be unified as one model, and it can be created in one time by engineers when designing the system. Besides, the algorithm to translate from vMSVL model to MSVL model is formalized, which provides a strong support for the popularizing the MSVL-based model checking technology in industry as well as promoting the quality and the development efficiency of software.

The rest of paper is organized as follows. In the next section, PTL and MSVL are briefly introduced. In Sect. 3, the visual modeling language vMSVL is defined. In Sect. 4, the algorithm to translate from vMSVL model to MSVL model is given. Finally, conclusions are drawn in Sect. 5.

2   Preliminaries

2.1   Projection Temporal Logic

In this subsection, the syntax and semantics of Projection Temporal Logic (PTL) are briefly introduced. More details can be found in paper [3,4].

Syntax. Let $Prop$ be a countable set of atomic propositions and V a countable set of typed variables. $B = \{true, false\}$ represents the boolean domain. D denotes the data domain of the underlying logic. The terms e and formulas P of PTL are inductively defined as follows:

$$e ::= d \mid a \mid x \mid \bigcirc e \mid f(e_1, \ldots, e_m)$$
$$P ::= p \mid e_1 = e_2 \mid \rho(e_1, \ldots, e_m) \mid \neg P \mid P_1 \wedge P_2 \mid \exists vP \mid \bigcirc P \mid (P_1, \ldots, P_m) \; prj \; P$$

where $d \in D$ is a constant, $a \in V$ a static variable, $x \in V$ a dynamic variable, $v \in V$ either a static variable or a dynamic one; $p \in Prop$ is an atomic proposition; f is a function and ρ a predicate both defined over D.

Abbreviation. The conventional constructs $true$, $false$, $\wedge$, $\rightarrow$ as well as $\leftrightarrow$ are defined as usual. Furthermore, we use the following abbreviations:

$$\varepsilon \stackrel{def}{=} \neg \bigcirc true \qquad\qquad \bar{\varepsilon} \stackrel{def}{=} \neg \varepsilon$$
$$\odot P \stackrel{def}{=} \neg \bigcirc \neg P \qquad\qquad P;Q \stackrel{def}{=} (P,Q) \; prj \; \varepsilon$$
$$\bigcirc^0 P \stackrel{def}{=} P \qquad\qquad \bigcirc^n P \stackrel{def}{=} \bigcirc \bigcirc^{n-1} P, \; (n > 0)$$
$$\Diamond P \stackrel{def}{=} true;P \qquad\qquad len(n) \stackrel{def}{=} \bigcirc^n \varepsilon$$
$$\Box P \stackrel{def}{=} \neg \Diamond \neg P \qquad\qquad keep(P) \stackrel{def}{=} \Box(\bar{\varepsilon} \rightarrow P)$$
$$skip \stackrel{def}{=} \bigcirc \varepsilon \qquad\qquad halt(P) \stackrel{def}{=} \Box(\varepsilon \leftrightarrow P)$$
$$\forall vP \stackrel{def}{=} \neg \exists v \neg P \qquad\qquad fin(P) \stackrel{def}{=} \Box(\varepsilon \rightarrow P)$$
$$P \| Q \stackrel{def}{=} ((P;true) \wedge Q) \vee (P \wedge (Q;true)) \vee (P \wedge Q)$$

Semantics. A state s is a pair of assignments (I_p, I_v), which I_p assigns each atomic proposition $p \in Prop$ a truth value in B, whereas I_v assigns each variable $v \in V$ a value in D. An interval (i.e., model) σ is a non-empty sequence of states, which can be finite or infinite. The length of σ, denoted by $|\sigma|$, is ω if σ is infinite, or the number of states minus one if σ is finite. We use notation $\sigma_{(i..j)}$ to mean that a subinterval $<s_i, \ldots, s_j>$ of σ with $0 \leq i \preceq j \leq |\sigma|$. The *concatenation* of a finite interval $\sigma = <s_0, \ldots, s_{|\sigma|}>$ with another interval $\sigma' = <s'_0, \ldots, s'_{|\sigma'|}>$ (may be infinite) is denoted by $\sigma \bullet \sigma'$ and $\sigma \bullet \sigma' = <s_0, \ldots, s_{|\sigma|}, s'_0, \ldots, s'_{|\sigma'|}>$. Let $\sigma = <s_0, s_1, \ldots, s_{|\sigma|}>$ be an interval and $r_1, \ldots, r_h$ be integers ($h \geq 1$) such that $0 \leq r_1 \leq r_2 \leq \ldots \leq r_h \preceq |\sigma|$. The projection of σ onto $r_1, \ldots, r_h$ is the interval (called projected interval) $\sigma \downarrow (r_1, \ldots, r_h) = <s_{t_1}, \ldots, s_{t_l}>$, $(t_1 < t_2 < \ldots < t_l)$, where $t_1, \ldots, t_l$ is obtained from $r_1, \ldots, r_h$ by deleting all duplicates. For example, $<s_0, s_1, s_2, s_3, s_4, s_5> \downarrow (0, 2, 2, 2, 4, 4, 5) = <s_0, s_2, s_4, s_5>$.

An interpretation, as for PTL, is a triple $\mathcal{I} = (\sigma, i, j)$, where σ is an interval, $i \in N_0$ and $j \in N_\omega$, and $0 \leq i \preceq j \leq |\sigma|$. We use notation (σ, i, j) to mean that a term or a formula is interpreted over a subinterval $<s_i, \ldots, s_j>$ of σ with the current state being s_i. Then, for every term e, the evaluation of e relative to $\mathcal{I}$, denoted by $\mathcal{I}[e]$, is defined by induction on the structure of the term as follows:

$$\mathcal{I}[d] = d, \text{ if } d \in D \text{ is a constant value}$$
$$\mathcal{I}[a] = I_v^i[a] = I_v^0[a], \text{ if } a \text{ is typed static variable}$$
$$\mathcal{I}[x] = I_v^i[x], \text{ if } x \text{ is typed dynamic variable}$$
$$\mathcal{I}[\bigcirc e] = \begin{cases} (\sigma, i+1, j)[e], & \text{if } i < j \\ nil, & \text{otherwise} \end{cases}$$
$$\mathcal{I}[f(e_1, \ldots, e_m)] = \begin{cases} nil, \text{ if } \mathcal{I}[e_h] = nil \text{ for some } h(1 \leq h \leq m) \\ \mathcal{I}[f](\mathcal{I}[e_1], \ldots, \mathcal{I}[e_m]), \text{ otherwise} \end{cases}$$

For a variable v (static or dynamic), two intervals σ and σ' are v-equivalent, denoted by $\sigma \overset{v}{=} \sigma'$, whenever σ' is the same as σ except that different values can be assigned to v. The satisfaction relation ($\models$) for PTL formulas is inductively defined as follows:

$\mathcal{I} \models p$ iff $I_p^i[p] = true$, for any given atomic proposition p.

$\mathcal{I} \models \rho(e_1, \ldots, e_m)$ iff ρ is a primitive predicate other than $=$ and, for all $h(1 \leq h \leq m)$, $\mathcal{I}[e_h] \neq nil$ and $\mathcal{I}[\rho](\mathcal{I}[e_1], \ldots, \mathcal{I}[e_m]) = true$.

$\mathcal{I} \models e_1 = e_2$ iff $\mathcal{I}[e_1] = \mathcal{I}[e_2]$.

$\mathcal{I} \models \neg P$ iff $\mathcal{I} \not\models P$.

$\mathcal{I} \models P \wedge Q$ iff $\mathcal{I} \models P$ and $\mathcal{I} \models Q$.

$\mathcal{I} \models \exists v P$ iff $(\sigma', i, j) \models P$ for some interval σ', $\sigma_{(i..j)} \overset{v}{=} \sigma'_{(i..j)}$.

$\mathcal{I} \models \bigcirc P$ iff $i < j$ and $(\sigma, i+1, j) \models P$.

$\mathcal{I} \models (P_1, \ldots, P_m)$ prj Q iff there exist integers $i = r_0 \leq \ldots \leq r_{m-1} \leq r_m \preceq j$ such that $(\sigma, r_{l-1}, r_l) \models P_l$ for all $1 \leq l \leq m$, and $(\sigma', 0, |\sigma'|) \models Q$ for one of the following σ':
(1) $r_m < j$ and $\sigma' = \sigma \downarrow (r_0, \ldots, r_m) \bullet \sigma_{(r_m+1..j)}$.
(2) $r_m = j$ and $\sigma' = \sigma \downarrow (r_0, \ldots, r_h)$ for some $0 \leq h \leq m$.

2.2 Modeling, Simulation and Verification Language

Modeling, Simulation and Verification Language (MSVL) is an executable subset of PTL. With MSVL, expressions can be regarded as the PTL terms and statements as treated as the PTL formulas. In the following, we briefly introduce the kernel of MSVL. For more deals, please refer to literatures [1,2].

Data Type. MSVL provides a rich set of data types. The fundamental types include unsigned character (char), unsigned integer (int) and floating point number (float). Besides, there is a hierarchy of derived data types built with the fundamental types, including string (string), list (list), pointer (pointer), array (array), structure (struct) and union (union).

Expression. The arithmetic expressions e and boolean expressions b of MSVL are inductively defined as follows:

$$e ::= d \mid x \mid \bigcirc e \mid \ominus e \mid e_1 + e_2 \mid e_1 - e_2 \mid e_1 * e_2 \mid e_1/e_2 \mid e_1 \% e_2$$
$$b ::= true \mid false \mid \neg b \mid b_1 \wedge b_2 \mid e_1 = e_2 \mid e_1 \leq e_2$$

where d is an integer or a floating point number; $x \in V$ is a static or dynamic variable; $\bigcirc e$ ($\ominus e$) refers to the value of expression e at the next (previous) state.

Statement. The elementary statements in MSVL are defined as follows:

(1) Immediate Assign $x \Leftarrow e \stackrel{\text{def}}{=} x = e \wedge p_x$

(2) Unit Assignment $x := e \stackrel{\text{def}}{=} \bigcirc x = e \wedge \bigcirc p_x \wedge skip$

(3) Conjunction $S_1 \ and \ S_2 \stackrel{\text{def}}{=} S_1 \wedge S_2$

(4) Selection $S_1 \ or \ S_2 \stackrel{\text{def}}{=} S_1 \wedge S_2$

(5) Next $next \ S \stackrel{\text{def}}{=} \bigcirc S$

(6) Always $always \ S \stackrel{\text{def}}{=} \square S$

(7) Termination $empty \stackrel{\text{def}}{=} \neg \bigcirc true$

(8) Skip $skip \stackrel{\text{def}}{=} \bigcirc \varepsilon$

(9) Sequential $S_1 ; S_2 \stackrel{\text{def}}{=} (S_1, S_2) \ prj \ \varepsilon$

(10) Local $exist \ x : S \stackrel{\text{def}}{=} \exists \ x : S$

(11) State Frame $lbf(x) \stackrel{\text{def}}{=} \neg \ af(x) \rightarrow \exists \ b : (\bigcirc x = b \ \wedge x = b)$

(12) Interval Frame $frame(x) \stackrel{\text{def}}{=} \square (\ \overline{\varepsilon} \rightarrow \bigcirc (lbf(x)))$

(13) Projection $(S_1, \ldots, S_m) \ prj \ S$

(14) Condition $if \ b \ then \ S_1 \ else \ S_2 \stackrel{\text{def}}{=} (b \rightarrow S_1) \wedge (\neg b \rightarrow S_2)$

(15) While $while \ b \ do \ S \stackrel{\text{def}}{=} (b \wedge S)^\star \wedge \square (\ \varepsilon \rightarrow \neg b)$

(16) Await $await(b) \stackrel{\text{def}}{=} \bigwedge_{x \in V_b} frame(x) \wedge \square (\ \varepsilon \leftrightarrow b)$

(17) Parallel $S_1 \| S_2 \stackrel{\text{def}}{=} ((S_1 ; true) \wedge S_2) \vee (S_1 \wedge (S_2 ; true))$
  $\vee (S_1 \wedge S_2)$

where x is a variable, e is an arbitrary expression, b is a boolean expression, and $S_1, \ldots, S_m, S$ are all MSVL statements. The immediate assignment $x \Leftarrow e$, unit assignment $x := e$, $empty$, $lbf(x)$ and $frame(x)$ are basic statements, and the left composite ones.

3   Structures of vMSVL

To make vMSVL be easily mastered by engineers in industry, the structural description components of vMSVL follow largely the flowchart notations described in [19]. We also introduce some notations to meet the modeling needs for concurrent systems.

The language vMSVL consists of fundamental notations and visual notations. The former are used to describe the attributes and the details of activities of the system to be modeled, and the latter are used to model the processing logic of the system in a graphical and hierarchical way.

3.1   Fundamental Notations

The fundamental notations of vMSVL include data types, expressions as well as elementary statements. The notations are nearly identical to that in C programming language.

Definition 1 (Data Type). The fundamental data types of vMSVL include character (char), integer (int) and floating point number (float), boolean (bool) and string (string). Besides, there is a hierarchy of derived data types including array (array(type)), pointer(type *) structure (struct), union (union) and enumeration (enum).

Definition 2 (Expression). Let d be a constant and x be a variable respectively. The arithmetic expressions e and boolean expressions b of vMSVL are inductively defined as follows:

$$e ::= d \mid x \mid e_1 \ op_1 \ e_2 \ (op_1 ::= + \mid - \mid * \mid / \mid \%)$$
$$b ::= true \mid false \mid !b \mid e_1 \ op_2 \ e_2 \ (op_2 :==< \mid \leq \mid > \mid \geq \mid ==)$$
$$b_1 \ op_3 \ b_2 (op_3 :==, \&\& \mid , \|)$$

where op_1 denotes the traditional arithmetic operators, op_2 are the relational operators and op_3 the logical operators

Definition 3 (Elementary Statement). Let $type$ be a data type and x be a variable. The Elementary Statement s of vMSVL are inductively defined as follows:

$$s ::= type \ x \mid type \ x = d \mid x = e \mid x = b \mid x = fun(e_1, \ldots, e_n) \mid s_1; s_2$$

where fun is a function with $n(n \geq 0)$ parameters.

3.2   Visual Notations

The visual notations of vMSVL are defined in Table 1. The major shapes used in vMSVL, i.e. flow line, process and decision, keep identical to that in classic flowchart [19]. Besides, we also make some necessary extensions for convenience of modeling complex concurrent system in a hierarchical way:

Table 1. Visual notations for vMSVL

Shape	Name	Description
→	flow line	Represents the control flow passing from one symbol to another.
(entrance shape)	entrance	Represents the entrance of a function. It contains the function name and parameters.
(exit shape)	exit	Represents the exit of a function. It may contain the return value of the function if it has.
(process shape)	process	Shows some fundamental statements are performed, e.g., "X = 1", "int Y"
(Ref shape)	reference	Denotes complex processing step which is detailed in a separate flowchart. It contains the name of the separate flowchart.
(Fun shape)	function call	Indicates a function being invoked and the function is modeled in a separate flowchart. It contains the name of the function and the possible arguments passed to the function.
(diamond shape)	decision	Represents where a decision is necessary. The decision is described as a boolean expression and contained in the symbol. The symbol has two arrows departing from it, one corresponding to Yes, and one corresponding to No.
(fork/join shape)	fork/join	Show the parallel flows. Note that all parallel flows start at a fork symbol and end at a join one.

- Replace the original terminal symbol with entrance symbol and exit symbol to explicitly represent the entrance as well as the exit of the function respectively.
- Add a new reference symbol to represent a complicated processing step which is detailed in another separate flowchart.
- Add a new function call symbol to represent calling a function which is modeled in another separated flowchart.
- Introduce a new fork/join symbol to represent the starting/ending of the parallel execution of several sub-flows. Note that although we employ a unified symbol to represent both the fork and the join of a parallel execution, it can be easily distinguished by checking the number of the ingoing and outgoing flow lines of the symbol. A fork symbol has only one ingoing flow line and several (≥ 2) outgoing flow lines, whereas a join one has several (≥ 2) ingoing flow lines and only one outgoing flow line.

3.3   System Modeling with vMSVL

The general system modeling strategy with vMSVL is similar to that with classic flowchart in software system design, i.e., describing each component of the system with a flowchart and assembling them into a complete system through function calls or references. Thus, a vMSVL system model may consist of many flowcharts, within which one must be explicitly declared as the entry of the model.

In the following, we give an example to show how to model with vMSVL. As shown in Fig. 1, we employ a parallel algorithm to compute $\sum_{n=1}^{5}(\sum_{i=1}^{n} i + n!)$. The whole model consists of three flowcharts describing three functions, among which function main is the entry of the program, functions sum and $fact$ execute in parallel to compute $\sum_{i=1}^{n} i$ and $n!$ respectively.

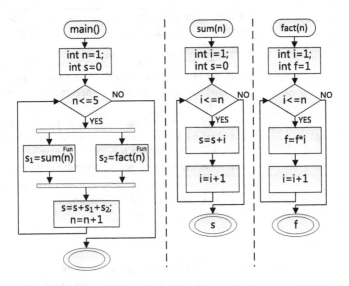

Fig. 1. System model for computing $\sum_{n=1}^{5}(\sum_{i=1}^{n} i + n!)$

3.4   Formal Definition of vMSVL Model

In vMSVL, a flowchart can be regard as a directed graph which node notations (notations except for flow line) are vertexes and flow lines are arcs between vertexes. Thus, a vMSVL system model is in fact the set of directed graphs.

Definition 4 (vMSVL Model). The node notation $Vertex$, flow line Arc, flowchart $FlowChart$ and the model $FCModel$ are defined inductively as follows:

$$
\begin{aligned}
Vertex &::= (ntype, ncontent) \\
Arc &::= (verFrom, label, verTo) \\
FlowChart &::= (verSet, arcSet, entryVer) \\
FCModel &::= (FCSet, entryFC)
\end{aligned}
$$

where *ntype* denotes the type of the notation and its values is given in Table 2; *ncontent* is an expression or an elementary statement contained in the notation; *verFrom* and *verTo* represents the coming from and ending at node notations of flow line respectively; *label* is the label on the flow line and it can only take the value of "YES"/"NO" in case of the flow line departing from a decision shape; *verSet* and *arcSet* are the sets of vertexes and arcs respectively; *entryVer* is the entrance of the flowchart; *FCSet* denotes the set of flowcharts and *entryFC* the entry flowchart of the model.

Table 2. The value of node notation type

Notation name	Value	Notation name	Value
entrance	NT_ET	exit	NT_EX
process	NT_PR	reference	NT_RF
function call	NT_FC	decision	NT_DC
fork/join	NT_FJ		

4   Translation of vMSVL Model into MSVL Model

In case of the vMSVL system model being created, the left work is to automatically translate it into the MSVL model. To this end, a formal definition of sMSVL Model is given, and a hierarchical syntax chart (HSC) is introduced to describe the syntax of the vMSVL model. Besides, the algorithms for translating vMSVL model into HSC and HSC into MSVL model are also formalized respectively.

4.1   Transition of vMSVL Model into Hierarchical Syntax Chart

On the whole, the execution of a flowchart is in fact sequentially traversing each node from the entrance to the exit, but the structures such as branch, loop and parallel violate the sequential traverse. So, we cannot transform these structures into MSVL code according to the traverse sequence directly. To solve the problem, we introduce a data structure, named Hierarchical Syntax Chart (HSC), to analyze the syntax of a vMSVL model.

Hierarchical Syntax Chart. The strategy of HSC representing the syntax of vMSVL model is to recognize each execution branch and organize them as a sequence of compound statements, and each compound statement contains a sequence of statements in the executing branch. The structure of HSC can be depicted as the figure in Fig. 2. In first level, the HSC is the sequence of compound statements of functions, and the function body, a compound statement, is the sequence of statements in the function body. If the compound statement includes if, while or parallel statements, their corresponding execution breaches are also

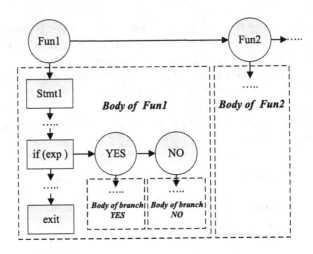

Fig. 2. Structure of hierarchical syntax chart

organized the sequence of compound statements, e.g. the *if* statement in the body of function *Fun*1.

According to the above analysis, the data structure of HSC is defined in C Language as follows:

```
/*type  of  the  statements*/
typedef enum{
      TYPE_COM,                /*Common  statement*/
      TYPE_IF,                 /*Branch  Statement*/
      TYPE_LOOP,               /*Loop  Statement*/
      TYPE_FORK,               /*Fork  Statement*/
      TYPE_JOIN,               /*Join  Statement*/
      TYPE_EXT                 /*Exit  Statement*/
}STMT_TYPE;

/*type for the  list of compound  statements*/
typedef struct  com_stmt{
      string stmt_name;
      stmt_node *first_stmt;
      com_stmt *next_com_stmt;
}com_stmt_node, *HSC;

/*type for list of statements*/
typedef struct  stmt{
      STMT_TYPE type;
      Vertex ver;
      com_stmt *first_com_stmt;
      stmt *next_stmt;
}stmt_node, *stmt_list;
```

In definition of struct *com_stmt*, member *stmt_name* is the name of the compound statement, which may be the name of a function or take the value of "YES"/"NO" representing a specific branch of a *if* or *while* statement; members *first_stmt* and *next_com_stmt* are two pointers pointing to first statement as well as the next compound statement respectively. In definition struct *stmt*, member *ver* saves the entity of a statement; member *next_stmt* points to the next statement; member *first_com_stmt* points to the first sub-compound statement and it takes effect only if the type of the current statement takes the value of TYPE_IF, TYPE_LOOP or TYPE_PAR.

Algorithm for Constructing HSC. For a given vMSVL model, the algorithm for constructing the HSC consists of the functions vMSVL2HSC, FC2ComStmt, DFS_Trans, Handle_Decision, Handle_Parallel and Handle_Branch. The functions are defined in pseudo C Language as follows.

Function vMSVL2HSC is the entry of the algorithm. It enumerates each flowchart in the given vMSVL model and calls function FC2ComStmt to translate it into a compound statement. All the compound statements obtained are concatenated into a complete HSC.

```
vMSVL2HSC(FCModel model){
    HSC hsc = NULL;
    Foreach fc in model{
        com_stmt_node cs_node = FC2ComStmt(fc);
        AddTail(hsc, cs_node);
    }
    return hsc;
}
```

Function FC2ComStmt translates a flowchart into a compound statement based on the strategy of deep first search (DFS) of a direct graph. To this end, two boolean arrays *visited* and *isParent* are employed to mark whether or not a vertex is visited as well as is the parent of the vertex currently visiting respectively. Besides, stack S is used to keep the flow control statement, i.e. *Decision* and *Parallel*, appearing in the traverse path.

```
FC2ComStmt(FlowChart fc){
    bool visited[]={false};
    bool isParent[]={false};
    InitStack(S);
    comp_stmt node;
    node.stmt_name= fc.entryVer.ncontent;
    node.first_stmt=DFS_Trans(fc.entryVer.nextVer,
                              visited,isParent,S);
    return node;
}
```

Function DFS_Trans constructs the body of a compound statement while deep first traversing a flowchart from the given vertex. If the vertex is visited (i.e., *visited*[*ver*] == *true*), which means a new branch is found, it calls function *Handle_Branch* to deal with an returns the result. Otherwise, the function marks the *visited* as well as *isParent* tags both be *true*. Subsequently, it creates a new statement node *newNode* with the current vertex *ver*. Further, the function recursively constructs the body of the compound statement according to the type of the vertex *ver*. If the type is a process (NT_PR), reference (NT_RF) or function call (NT_FC), it calls DFS_Trans to deal with the left part of the flowchart. If the type is a decision (NT_DC) (w.r.t. fork/join (NT_FJ)), the function calls Handle_Decision (w.r.t. Handle_Parallel) to process. Finally, the function removes the vertex *ver* from the traverse path (*isParent*[*ver*] = *false*).

```
DFS_Trans(Vertex ver, bool visited[], bool isParent[],
          Stack S){
    if(visited[ver]==true){
        return Handle_Branch(ver, isParent, S)
    }
    visited[ver] = isParent[ver] = true;
    newNode.first_com_stmt = NULL;
    newNode.ver = ver;
    switch(ver.ntype){
        case NT_PR or NT_RF or NT_FC:
            newNode.type = TYPE_COM;
            newNode.next_stmt = DFS_Trans(ver.nextVer,
                          visited, isParent, S);
            break;
        case NT_EX:
            newNode.type = TYPE_COM;
            break;
        case NT_DC:
            Handle_Decision(newNode, ver, S);
            break;
        case NT_FJ:
            Handle_Parallel(newNode, ver, S);
    }
    isParent[ver]=false;
    return newNode;
}
```

Function Handle_Branch is designed for processing a new-found execution branch in a compound statement. The following tow cases must be considered: (1) The branch is the body of a *loop* statement. It can be handled by checking whether the DFS of the flowchart goes into a parent node in the traverse path (i.e., *isParent*[*ver*] == *true*). (2) The branch is the body of a *if* construct. In the latter case, the vertex *ver* is the meeting point of the two branches of *if* construct. However, we cannot recognize which vertex is the last one in traversing the first branch of *if* construct. So, the vertexes in the first branch and the vertexes after the branch are all treated as body of the first compound statement of *if* construct. With meeting point *ver*, we separate the statements after the first branch with function Split and concatenate them as the statements next to the *if* construct in the top of the stack *S*.

```
Handle_Branch(Vertex ver, bool isParent[], Stack S){
    nodeTop=GetTop(S);
    if(isParent[ver]==true){      //Find a loop
        if(ver.ntype!=NT_DC){
            ThrowError("Invalid loop construct!");
        }
        nodeTop.type = TYPE_LOOP;
        return NULL;
    }else{   //Two branches of an if construct meet
        left = Split(nodeTop.first_com_stmt, ver);
        nodeTop.next_stmt=left;
        return left;
    }
}
```

Function Handle_Decision is designed for handling if/while constructs. Initially, it set the type of new node to TYPE_IF and push it into the stack *S*. Subsequently, it deals with the "YES" branch of the construct by calling function DFS_Trans and check the result. If the construct is a loop (i.e., *newNode.type* == TYPE_LOOP), in such case the body of the loop has been recognized and we pop it from the stack *S* and treat the "NO" branch of the construct as the successor the loop construct. Otherwise, we treat the "NO" branch as the another compound statement of the construct.

```
Handle_Decision(stmt newNode, Vertex ver, Statck S){
    newNode.type=TYPE_IF;
    push(S, newNode);
    //process YES branch
    newComStmtYes.stmt_name = "YES";
    newComStmtYes.next_com_stmt = NULL;
    newComStmtYes.next_stmt = DFS_Trans(
        GetBranch(ver,''YES''),visited,isParent,S);
    newNode.first_com_stmt = newComStmtYes;
    if(newNode.type==TYPE_LOOP){
        Pop(S);
        newNode.next_stmt = DFS_Trans(
            GetBranch(ver,"NO"),visited,isParent,S);
    }else{ //Process NO brance
        newComStmtNo.stmt_name = "NO";
        newComStmtNo.next_com_stmt = NULL;
        newComStmtNo.next_stmt = DFS_Trans(
            GetBranch(ver,"NO"),visited,isParent,S);
        newComStmtYes.next_com_stmt = newComStmtNo;
        Pop(S);
    }
}
```

Function Handle_Parallel is designed for handling Parallel constructs. Firstly, we employ the function GetAdjArcsCount to count of the adjacent arcs departing from vertex *ver*. If the result equals 1, which indicates the construct is a join one, then we cache the successor vertex of the join construct as the next statement of the fork statement in the top of stack S. Otherwise, we create a new statement with the type TYPE_JOIN, push it into the stack S, and then recursively create the compound statement for each branch of the fork construct. In case of all the branches having been handled, we popup the parallel statement *nodeTop* from the stack S and further deal with the left part of the flowchart beginning at the cached vertex in *nodeTop*.

```
Handle_Parallel(stmt newNode, Vertex ver, Statck S){
    if(GetAdjArcsCount(ver)==1) {//Join
        nodeTop=GetTop(S);
        if(nodeTop.type!=TYPE FORK){
            ThrowError("Invalid parallel construct!");
        }
        if(nodeTop.next_stmt!=NULL){
            tmpNode.type = TYPE_JOIN;
            tmpNode.ver = ver.nextVer;
            nodeTop.next_stmt = tmpNode;
        }
    }else{   //Fork
        newNode.type=TYPE_FORK;
        push(S, newNode);
        foreach adjVer in GetAdjVexSet{
            newComStmt.stmt_name = "PAR";
            newComStmt.next_com_stmt = NULL;
            newComStmt.next_stmt = DFS_Trans( adjVer,
                visited, isParent, S);
            AddTail(newNode, newComStmt);
        }
        nodeTop = Pop(S);
        nodeTop.next_stmt = DFS_Trans(
            nodeTop.next_stmt.ver, visited, isParent, S);
    }
}
```

In the following, we illustrate how the algorithm vMSVL2HSC works by translating the vMSVL model shown in Fig. 1 into its HSC. For simplicity, we only give the details of transforming the flowchart of function *main* into HSC. Further, for convenience of explanation, we add a number in parentheses as the extra mark to each vertex in the flowchart of function *main* as shown in Fig. 3(a). According to the algorithm vMSVL2HSC, the constructing process of HSC for function main is as follows:

(1) Initially, a compound node <1>, as shown in is created according to the entrance vertex (1) of the flowchart of main.

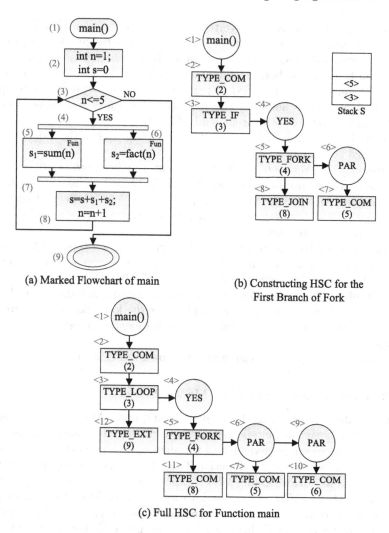

(a) Marked Flowchart of main

(b) Constructing HSC for the
First Branch of Fork

(c) Full HSC for Function main

Fig. 3. Constructing process of HSC for function main

(2) Then, following the DFS used in function DFS_Trans, vertexes (2) and
(3) are met in sequence and two statements <2> and <3> are added
correspondingly to the body of compound node <1>.

(3) Since vertex (3) is a decision vertex, according to function Handle_Decision,
the corresponding statement <3> is pushed into the Stack S, and a new
compound node <4> is created to deal with the "YES" branch of the
decision vertex.

(4) In constructing the body of compound node <4>, vertex (4) is met and a
new statement <5> is added.

(5) Because vertex (4) is a fork vertex, according to function Handle_Parallel, the corresponding statement <5> is pushed into the Stack S, and a new compound node <6> is added to handle the first branch of the fork vertex.

(6) In constructing the body of compound node <6>, vertex (5) is met and a new statement <7> is added. When the join vertex (6) is met, a temporal statement <8> is added as the successor of the fork statement <5>. At this time point, the HSC is shown in Fig. 3(b).

(7) Similarly, the compound statement for the left branch of the fork statement is added to statement <5>.

(8) After all the branches of the fork statement have been processed, statement <5> is popped up from the stack S and the cached vertex (8) is obtained. Beginning with vertex (8), the left part of the "YES" branch of vertex (3) is continuously constructed and a new statement <11> is added as the successor of statement <5>.

(9) Following the DFS path, the departing arc of vertex (8) points to a parent node (3), according to function Handle_Branch, a loop statement appears and the type of statement <2> is set to TYPE_LOOP. Further, the full body of the loop statement has been constructed and the "NO" branch of node (3) represents the statements after the loop. So, a new statement <11> corresponding to vertex (9) is added as the successor of statement <2>.

(10) So far, the full HSC is constructed as shown in Fig. 3(c).

4.2   Transforming from HSC to MSVL Model

For a given HSC, the algorithm for transforming it into a MSVL model is defined in pseudo C Language as follows. Within the algorithm, the called function Get-Variables is used to compute the list of variables appearing in the variable statements of a statement node; the function Trans_Exp is used to convert a vMSLV expression into its corresponding MSVL expression; and function Trans_Stmt is used to convert a vMSLV statement into its corresponding MSVL statement. With aid of the translation rules of expressions and statement given in Table 3, it is readily to formalize the three functions. So their code is omitted here.

Table 3. Transformation Rules for expressions and statements

Type	vMSVL	MSVL
Arithmetic expression	e	e
Boolean expression	$b_1 \&\& b_2$	$b_1\ and\ b_2$
	$b_1 \| \| b_2$	$b_1\ or\ b_2$
Elementary Statement	$x = e$	$x := e$
	$type\ x = d$	$type\ x\ and\ x \Leftarrow d\ and\ empty$
	$s_1; s_2$	$s_1\ and\ S_2$

```
//Entry of the algorithm
HSC2MSVL(HSC hsc){
    p = hsc;
    string code;
    while(p){ //Deal with each function
        code = code + p.name + CompStmt2MSVL(p);
        p = p.next_com_stmt;
    }
    return code;
}


//Translating the body of a compound statement
CompStmt2MSVL(com_stmt comStmt){
    p=comStmt.first_stmt;
    varList=GetVariables(p);
    string body;
    while(p){
        body = body + Stmt2MSVL(p);
        p = p.next_stmt;
    }
    return"frame("+ varList+")and("+ body +")";
}


//Transform a statement
Stmt2MSVL(stmt node){
    switch(node.type){
        case TYPE_COM:
            return Trans_Stmt(node.ver.ncontent);
        case TYPE_LOOP:
            return"while("+Trans_Exp(node.ver.ncontent)
            +"){"+CompStmt2MSVL(node.first_com_stmt)+"}";
        case TYPE_IF:
            return"if("+Trans_Exp(node.ver.ncontent)+"){"
            + CompStmt2MSVL(node.first_com_stmt)
            +"}else{";
            + CompStmt2MSVL(node.first_com_stmt.next_com_stmt)
            +"}"
        case TYPE_FORK:
            string fork = CompStmt2MSVL(node.first_com_stmt);
            p = node.first_com_stmt.next_com_stmt;
            while(p){
                fork = fork + "||" + CompStmt2MSVL(p);
                p = p.next_com_stmt;
            }
            return fork;
    }
}
```

For instance, if we transform the HSC of function main given in Fig. 3(c) with algorithm HSC2MSVL, the result MSVL code is as follows.

```
function main( ){
    frame(n , s ) and (
        int n and n <==1 and empty;
        int s and s <==0 and empty ;
        while (n<=s ){
            s1 := sum(n)||s2 := fact(n);
            s := s + s1 + s2 ;
        }
    )
}
```

5   Conclusion

In this paper, we present a visual language vMSVL for modeling the system to be verified in a visual and hierarchical way, and formalize the algorithms for automatically translating vMSVL model to MSVL model. The introduction of vMSVL will facilitate the popularizing of the MSVL-based model checking technology in industry as well as promoting the quality of software. In the near future, we will enrich the vMSVL with semaphore and projection notations to have a more powerful support for modeling concurrent systems. Besides, we will develop the vMSVL based visual modeling tool and apply the method to verify more complex concurrent and distributed system, such as operating system, cloud computing, etc.

References

1. Duan, Z., Yang, X., Koutny, M.: Framed temporal logic programming. Sci. Comput. Program. **70**(1), 31–61 (2008)
2. Duan, Z., Koutny, M.: A framed temporal logic programming language. J. Comput. Sci. Technol. **19**, 333–344 (2004)
3. Duan, Z.: An extended interval temporal logic and a framing technique for interval temporal logic programming. Ph.D thesis, University of Newcastle Upon Tyne, May 1996
4. Duan, Z.: Temporal Logic and Temporal Logic Programming. Science Press, Beijing (2005)
5. Duan, Z., Tian, C., Zhang, L.: A decision procedure for propositional projection temporal logic with infinite models. Acta Inf. **45**(1), 43–78 (2008)
6. Tian, Z.D.C.: A practical decision procedure for propositional projection temporal logic with infinite models. Theoret. Comput. Sci. **554**, 169–190 (2014)
7. Tian, C., Duan, Z., Zhang, N.: An efficient approach for abstraction-refinement in model checking. Theoret. Comput. Sci. **461**, 76–85 (2012)
8. Duan, Z.: Modeling and Analysis of Hybrid Systems. Science Press, Beijing (2004)
9. Wang, M., Duan, Z., Tian, C.: Simulation and verification of the virtual memory management system with MSVL. In: CSCWD 2014, pp. 360–365 (2014)

10. Cui, J., Duan, Z., Tian, C., Zhang, N., Zhou, C.: Model checking μ C/OS-III multi-task system with TMSVL. In: Butler, M., Conchon, S., Zaïdi, F. (eds.) ICFEM 2015. LNCS, vol. 9407, pp. 187–200. Springer, Cham (2015). doi:10.1007/978-3-319-25423-4_12

11. Yu, Y., Duan, Z., Tian, C., Yang, M.: Model checking C programs with MSVL. In: Liu, S. (ed.) SOFL 2012. LNCS, vol. 7787, pp. 87–103. Springer, Heidelberg (2013). doi:10.1007/978-3-642-39277-1_7

12. Bin, Y., Duan, Z., Tian, C.: Bounded model checking of traffic light control system. Electr. Notes Theor. Comput. Sci. **309**, 63–74 (2014)

13. Shu, X., Duan, Z.: model checking process scheduling over multi-core computer system with MSVL. In: Liu, S., Duan, Z. (eds.) SOFL+MSVL 2015. LNCS, vol. 9559, pp. 103–117. Springer, Cham (2016). doi:10.1007/978-3-319-31220-0_8

14. Ma, Q., Duan, Z., Zhang, N., Wang, X.: Verification of distributed systems with the axiomatic system of MSVL. Formal Aspects Comput. **27**(1), 103–131 (2015)

15. Zhang, N., Duan, Z., Tian, C.: A cylinder computation model for many-core parallel computing. Theoret. Comput. Sci. **497**, 68–83 (2013)

16. Shu, X., Duan, Z.: Extending MSVL with semaphore. In: Dinh, T.N., Thai, M.T. (eds.) COCOON 2016. LNCS, vol. 9797, pp. 599–610. Springer, Cham (2016). doi:10.1007/978-3-319-42634-1_48

17. Tian, C., Duan, Z.: Expressiveness of propositional projection temporal logic with star. Theoret. Comput. Sci. **412**(18), 1729–1744 (2011)

18. Duan, Z., Tian, C.: A unified model checking approach with projection temporal logic. In: Liu, S., Maibaum, T., Araki, K. (eds.) ICFEM 2008. LNCS, vol. 5256, pp. 167–186. Springer, Heidelberg (2008). doi:10.1007/978-3-540-88194-0_12

19. Strong, H.R.: Translating recursion equations into flowcharts. J. Comput. Syst. Sci. **5**(3), 254–285 (1971)

Author Index

Printed in the United States
By Bookmasters